Forgetful Memory

FORGETFUL MEMORY

Representation and Remembrance
in the Wake of the Holocaust

MICHAEL BERNARD-DONALS

STATE UNIVERSITY OF NEW YORK PRESS

Published by
STATE UNIVERSITY OF NEW YORK PRESS, ALBANY

© 2009 State University of New York

For information, contact State University of New York Press, Albany, NY
www.sunypress.edu

Production, Laurie Searl
Marketing, Anne M. Valentine

Library of Congress Cataloging-in-Publication Data

Bernard-Donals, Michael F.
   Forgetful Memory : representation and remembrance in the wake of the Holocaust / Michael Bernard-Donals.
       p. cm.
   Includes bibliographical references and index.
   ISBN 978-0-7914-7671-0 (hardcover : alk. paper)
   ISBN 978-0-7914-7672-7 (paperback : alk. paper)
1. Holocaust, Jewish (1939–1945)—
Influence. 2. Holocaust, Jewish (1939–1945)—Historiography. 3. Holocaust, Jewish (1939–1945)—Moral and ethical aspects. 4. Memory—Social aspects. I. Title. II. Title: Representation and remembrance in the wake of the Holocaust.
   D804.348.B474 2008
   940.53'18—dc22

                                                                                    2008003113

10   9   8   7   6   5   4   3   2   1

Contents

Figures

Acknowledgments

This book began with a question—why have memory and history been at odds since 1945—that I asked in 2000 at the Institute for Research in the Humanities, which had granted me a semester's fellowship. My colleagues at the Institute, and many more since that time, have pushed me to consider the methodological implications of that question—what we mean by history, and how writing and history require a certain kind of memory—that have made this book far richer. Since asking that initial question, I have also been invited to investigate the implications of forgetful memory in several different contexts—on the ethical implications of forgetfulness in Levinas's thought, at a conference on Rhetoric, Politics, and Ethics at the University of Ghent in the Netherlands; on the specifically Jewish facets of memory and forgetfulness at a conference on modern Jewish Literature sponsored by the Universities of Ghent and Antwerp; and on the relation of ethics and politics in Levinas's thoughts about Israel since the Holocaust at the first annual conference of the North American Levinas Society at Purdue University. I'm deeply grateful to my friends and colleagues at those conferences and at others—especially Diane Davis, Richard Glejzer, Diana George, Steve Mailloux, David Metzger, and Cliff Spargo—whose thoughtful questions and *engagement* have helped push this project along, sometimes when I thought it had stopped in its tracks. Jeffrey Carter, at the L'Enfant Plaza archive of the U.S. Holocaust Memorial Museum, was incredibly helpful as I sorted through boxes of material that eventually became the center of the book's seventh chapter. I could not have started, let alone completed, the book's sixth chapter without Ethan Witkowsky's incredibly helpful questions, insights, and superb research skills. My colleagues in the Department of English at the University of Wisconsin have been incredibly patient with me, particularly during my term as chair, as I wandered off to deliver portions of this book as papers at conferences and to pore through archives, leaving the business of the department, from time to time, in their hands. James Peltz at SUNY Press is, as always, generous of his time and good humor, and Laurie Searl has been incredibly patient as the editor for this project. Finally, my students' voices may not be audible to those reading this book, but they are always present in my ears, as they have been—along with those of my family—what's kept my perspective.

Portions of this project have appeared in print before. A version of chapter 3, "If I Forget Thee, Jerusalem," appeared in *After Representation: Literature and the Holocaust*. Chapter 4, "Memory and the Image," appeared in a different form in *College English* in 2004; chapter 5, "'Thou Shalt Not Bear False Witness,'" was published in a slightly revised form in *PMLA* in 2001; portions of chapter 7, "Conflations of Memory," appeared in *The New Centennial Review* in 2005; and an early version of chapter 8, "Difficult Freedom," appeared in *diacritics* in 2007.

I'm very grateful to Bracha Lichtenberg Ettinger, for permission to reprint a portion of "Autiswork"; to Serge Klarsfeld, for permission to reprint photographs from his monumental *French Children of the Holocaust*; and to the Bildarchiv Preussicher Kulturbesitz in Berlin, for permission to reprint images from their archives, all of which appear in chapter 4.

PART I

Memory and Forgetting

ONE

On the Verge of History and Memory

SPEAKING OF THE troubled relation of memory to history, Yosef Yerushalmi says of the contemporary moment that "perhaps the time has come to look more closely at ruptures, breaches, breaks [in history], to identify them more precisely, . . . to understand that not everything of value that existed before a break was either salvaged or metamorphosed, but was lost, and that often some of what fell by the wayside became, through our retrieval, meaningful to us" (*Zakhor* 101). Writing at the conclusion of a century that was to witness one of the most profound breaks in all of history let alone Jewish history, his is an understandable call. It is not just the call to understand the ways in which what has been lost to memory affects the writing both of testimony and of the histories that make use of it as its raw material. It is also a call to understand the ways in which that effort at retrieval—sometimes exceedingly selective, sometimes careless or mightily subjective—creates something other than memory, something new, and something perhaps tenuously related to what took place.

I want to make the case that memory and forgetfulness are facets of the same phenomenon of understanding: the occurrence of events begins interminably to recede into an inaccessible past at the very moment of occurrence, while the event's passage into language—into any knowledge that we might formulate of the occurrence—makes of the occurrence something (narrative, testimony, history) *other* than the event. The narrative of the event and the irretrievable event itself may, in Emmanuel Levinas's terms, approach one another, but they are of an altogether different order; and—nonetheless—the event intrudes upon the witness's ability to place it into the fabric of narrative, tearing it, or tugging at it, haunting the narrative and the witness both. My aim is to explore this phenomenon, particularly the representations that are produced, as a kind of "excess" of the event, which haunt both the one who was there and the one who only catches a glimpse of the event secondhand.

I'm particularly interested in events that might be called traumatic, or what Yerushalmi called, in the realm of history, "breaks" in the fabric of the known. In fact, it may well be the case that the passage of the occurrence from event to experience is confounded by that void of memory (the disappearance of the event) that insinuates itself in the midsts of that passage. The path from event to experience, from what happened to knowledge of what happened, is a discursive one: to make events available at all—to make them historical—one has to speak them. But this passage from witness to testimony or from the immemorial event to memory, is an impossible one if we think of it as recuperation or redemption of the event. Of course, the Holocaust is the most obvious instance of an event that seems to stand in the way of recollection—Agamben has made the case, troublingly, that the event can only be recuperated by those who, in his terms, speak for the dead (an impossible task)—and that produces a crisis of representation for memory. The Holocaust, as a break, functions doubly in this book: it is at once the historical instance that, in Blanchot's words, "ruined everything," that forced us to decisively change how we think of history and its relation to memory (see LaCapra); and it also haunts our accounts of how memory and its object— our representation of events and the events themselves—come into contact with one another since 1945.

It was Emmanuel Levinas—the philosophical touchstone of this project—that most obviously revolutionized the philosophical foundations of remembrance. In *Totality and Infinity* and in *Otherwise than Being*, he argued that the individual's engagement with others and the individual's representation of those engagements (events and the memory of events) cannot be made commensurate, but that their relation produces a kind of void or excess. For Levinas, this void is always associated with the "break" of the Holocaust. But it's a void that is productive of a positive ethics. If the relation of memory and forgetfulness is less a matter of extremes or opposition and more a matter of simultaneity—as Levinas has laid out—then the passage from event to experience, witness to testimony, might be less a passage than a crux, a point in time that annihilates time and that forces upon the witness both the imperative to speak and the knowledge that to speak the experience and to act in the face of that experience is both impossible and impossible to avoid. This is precisely the ethical moment implied by Levinas's simultaneous imposition of what he calls "the saying" and "the said": faced with the enormity of the event we are compelled to act and to make that action knowable to and oriented toward an other through speech (what is said), and yet we realize that anything said or represented reduces that enormity to a language or a medium that can't quite contain it. And yet the event itself is completely lost—both to history and to memory—unless it is said. Just as saying and said cannot exist without one another, neither can memory and forgetting so exist.

Notions of memory that take as their task a full or even partial recuperation of events in the name of knowledge will always fail in that task: because the event disrupts our ability to, in Kant's terms, bring it under a concept adequate to the experience itself, there is no way the event could be said to be redeemed. What I'm calling forgetful memory comes as an involuntary and unbidden flash of the event that disrupts collective memory and history (that sees it, in other words, as a variety of *anamnesis* rather than as *mneme*, as a marker of what has been lost rather than as a representation of what can be remembered). If it is true that disastrous or traumatic events are themselves paradigmatic for the source of memory—if it is true, in other words, that Levinas's witness is someone who feels the weight of the event bodily and not just intellectually or existentially—then it may be useful to think of watershed events as found in the historical or cultural record as prooftexts for a forgetful memory.

I'll examine, among other questions, how what we see (and forget) influences what we can say and write about disastrous events; what narratives of witness give us access to; and whether the priority of events to their remembrance—and their inherent susceptibility to forgetting—impoverishes or enriches a survivor's capacity to remember events or to act as an eyewitness. Taking the work of Amos Funkenstein, Pierre Vidal-Naquet, Pierre Nora and others as its point of departure, the book explores the ways in which what Maurice Blanchot calls "the immemorial" affects memory since the Holocaust, a fabric of narrative and of images several thousand years old—and punctuated by injunctions to remember—that has been profoundly affected by the destruction. But instead of seeing testimonial accounts of disasters as a record of the events that, taken one by one, can be understood as "exile," or "pogrom," or "Final Solution," I'll make the case that such accounts indicate not only a loss of life or of culture or of family, but also a site where the event is replaced by a representation that bears a vexed relation to the event itself. I want to take up Yerushalmi's challenge to explore how the current, post-Holocaust generation sees the "uses of forgetting" found in sacred and secular literature, legal writing, and memorial, testimonial, and historical writing and other media.

I intend to do so by tracing how our accounts of events, in memory, reshape not just narrative consciousness but also our view of more traditional definitions of witness, testimony, and history. Witnessing is the act of seeing as we are confronted with or involved in a set of circumstances; testimony is what we say about those events. What intervenes between these two acts—one spontaneous and the other intentional—is memory and its opposite, forgetting. What Kant suggested two hundred years ago is relevant here: the occurrence of events is presented to consciousness by translating it into already-existing concepts and categories. As this process takes place, aspects of the event that are felt bodily may be lost to reason and speech. Specifically,

I'm interested in the double process of retrieval and loss—memory and for-getting—that lies at the crux *between* witness and testimony. Representations of what has been seen by witnesses are problematic not only because the wit-nesses has trouble finding the words to render the experience; they are prob-lematic also because in the process of witnessing and testifying they exchange the event-as-memory for consciousness of the event, the event-as-knowledge. In the process of remembering the event for history, the witness elides aspects of the event that aren't available as testimony or as representation, aspects that—for the reader or second-hand witness—may well be overlooked.

In an essay originally published as a review of Yerushalmi's *Zakhor*, Pierre Vidal-Naquet notes that "In Hebrew, 'zakhor' signifies 'remember.' In the Jewish tradition, remembering is a duty for those who are Jewish: 'If I forget thee, O Jerusalem . . .' What exactly must be remembered?" (58). He links Yerushalmi's book to Aharon Megged's novella *Yad Vashem*, explaining that the novel is in part about the conundrum of understanding the relation of the family's history in eastern Europe while insisting on a place in Eretz Israel. The couple's immediate problem is finding a name for their child that places him at once in Israel and nonetheless doesn't offend a grandfather who is a refugee from eastern Europe. The problem of remembering, suggests Vidal-Naquet, is the problem of the object of remembrance and the name: *yad vashem*, the monument and the name. While we attach names to objects, and see objects as mnemonics for that which is irrevocably lost—like the six mil-lion in Europe, or, in the case of Megged's grandfather, the connection to a decimated Ashkenazi culture—what has been lost and what is absent exerts a terrible pressure upon both monument and name, and insinuates itself between the two. "What exactly must be remembered?" Vidal-Naquet answers: "Aharon Megged's novella clearly shows that one can choose between memories," though the conundrum of Yerushalmi's thesis about memory and its connection to the break or rupture is that we may, in fact, not be able to choose at all; the choice comes, unbidden and out of our direct control. If there's any clearer indication of this, it's Vidal-Naquet's implicit connection of Yerushalmi and Proust, and his call for an integration of his-tory and memory that does not draw strict lines of demarcation between them. And both men, the historian and the novelist, are in the end writers: our challenge since 1945, he suggests, is of "setting memory in motion, of doing, in short, for history what Proust did for the novel. This is no easy task . . ." though in accomplishing it we understand that "writing history is also a work of art" ("The Historian and the Test of Murder" 140).

Vidal-Naquet, with the Holocaust revision industry on his mind, is con-cerned with the language of history and its tendency to reduce events to collectivities. What happens to an individual in Auschwitz, what is remembered and written as testimony, is collected together with all other such remembrances and taken as an amalgam, and we say that such and such happened in Auschwitz (or maybe more insidiously, we know that such and such happened there). Any discrepancy among the testimonies—the memories—of those who were there are taken as errors or lies by the deniers, and is used to impeach the knowledge of the atrocities: the raw material that acts as its foundation is, after all, riddled by inaccuracy, or dishonesty, or forgetfulness. The paradigm for history's flattening of memory is Thucydides' account of the "disappearance" of the Helots at the hands of the Spartans in 424 BCE. "To constitute the two thousand helots as a historical whole when each helot had his own life and his own death, one obviously must construct the set 'helots.' To us, this would seem to go without saying; it would seem to be, as one says, 'obvious,' but in reality it is not so, any more or any less than the set 'Jews' or the set 'National Socialist Germany'" ("The Holocaust's Challenge to History" 144). The construction of the set by history doesn't allow any language at all to indicate the experiences of the individuals. There is no room, in other words, in a collective memory that would stand in for history for individual memory (anamnesis) to intrude or interrupt the narrative. Certainly the reality of the individual experiences do intrude upon Thudydides' text, as Vidal-Naquet tells us by pointing attention to the word "each" as it refers to the helots: "shortly thereafter, they were made to disappear, and no one knew in what manner each of them had been eliminated" (Thucydides, IV: 80, 1–4; cited in *Assassins of Memory* 100). The attempt by the historian to write a memory that eliminates the individual memory, what at memory's foundation is lost (the manner of death and the quality of suffering), is foiled by language's uncanny ability to register just that absence.

But Vidal-Naquet worries that this isn't enough in the face of efforts by the denial industry to foreground the narrative over the silence of the victims. And so he points approvingly to Claude Lanzmann's *Shoah*, a film that foregrounds the individual, forgetful memory. In fact, if anything Lanzmann's film puts the narrative of the Shoah—the language and images we now take for knowledge, and have as a storehouse of collective memory—entirely in the background; Vidal-Naquet sees *Shoah* as something almost mad: it is "a historical work where memory alone, a memory of today, is called upon to bear witness" ("Holocaust's Challenge" 150). Lanzmann's film is an instance whereby those who saw and experienced the atrocities are given an opportunity to recall those events and to have a chance to speak precociously: to produce a language that is at once both a presentation of the object of memory, and which is at the same time a presentation of the object's loss and of that loss's effect upon the witness. The film is admirable because it places together, in an almost jarring fashion, *yad vashem*, the monument and the name— Simon Srebnik in peaceful fields outside Chelmno, fields where forty years earlier he exhumed and burned bodies; Simon Prodchlebnik nonchalantly telling Lanzmann that the trucks that were used to gas members of his town are very like those that deliver cigarettes to stores in his current hometown of Tel Aviv. Between mneme, the narrative of the Holocaust that we and the witnesses have clearly at their disposal as collective memory, and anamnesis, the flash of recall sparked by a name or a smell or sight, comes the disaster: a memory that is not a representation but a moment of seeing without knowing, a moment perhaps of witness, but a moment that annihilates both past and present and creates, instead, a presence that can only be made available for the viewer of the film, or the reader of testimony, through a speaking or writing that is precocious, out of control, and utterly troubling. Lanzmann has made a film that manages to "search for time lost as at once time lost and time rediscovered." He finds memory "[b]etween time lost and time rediscovered," and he finds it there as "the work of art" (150). For Vidal-Naquet, *Shoah* is a work of memory precisely because it navigates between yad vashem, the monument and the name, mneme and anamnesis, and understands that what lies between them is a void of memory, the destroyer of history, and the language that gives them all a palpable presence.

Vidal-Naquet sees the cause for this absence or forgetting in the intransigence of events, an intransigence that is different from the durability or presence of objects, things. It is an intransigence that exerts itself upon narratives that try to flatten them into collective memory, or render them as things: The Holocaust, The Diaspora, Auschwitz. "A historical discourse is a web of explanations that may give way to an 'other explanation' if the latter is deemed to account for" the heterogenousness of events in a more satisfactory manner (*Assassins of Memory* 97). It is the unreasonableness of events, their inability to fit paradigms, that is so damnably hard to account for in historical writing; and it is this unreasonableness—the apparent contradiction of an event's presence in memory and its simultaneous disappearance into an "irreducible opaqueness"—that compels writing. And it is writing (of a certain sort) that is best suited to rendering this opaqueness, memory and its converse. "The historian writes; he conjures up a place and time, but he himself is situated in a place and time, at the center of a nation, for example, which entails the elimination of other nations. As a writer, he has depended at length solely on written texts, which has simultaneously entailed the elimination of oral or gestural manifestations, the booty of anthropologists" (*Assassins of Memory* 110). But if the historian doesn't recognize that "oral and gestural manifestations," as well as the storehouse of rhetorical figure, are elements of the real, then we lose the connection with "what might be called, for lack of a better term, reality," and we are immersed then "in discourse, but such discourse would no longer be historical" (111). I'd go further, and suggest that unless a historian recognizes the demands of reality as well as the demands of writing, he is certainly writing historically but he is not accounting for memory. This, after all, was what *Shoah* did most notably: it insisted upon the place and the name—mneme, the discourse of "The Holocaust," and anamnesis, the flash of that which is absent—and allowed the two, together, to produce a memory in the viewer and the witness both.

David Krell explains that when one writes, one is "always writing on the verge of both remembrance and oblivion" (1). He goes on to wonder "whether writing is a metaphor for memory or memory a metaphor for writing" (4), and suggests that in the end untangling the relationship of memory and forgetfulness will require an understanding of writing, and how our understanding of it was influenced by the Greeks. Writing on the verge of memory and forgetfulness is not unlike Blanchot's thesis that "to write . . . is to be in relation, through words and their absence, with what one cannot remember" (121); and it is not unlike Aristotle's question, "How then does one remember what is not present? For this would imply that one could also see and hear what is not present" (450b 19). For Aristotle the question was how the feeling of memory was related to the object that called the feeling to mind if the object were forever lost; for Blanchot the question is how that feeling may be made palpable to the witness if not through a kind of writing or inscription. It was Aristotle who most plainly made the distinction between mneme and anamnesis, memory and recollection, where memory is the making present of something absent, while recollection is a type of kinesis or movement, a motion or animation in which what is absent becomes suddenly present but as process. "For recollection is the inherence of the power of presencings [or the presence within of the power that stimulates changes]. And this in such a way that the man is moved of himself and because of the motions that he has" (452a 10). The point, again, is that memory in this sense doesn't make the object or event present but—at best—brings events that are lost in time to a present time, but the events are not made present as such but as movement. The person brought to memory does not experience the presence of an object or event—as if it were possible to relive the experiences of Auschwitz, or the privations of the ghetto, or the horribly uncomfortable feeling as you listen to your parents' stories again and again—but is brought to a nexus, a juncture comprised not by a convergence of objects or events but a concavity of experience, a void. In Krell's terms, "*kinesis* . . . here means a gradual or perhaps quite sudden coming-to-presence or self-showing of an absent being that till now was also absent from memory" and what occurs is a "nexus or node—the origins of what Dilthey, Heidegger, and Merleau-Ponty will much later call the *Zusammenhang des Lebens*, the 'holding together' or cohesion of life" (19).

Anamnesis as distinct from mneme, then, is the creation of a nexus or crux through movement; memory as making present is here supplemented by a memory as absence or forgetting, a sense that what is not present is what in fact makes memory possible. For Aristotle, to have motion one must also have a starting point, an *arche*. This origin isn't found at the beginning as one would expect—as the origin of history, we presume, comes at the point where writing begins—but in the middle (452a 17). The origin of movement, of memories, is more like the midpoint of an amalgam of points, what Krell calls a *"ruling center* of a particular constellation of memories." "Aristotle intends to describe in kinesis not a linear movement from starting-point to end-point, like strings on a pearl or the events of a narrative, but a kind of back-and-forth movement from ruling center to adjacent, contiguous memories" in multidimensional space (Krell 19). It is a constellation organized by habit—by knowledge—but the movement itself is ungoverned by order. The move-ment—the absent origin, absent source of memory—is like the kernel that troubles the shell, like the event that haunts the survivor or the witness and compels her to testify and to speak in a language that is only partly, if at all, under her control. The flash of recollection, anamnesis, is not the making present of the event, then, but an incessant movement, a compulsion to speak. But "what do we remember?" What we remember is not the event itself; instead we bring to mind a sense that among all the knowledges we have at our disposal and through which we've ordered what we call our lives there is a crux, a void, that risks throwing all this order into disarray. That sense risks rendering the distinctions we've made between events that occur at different times—at different points in history, or at different stages of a nar-rative we've cobbled together to call collective memory—undistinguishable. But it is also has the potential effect of making out of all this disorder a kind of disastrous wholeness, a sense that "life is from hence permeated by an uncanny and thoroughly disruptive unity" (Krell 21). The point of origin—the lost memory—is the origin of writing as well.

But the most effective writing-as-memory, writing on the verge of memory and oblivion, is writing that is plainly indicative. Aristotle, won-dering about the same thing Vidal-Naquet does ("what is it that we remem-ber?"), asks:

> Does one remember the pathos or that from which the pathos came to be? . . . If pathos is like an imprint or a trace in us, why should the percep-tion of this very thing be the memory of something else and not simply of itself? (450b 11ff.)

The answer lies partly in the action of anamnesis—the action of the soul in memory "inscribes a kind of imprint of what is perceived" (450a 30)—which is seen as a kind of inscription or imprint, but not the kind normally associated with writing. Memory both is and is not a representation; it pre-sents (*darstellung*) what cannot be represented (*vorstellung*). But the answer also lies partly in seeing writing as, in Blanchot's terms, the disaster, that action of language that brings to mind the event's other, what precedes even our knowledge of the event.

The question of how fully a state of affairs can be rendered discursively is especially pressing in the case of historical discourse, in which the veracity or coherence of eyewitness testimony is one of the pillars on which the historical reality or truth of events rests. But while testimony may serve as evidence, it is not necessarily the best indication of the nature of events. Inherent in Holocaust testimonies, like other testimonies of trauma, are the "anguished memories" that make themselves apparent in survivor's attempts to write the disaster of their experiences during the events of the war. Lawrence Langer's point, in *Holocaust Testimonies*, is that the distance between what has been witnessed and what can be committed to testimony— what was seen and what can be said—is often wide and always palpable: not only in the witness's statements but in the shrugged shoulders, the winces, the tears, and the silences that punctuate the oral testimonies and that are aestheticized but not domesticated in the written language of figure. On extrinsic criteria, the worth of a discourse, regardless of its ability to produce knowledge or to accurately record an event, can always be called into question if we can impeach the character or the veracity of a speaker who cannot tell us precisely what happened in terms we can recognize. How could what they say be possible, we might ask? On intrinsic criteria, a testimony would have to agree with or at least corroborate a good deal of other eyewitness testimony of the Holocaust in order to tell a certain truth. It would have to represent a reality to which other witnesses have testified and which is internally coherent. (See Carlo Ginzburg's and Martin Jay's essays on the problems of verifiability of witnesses in the case of disasters like the Shoah.) Holocaust testimony is often both extrinsically incredible (the events to which the witness testifies seem impossible, unreal) and intrinsically incoherent (exhibiting gaps, silences, and disjunctions).

On an "indicative" criterion, what matters is a written account's ability to make readers "see" an issue or an event that exceeds language's ability to narrate it. In terms of kairos, rather than providing the criteria that would secure appropriate reactions from an audience based upon the constraints of time and place in which they find themselves, such a discourse would explode time and place, and indicate what Dale Sullivan calls a "fullness of time" that lies beyond any definable historical situation. An "indicative" (or "epideictic") criterion can be found in the Platonic corpus: there writing is granted the ability to indicate (though perhaps not produce) knowledge, and to the extent that it manages to indicate what lies beyond the contingencies of the world the speaker may be considered of better or worse character. In *Phaedrus* and *Gorgias*, Plato suggests that language leads speaker and listener to Truth by indicating rather than by producing it. Socrates' second speech on love (*Phaedrus* 244a–257b) figurally represents the cosmology whereby an investment in love and beauty brings souls closer to their point of origin; it does not produce knowledge of that cosmology. But the figural effect of the speech—as well as the object of representation itself, a mnemonic whereby the soul is perfected as it glimpses an object that reminds it of its former perfection—indicates what lies beyond the contingencies of the world (where, in the *Gorgias* [469b–c], Socrates imagines the possibility of a state of affairs in which he may neither do nor suffer harm). The relation between truth as content and what lies beyond truth—what might be called, in psychoanalytic terms, the "real"— is the matter at issue in the debate, late in the *Phaedrus*, on the value of writing. When, in Socrates' retelling of the myth of the origins of writing, Ammon charges writing not as a drug for memory, but for reminding (275a), he is making a claim similar to the one Socrates makes in his second speech on love about the perfection of the soul: that in seeing the beauty of the lover, the soul is reminded of its origin in perfection and is compelled to return there (249b–e). Writing cannot bring the object of knowledge to the reader, any more than the lover can bring about the perfection of the soul. But writing does (in Socrates' words) *remind* the reader of it, though it does not represent the object. In fact, the conundrum for Plato's Socrates is whether rhetoric produces truth or an image of truth, and most readers of the *Phaedrus* suggest that the best it can do is the latter. What writing, and ideally rhetoric, can do, however, is indicate that which is "really written in the soul" (278a), what lies at the source of language—what lies at its point of origin but to which language does not provide unfettered access.

It is precisely this relation between language and the events that precede or lie outside it—between writing and the disaster—that occupies Blanchot's attention in *The Writing of the Disaster*. There Blanchot makes clear that experience is a state of being that requires knowledge. The occurrence of the event in which a person is implicated and sees herself as such *precedes* experience. It is immediate: "not only [does it] rule out all mediation; it is the infiniteness of a presence such that it can no longer be spoken of" (24). In the occurrence of the event, the individual is "expose[d] to unity": in order to render the occurrence as an experience at all—in order for the occurrence to be seen as an event—the individual becomes defined as a subject. She becomes an "I" over against which the event can also be identified, given attributes, and finally named. At the moment the individual recognizes the occurrence of the event as an experience, and herself as the subject of experience, the event "falls in its turn outside being" (24). Experiences, recognized by the witness and named, are nonetheless haunted by their status as events, and "the names [are] ravaged by the absence that preceded them"— the event now lost to memory except as a name—and "seem remainders, each one, of another language, both disappeared and never yet pronounced, a language we cannot even attempt to restore without reintroducing these names back into the world" (58).

There is a bodily element to this kind of memory, the indicative facet of language or discourse that insinuates what precedes experience or knowledge into the narrative fabric of history or memory. Arguing against a Baudrillardian pleasure that seems inherent in a theory of indication, Edith Wyschogrod wonders whether there isn't something in memory—in the aguished winces or tears—that works against pleasure. She cites, in *The Transparency of Evil*, this passage:

> Auschwitz and the final solution simply cannot be expiated. Punishment and crime have no common measure here, and the unrealistic character of the punishment ensures the unreality of the facts. What we are currently experiencing is something else entirely . . . a transmission from a historical stage into a mythical stage: the mythic—and media led reconstruction of these events. (92)

There is, apparently, no way to see, as Vidal-Naquet wishes to, the intransigence of the real beyond the proliferation of discourse.

But if we see the real as precisely those gaps or breaks in testimony—in the kinesis of memory, the precociousness of speech that seems to work its way out of the mouths of the witnesses in spite of their desire to flatten the narrative and simply "say what they saw"—then a language of indication doesn't "go all the way down" in Rorty's terms but in fact stops at the crux of memory which in very real terms involves suffering. Inasmuch as Roskies' ghetto poets, Lanzmann's survivors, and the key-bearing Moroccans who may or may not carry with them a palpable reminder of loss all make memory present with a sign, it is evidence of, in Aristotle's terms, a potentially painful "movement of himself," or in Plato's of what is "truly written on the soul." It is evidence of "*bodily pain*," which "*is the limiting condition of the hyperreal*" (Wyschogrod 180; original italics).

Caruth's point in "Unclaimed Experience" and in her book of the same title is that history and trauma bear an indissoluble connection with one another. We consider history as that which can be preserved as a memory and written, but the event that serves as the object of history, that which happens, is erased or blotted out. Blanchot's argument about the "immemorial" nature of the disaster suggests that once an experience occurs, it is forever lost; it is at this point—"upon losing what we have to say" (Blanchot 21), the point of forgetfulness—that writing begins. Forgetfulness is the source of memory. The "victim of [trauma] was never fully conscious during the [event] itself: the person gets away, Freud says, 'apparently unharmed'" (Caruth 187). The witness saw, but *only* saw, the deed or the circumstance that presented itself as trauma; the traumatic circumstance was never fully known—and hence could not be remembered—at all, and what follows is a profusion of language. What we read in survivor testimonies is the displacement of the traumatic event—the historical event, lost to memory—by the language of the testimony, the sometimes broken, sometimes contradictory stories of the camps, or of hiding, or of the aftermath. But it is a language that is disrupted by that event, the language of repetition, in which the event is narrated over and over again but in language that may not be obviously associated with the event at all. "When a discourse *holds* in some way, it is . . . because it has been opened upon the basis of some traumatizing event, by an upsetting question that does not let one rest . . . and because it nevertheless resists the destruction begun by its traumatism" (Derrida, *Passages* 381; original italics). Re-membering is a sense of what has been dismembered, that which is not whole, which doesn't obey the rules of logic or knowledge, and what is not fully present.

This truly is a forgetful memory, in which the making present of what is irretrievably past acknowledges that absence. Speaking of Augustine, who—in the *Confessions* (X 16–26)—is at pains to understand how to remember forgetfulness, Edith Wyschogrod writes that "forgetfulness appears to be more than a mere privation of the being of memory but takes on a density of its own" (186). The problem this presents for Augustine is that it gives to absence—oblivion—a palpable presence. Augustine recognizes that "forgetting is an absence of objects which once may have been present. Augustine can then hope that some remnant of a particular absent object will show itself. Failing such an appearance, there is only oblivion" (187). But it is possible to see that absence as being indicated by a sign which is itself a trace of what is missing. That is, what Augustine had not quite been able to theorize (oddly enough, given his predisposition to neoplatonism) is an indicative writing that created a space not for oblivion (pure negativity) but for a fullness that is marked as absence. Like trauma, oblivion might better be seen as an *arche*-event that was never fully present and, as void, has been repressed and transformed into a symptom (see Wyschogrod apropos Lacan, 188). The source of memory is lost and breaches speech; it is not language but is lodged within language, as oblivion is lodged within language and made present through it. Breaching speech is only possible through the trace, the "arche-phenomenon of memory" in Derrida's terms, without which there could be no writing at all. The trace is "the non-presence of the other inscribed within the sense of the present" (*Of Grammatology* 70–71), a collapse of space and time into itself, creating a space, a void. Indicative writing, a writing that indicates memory as the break, is a kind of incision, a commingling of inside and outside that is written on the heart as much as (in *Phaedrus*) one's soul: "I will put my law, [the Torah] within them and I will write it on their hearts" (Jeremiah 31:33)

The source of memory is a crux (in Merleau-Ponty, *creux*) that "has everything to do with memory: *se creuser la tete* means to make a great effort to recall something" (Krell 93). In *The Visible and the Invisible*, Merleau-Ponty writes that the crux "is a pit or hollow that opens of itself in the otherwise too solid flesh of the world, a concavity that allows there to be visibility" (193). But it is also "a certain interiority, a certain absence, a negativity that is not nothing" in a palpable embodiment of ideas. Merleau-Ponty is attempting to describe, perhaps no better than Augustine and Plato but certainly no worse, the bodily, almost painful sense that comes with the unbidden memory, a sense that there is something—the opacity of the event—that language indicates but whose source is maddenly difficult if not impossible to locate in time and space. The true problem of memory is

> how at each instant [consciousness's] former epxeriences are present to it in the form of a horizon which it is able to reopen, if it takes that horizon as its theme, in an act of reminiscence, but which it can also leave "at the margins." . . . To remember is not to restore under the gaze of consciousness a tableau of the self-subsistent past; it is to ensconce oneself on the horizon of the past and to unfold little by little the perspectives contained there until the experiences bounded by that horizon are, as it were, lived anew in their temporal place. (*Phenomenology of Perception* 30)

Memory involves a collapse of time, and involves a bodily "attempt to reopen time, starting from the implication of the present, and only in the body, being our only permanent means of 'adopting a stance'" (*Phenomenology of Perception* 211). Like Aristotle's kinesis, and Plato's indication, memory here involves a midpoint between representing fully a presence of the event in its cultural or collective sense (mneme) and the flashing forth in the present that which is altogether lost (anamnesis), a shuttling back and forth that produces and is related to bodily pain, and that indicates a sense of profound and traumatic loss. Memory as crux is both a presence and an absence that limits being and is its guarantor (Krell 95).

What all of this suggests is that we should give up on the idea of memory as a kind of representation. Instead, we should see memory as an intersection of remembrance and oblivion, a troublesome presence that is forgotten but guaranteed by the event's loss. Memory truly is on the verge: the past can make itself bear painfully upon the present but it can't be brought into the present in representation, or mimetically. What this means is that the only vehicle for memory is the body, as it is inscribed by the event and calls for its inscription—its indication—but that doesn't quite have the tools for it. Memory is indexical insofar as it is a convergence of collected, collective memories, and of histories, that provide a way to know a memory's *environs*, but it is indexical in that it allows you to read only that which is concealed by its own shorthand, in its breathlessness. We should think of memory as a kind of writing, in that events may be indicated rather than recollected, indicated from one body onto another.

TWO

Ethics, the Immemorial, and Writing

Saying . . . is a way of signifying prior to any experience. It is pure witnessing.

—Levinas, "God and Philosophy"

Reality is not a matter of the absolute eyewitness, but a matter of the future.

—Lyotard, *The Differend*

Thought cannot welcome that which it bears within itself and which sustains it, except by forgetting.

—Blanchot, *The Writing of the Disaster*

Names . . . seem remainders, each one, of another language, both disappeared and never yet pronounced, a language we cannot even attempt to restore without reintroducing these names back into the world, or exalting them to some higher world of which in their external, clandestine solitude, they could only be the irregular interruption, the invisible retreat.

—Blanchot

IN THE FRONT MATTER of Emmanuel Levinas's most mature philosophical work (*Otherwise than Being*, hereafter abbreviated *OTB*), the reader will find a dedication to the memory of the six million victims of the Holocaust, and to the six members of his family who remained in Lithuania during the war and were killed either by the Nazi *Einsatzgruppen* who followed the Wehrmacht during the invasion of the Soviet Union or by pro-Nazi Lithuanian antisemites. This shouldn't be surprising, since Levinas refers to the Holocaust in his writing fairly frequently, at times obliquely and at other times—particularly in his essays on Judaism and on history (the work collected in *Difficult Freedom* and the book *In the Time of the Nations*)—more explicitly. In all his work, the Holocaust seems to press on Levinas as a memory, as a trace of what has receded irrecuperably into the past. In "Signature," the essay that closes *Difficult Freedom*, he writes that his biography "is dominated by the presentiment and the memory of the Nazi horror" (291). To cite just two examples, the essay that concludes *Proper Names* functions as an extended metaphor of the conditions that led to the annihilation of European Jews in the name of *Volksgemeinschaft*; and "The Name of a Dog; or, Natural Rights" (in *Difficult Freedom*) is a recollection of Levinas's internment in camp 1492, in which his nameless condition—in which he was "stripped . . . of [his] human skin" (153)—was paradigmatic of the anonymity of the subject. The connection between the ethics established in Levinas's writing and the Holocaust has been well established by writers such as Colin Davis, Jacob Meskin, and Robert Eaglestone, among others.

My point in this chapter, however, is not to join those who wish to connect Levinas's philosophy to the Holocaust. Instead it is to make clear how Levinas's notion of ethics is inextricably linked to a notion of the *memory*—or perhaps more specifically, of the tension between memory and *forgetting*—tied to the disaster of the Holocaust. I'll argue that Levinas establishes a theory of *post-Holocaust memory*, though it's a forgetful memory, that works through writing oriented toward a future rather than toward the irrecuperable, immemorial event. Levinas juxtaposes memory as *mneme* and memory as *anamnesis*—of memory as a fullness of time and memory as a rupture of time—and the result is that mneme and anamnesis fall "out of phase with one another," yielding a trace or an excess of memory.

I also want to examine the relation between Levinas's writing on memory in *Otherwise than Being* and some of his other work, and among that work and Blanchot's *The Writing of the Disaster* and Lyotard's *The Differend*—both works whose point of departure is the Shoah and which take as their founding question the possibility of remembering or witnessing the events that comprise it—to lay out a theory of memory for a post-Holocaust ethics, a theory that begins with the impasse between knowledge and non-knowledge, and the surplus of knowledge (knowledge's trace) that is produced in that impasse. While Levinas himself doesn't work out a theory of memory as such in this work or any other, it's there nonetheless. Understanding his idea of memory is crucial for any analysis of his work on ethics, particularly a post-Holocaust ethics. Essentially, Levinas juxtaposes a memory based in historical understanding—in the sweep of collective "saids" or narrative accounts that become regularized and taken for the event itself in the event's wake—with a moment of saying in which the witness sees the event prior to experiencing the event as an event, prior to his ability to know it as an event at all.

It is a juxtaposition of memory as mneme, and memory as anamnesis—of memory as a fulness of time and memory as a rupture of time—in which the two fall "out of phase with one another." In that moment—the moment in which the memory and the event are dissociated—the witness is forced into language, forced to speak a memory that isn't a memory at all, and produces not so much an account of events, a testimony, as an account of the rupture of language and the void of memory. Speaking doesn't provide an account of past events; it provides a glimpse of the destruction of memory. What is important in the witness's testimony is not the account of the event but the moment that compels it, a moment that is both radically open and oriented to the future and doomed to foreclosure in the utterance that follows. What Levinas offers is an idea of memory in which the moment of saying—of the event prior to knowledge and immemorial—compels human activity and discourse and founds ethics.

IN MEMORIAM

Memory after Auschwitz weighs heavily on Levinas in the dedication page of *Otherwise than Being* (see, for three examples, Trezise 358; Eaglestone, Holocaust 254; Herzog 342–3). The two dedications that appear there, related in their scope but very different in their language and their willingness to name individuals, indicate *two* memories, two ways of remembering. Between these two dedications is a trace of memory, a notion that is integral to the task of living—and of bearing witness—after the Holocaust. I want to spend some time with these dedications, because it seems to me they mark, in palimpsest, the relation between naming, post-Holocaust memory, and ethics that is foundational to Levinas.

The first dedication, which appears at the top of the page in French (and translated into English in the book's American edition), reads as follows: "To the memory of those who were closest among the six million assassinated by the National Socialists, and of the millions on millions of all confessions and all nations, victims of the same hatred of the other man, the same anti-semitism" (v). The second, which appears at the bottom of the page, is in Hebrew, and is untranslated. It begins with the word for the imperative to remember, *l'zachor*, and reads in part "To the memory of the spirit of my father, Yehiel, son of Avraham Halevi, my mother Devorah, daughter of Moshe," goes on to name his two brothers and his wife's mother and father, and ends with the abbreviation—found on many tombstones in Jewish cemeteries—that stands for the imprecation "May their souls be bound up in the bond of eternal life." Those closest to Levinas, members of his family, are named only in the second dedication, and then only in Hebrew. And the two dedications also reflect distinct traditions—one European and secular, one Jewish and religious—and thus two distinct manners of saying: one that is comfortable with the well-worn terms "six million," "hatred," "National Socialists," "anti-semitism," and another that refuses the political in favor of the *heimish*, a manner of speaking that is as intimate as a blessing in a synagogue. In these two dedications reside two distinct memories, two attempts to remember and to speak memory. Yet in neither one of them can the reader see or recall those individuals invoked by Levinas. In speaking their names in a manner that disrupts the act of naming by forcing together two languages and two traditions that do not fit neatly together, the dedications *indicate* a site of the immemorial.

In these dedications, Levinas gives a palpable presence both to the names that are substituted for the events of history and the effect of the events themselves; to what has been written and what is "antecedent to the verbal signs it conjugates, to the linguistic systems and the semantic glimmerings," a "foreword preceding languages" (*OTB* 5). The antecedent or foreword of history—as in the case of the foreword whose language precedes the text—is made present for the witness or reader, but not as knowledge. Events occur in the presence of the witness, the witness sees the events, but what happens *precedes* the witness's ability to say what happened, to transform the event into experience, and to provide a means by which to make it known to others who weren't there. Between the names through which we *know* what happened—the names of the six million, the Holocaust, or even of those individuals closest to us of blessed memory—and the event itself, is the trace, what Maurice Blanchot called "the disaster."

Derrida saw the idea of "the trace" as the single most important facet of Levinas's work, and in *On Grammatology* calls it the center of his critique of traditional philosophy (70). In "On the Trail of the Other," Levinas connects the trace to the asynchronous temporality of the other. There is, in every sign or word—in every utterance on the page or that hangs in the air between interlocutors—a trace of the moment of utterance, of "the passage of the person who left the sign" (44–5). The trace is the imprint of both the other who spoke, and of the moment of speaking, both of which are lost irrevocably and yet which are made present—but aren't "represented"—in the utterance itself. The trace is also the mark of human contact, something integral to language but which can't be boiled down to the sign. The other is nonsynchronous because its trace is fleeting and is lost before it can be known. The trace is evidence of what Levinas called "inflexions of forgotten voices" (*OTB* 26) which seem to haunt the margins of language and confound the speaker who tries desperately to recall those voices to memory. That is, the utterance and the moment of understanding the utterance are distinct both qualitatively and temporally: the moment of contact between individuals is materially real, lived, and uninterpretable, while the moment of understanding is interpretive, rational, and—at least in Derrida's reading of it—mainly textual. The trace—as apparent to the witness—is upon language and knowledge, but language and knowledge as such are already separate from it. The move from event to experience, from what happened to a recollection of what happened, involves a withdrawal—a forgetting—that compels language. It is on the loss of the event that we are compelled to say what we saw; but it is that loss that dooms language, as Levinas's "said," to failure. The disaster of the event destroys the experience that might have stopped at the word.

The otherwise than being, made evident in the trace, cannot be homogenized and recuperated by (or as) history. It is present in history, however, and it confounds both history and memory (as mneme). For Levinas, both history and memory refer to a universal past—a past both known and knowable—to which he opposes an irrecuperable moment, an anachronism (time out of time), that lies at the heart of human memory and that compels human action. He opposes, in other words, history as a repetition of the same—events call to mind other events; ritual and liturgical celebrations reenact founding moments in history—with a temporality that repeats with a difference or surplus, in which events cannot be made commensurable with the narrative accounts we produce for them or their liturgical reenactments. Their juxtaposition produces a trace that can't be converted into a category or concept and return to the self that originated them. This trace—the excess of signification, not unrelated to the real made present in Lacan's *objet petit-a*—is what troubles the speaking subject, the witness to events, and compels him to speak, though *of what* he speaks is sometimes uncertain.

The encounter with the other produces a "fecundity," in which the attempt to fuse the self with the pronominal "I" through which it would speak itself fails, and whose byproduct is the nagging sense that there's something left to be said. In *Totality and Infinity* (227–85), Levinas likens the surplus produced through otherness to an offering, as a child is the offering of a father. It offers both a continuity of the self living into the future, and a radical discontinuity (in that it will continue as an entity entirely separate from its point of origin). Like the discontinuity of fecundity, in which the self can never return to its point of origin, so the memory of an event can never recover the event. Human action, whether we want it to or not, always plunges us farther into a future that simply can't be foreseen. Memory (the "lost time" of Proust's title) is just such a discontinuity, a positive relation to the infinity of the future, something that enables what Susan Handelman calls a "*nonnostalgic*, nonfated, nonmythical relation to the past" (207), one that offers the *possibility*—though certainly no guarantee—of redemption (see *Totality and Infinity* 282–3). The excess produced through fecundity is both related (through an unlocatable origin) and unrelated (because it is noncoincident with that origin) to the event that founds it. If we think of this excess as memory, then excess takes precedence over (and disrupts) any representation that tries to recuperate lost time. The surplus of memory acts upon the past, and provides the potentially redemptive moment by opening up time and compelling action (see *Totality and Infinity* 284–5). The production of fecundity works against a repetition of the same, the handing down of tradition through collective memory and establishes instead a discursive orientation to the other that produces language that is perhaps only tangentially related to the past as remembered collectively. The trace, in other words, requires a turn to ethics because it is this gesture (the non-word that indicates both the encounter with the other and its orientation to the future) that compels speech.

But the moment that compels and precedes writing—the event lost to memory—is available through writing itself *as experience*. Memory dispatches the nuance of what happened to the margins of the narrative that we fix on to recover it, and whatever path we take to try to be mindful of the event is deflected by the name we give it. It is to—*toward*—the memory of the six million that the names of the dead proceed; but the traces of the lives of Yehiel son of Avraham Halevi and the others whose names are recited in the dedication of the book cannot be recuperated except as they disturb our determined effort to (perhaps too easily) equate these dead with the memories of our own. The failure of the attempt to name them in order to capture the traces of the lives disturbs the narrative and the names themselves, and Yehiel ben Avraham Halevi forces us to realize that those closest among the six million renders "the six million" impossible to recall.

The event's relation to the experience is intimately tied to the vexed relation of saying and said, and to the fraught relation between mneme and anamnesis. In *Otherwise than Being*, Levinas turns his attention from the idea of the trace to how the trace is made evident in language: in the saying and the said (*le dire et le dit*). While the two categories reflect different aspects of being, they are coincident in at least this way: saying is only available in the said. Susan Handelman calls saying

> a "language before language," prior to ontology, "origin," and representation, an-archic—and so unknowable, or prior to all philosophical consciousness. But this "saying" necessarily shows and "betrays itself" in the "said"—the realm of language as the set of signs which doubles being, which re-presents, synchronizes, names, designates, and which "consciousness" grasps, manipulates, thematizes, brings to light, remembers, and in which we discuss and define this "saying." (233)

Any utterance that purports to convey a sense of what happened—that speaks a memory—both makes present its narrative and undoes that narrative by betraying what can't be said. Even the simplest discursive operation, in which we liken a word to a synonymous word—or even a word to itself (as in Levinas's description of substitution, in which "A is A," reveals a nonidentity)—brings to the surface an element of the event, of the real, that falls out of the equation and returns to haunt it (see *OTB* 114). The closest among the six million and those who are named in loving memory unsay one another; the French dedication to memory and the Hebrew recitation of the names of the dead can't be made equal. Their juxtaposition produces an element of memory, the "inflexions of forgotten voices" (Levinas 26), that can't be contained in either. This juxtaposition is potentially horrifying. These voices, as they come unbidden, can be heard in the relation—the crux—between saying and said, and are suspended between memory as recollection (mneme) and memory as the fleeting but ungraspable image (anamnesis).

To say that the incommensurability of the event and the name, the saying and the said, is potentially horrifying is to recognize the bodily effect of Levinas's notion of ethics, and the palpable weight of the responsibility that comes with the obligation to speak. What lies beyond Being, for Levinas, isn't some transcendent state of elevation; quite to the contrary, the excess that results from the noncoincidence of being—through language—imprints itself on the body as pain, aging, suffering, and trauma. The moment of saying, in which the subject, painfully aware that what she says can't be made coincident with what she sees or with what has happened, gives way to an uncontrollable, non- (or extra-) rational speaking. It's a moment of radical exposure, in which the subject incarnates herself as a "ruin . . . of being and time" (*OTB* 9), a ruin of the essential, self-identical subject. Speaking not only ruins being, but time as well: history is no longer what happened, but the divergence of what happened from the language in which it could be made known, and it falls to ruins at the moment of saying as well (see *OTB* 108). Not only is the self exposed and wounded at the moment of saying—laid bare as noncoincident, out of phase with itself—but the event is so exposed as well. It is exposed as a material quantum, a conflation of quotidian, mundane, and innumerable bits that can't be subsumed to rationality or to knowledge but which make themselves most clearly visible in their disruption of rationality and knowledge. The moment of saying disrupts history to the extent that it throws open the moments we'd try to recollect, and forces our attention to what can't be remembered or said.

To speak memory is to bear witness. To utter the word "I" is essentially to open oneself up to another: "The word 'I' means *here I am*, answering for everything and everyone" (*OTB* 114), and the act of witnessing is something that—at least for Jews—is required in every moment. In an essay on Franz Rosenzweig, whose work influenced Levinas deeply, he calls this demand one that comes of love: what is demanded by God isn't that humans love the divine, but that humans open themselves up to one another as a demand of love: "the eminent role of the *mitzvah* in Judaism signifies not a moral formalism, but the living presence of divine love that is eternally renewed" and renewed "*today*, even though Mount Sinai belongs in the past" (*Difficult Freedom* 191). The individual is compelled to see, to participate in the world, and

to realize that his participation compels testimony: to be involved in the
world is to become responsible for speaking for yourself and for that participation; and to speak is to make yourself present to others. Saying what you've
seen—or even making yourself present by saying "here I am"—requires an
offering and the assumption of a risk: that making yourself visible ("here I
am") will bring your persecution.

THE VOICE OF THE WITNESS

Now we can turn to the related sets of terms, and take them in order:
event/experience, saying/said, and witness/testimony. Early on in *Othewise
than Being*, Levinas distinguishes between Being and interest on the one
hand, and what can't be so easily understood as being and disinterest on the
other hand, and suggests that the interest of Being is connected to "egoism,"
the understanding that the pronominal "I" and the subject herself are identical, and that in uttering the name of the first one has made herself fully present and knowable. To this sort of Being, Levinas links the conventional
understanding of memory, a memory connected to and which comprises history. It is a memory in which past events can be recuperated fully and known,
like Benjamin's moments of time strung one next to the other like pearls on
a necklace (see "Theses on the Philosophy of History" 256–7), and that presents itself in full: it is a fullness of memory "always assembled, present, in a
present that is extended, by memory and history, to the totality determined
like matter, a present without fissures or surprise" (*OTB* 5). Because there's
nothing to surprise the witness here—the historian, the reader—history is
driven by interest, by a compulsion to know that insists on the durability, the
recuperability, of the event, a durability made evident by the intransigence of
the names provided for it.

Levinas here tries to distinguish between the names that are substituted
for the events of history and the events themselves; between what has been
written what is "antecedent to the verbal signs it conjugates, to the linguistic systems and the semantic glimmerings," a "foreword preceding languages"
(5). The antecedent or foreword of history—as in the case of the book whose
language is preceded by the foreword or the preface—is palpably present and
before the witness or reader, but presents itself prior to knowledge. Events
occur in front of the eyes of the witness, the witness sees the event—it happens in front of him, to him—but what happens precedes the witness's ability to say what happened, to transform the event into experience, and to
provide a means (a "said") by which to make it known to others who weren't
there. The difference between the names through which we know what happened—the names of the six million, of the Final Solution, the Holocaust,

or even those individuals closest to us of blessed memory—and the event itself is the difference between the event, what Blanchot calls the disaster, and experience.

Blanchot puts it this way: the event as it is lived can't be understood as experience; rather, it is "already non-experience" once it has withdrawn from the "present of presence." The event, transformed as experience, produces an excess, "and affirmative though it may be, in this excess no experience occurs. . . . [T]here cannot be any experience of the disaster, even if we were to understand disaster to be the ultimate experience. This is one of its features: it impoverishes all experience, withdraws from experience all authenticity" (50–51). The disaster—the event as it occurs and imprints itself upon the witness—may imprint itself, as a trace, upon language and knowledge, but language and knowledge as such are already separate from it. The disaster—the event—withdraws authenticity from experience insofar as experience is an attempt to regularize the event, to (in Kantian terms) bring it under a concept, to make it known. "Authenticity," the trace of the event, is withdrawn, but it returns as surplus, as the fissure and the surprise, as the memory that isn't so much a recollection as it is a loss. In this sense, the move from event to experience, from what happened to a recollection of what happened, is a withdrawal—a forgetting—that compels language: "It is upon losing what we have to say that we speak—upon an imminent and immemorial disaster—just as we say nothing except insofar as we can convey in advance that we take it back, by a sort of prolepsis, not so as finally to say nothing, but so that speaking might not stop at the word" (Blanchot 21). It is on the loss of the event that we are compelled to say what we saw; but it is that loss that dooms language, as the "said," to failure. The disaster of the event destroys the experience—the language or representation through which memory is made present—that might have stopped at the word. It is this relation—what Blanchot calls the writing of the disaster, the speaking that comes on the heels of the event's loss to memory—between the saying and the said that is an important crux for memory.

But the moment that compels writing isn't negated, completely lost. The moment that compels and precedes writing—the event lost to memory; the disaster, in Blanchot's terms—is only available through the writing itself (as experience). Whatever writing results from this movement from event to experience deforms the event irrecuperably, just as history inevitably destroys the contours of the events it purports to describe, and just as memory dispatches the nuance of what happened to the margins of the narrative the we fix on to recover it; whatever path we take to try to be mindful of the event is deflected by the name we give it.

Saying is the condition of encountering the other, a location prior to discourse—a location outside of time and place, outside knowledge and experience—in which the plenitude of possible options or ways of seeing and speaking are radically open and unmanaged by (and so disruptive of) knowledge. Like Geoffrey Galt Harpham's understanding of the moment in ethics in which the subject has the array of possible choices before her and in which she knows that any choice is the foreclosure and loss of this plenitude, saying is the moment in which the subject sees plainly what lies before her but in which she is also painfully aware that any move she makes or word she utters (in "the said") names the event and in so doing destroys it.

It is at the crux between saying and said—between the events as they occur and the necessarily doomed operation involved in recuperating them in memory—that the urgent task of philosophy for Levinas becomes most clear: the need, in Handelman's terms, to continually *unsay* the said (Handelman 233). Any utterance that purports to convey a sense of what happened—that speaks a memory—both makes present its narrative and undoes that narrative by betraying what can't be said. Every utterance contains a moment of what Blanchot calls "writing," the moment that "precedes every phenomenon, every manifestation or show: all appearing" (Blanchot 11). While the actual act of inscription—putting words to paper, uttering descriptions of what one saw—inevitably omits aspects of the real, writing in Blanchot's sense, or saying in Levinas's, simultaneously "bring[s] to the surface something like absent meaning, . . . welcome[s] the passive pressure which is not yet what we call thought" (Blanchot 41), and leaves a mark or trace—an excess—of the irreducible event.

It's worth noting here—though it's something I'll examine in more detail in a later chapter—that the physical discomfort associated with saying is a kind of withdrawal. If "matter is the very locus of the for-the-other," and "the way signification shows itself before showing itself as a said in the system of synchronism" is a "giving [of] his skin" (*OTB* 77), then saying is a process of turning the self—and the materiality of the self and of the body—inside out. The feeling of being "ill at ease in one's own skin" is an "entry inwards," "not a flight into the void, but a movement into fullness, the anguish of contraction and breakup," a "recurrence by contraction" (*OTB* 108). The withdrawal that Levinas takes to be part of being—the noncoincidence of event and memory, origin and lived life—is related to our material existence, and forces us to recognize that it can't be pinned down to what we know. More to the point, withdrawal, noncoincidence, is traumatic: signification and writing—making manifest the beyond of being; saying what one has seen—is produced "not in elevated feelings, in 'belles lettres,' but as in a tearing away of bread from the mouth that tastes it, to give it to the other. Such is the coring out [denucleation] of enjoyment, in which the nucleus of the ego is cored out" (*OTB* 64). Such a "trauma theory of language" and subjectivity depends upon the exposure involved in the moment of utterance—the opening of the self, and of history, to the unforseen. It depends, in other words, upon a witness, but one "that does not thematize what it bear witnesss of, and whose truth is not the truth of representation, is not evidence" (OTB 146). Because the speaking subject—the one who says what he saw or what happened; the witness—is mired in the language to which he has access, and because the material, quotidian occurrences can't be made to coincide with that discursive material, there is a risk involved in witnessing: the risk of taking the utterance as fact, as history, or (what amounts to the same thing) as knowledge. There will always be the risk to the witness that the opening of the self for the other—that the act of witnessing—won't be returned in kind; that it will be rebuffed, or misunderstood, or go unheard altogether. There is no redemption that comes automatically with the act of witnessing; "my substitution for the other (in the first person as the unique, responsible 'I') does not constitute in any way a reciprocal demand for the other to substitute her- or himself for me" (Handelman 258). The witness runs the risk—a risk made apparent years ago by Lyotard as the "wrong" perpetrated by the deniers in France and made all the more palpable and urgent by the likes of Ernst Zundel in Canada and the Institute for Historical Review in the United States—that either the word will be taken for the event or what she says of the event will be taken as a lie and as an opportunity for persecution (see OTB 126). This makes the act of witnessing all the more traumatic: not only has the witness seen what she's seen, and not only does she admit to a physical discomfort—an illness of ease inside her own skin—in saying what she saw knowing full well that what she says may be ignored; it is also quite possible that she'll also be persecuted for what she has to say, that it will be taken for a lie, or for bad faith, by people who are themselves shaken by the utterance, the act of witness, by the excessive nature of the "inflexions and forgotten voices," their fissures and surprises.

But the witness doesn't have a choice. "Saying opens me to the other, but in this sign, it signifies the very donation of the sign. . . . This is a saying bearing witness to the other of the infinite. . . . It is pure witnessing, a way of signifying prior to any experience" ("God and Philosophy" 74). While here Levinas is talking about God, he describes the act of witnessing more broadly as approximating the incomprehensible, as a language that exceeds its ability to make clear the object of discourse. But the

> witness is not reducible to the relation that leads from an index to the indicated. That would make it a disclosure and a thematization. . . . It is [, rather,] the meaning of language, before language scatters into words, into themes equal to the words and dissimulating in the said the openness of the saying exposed like a bleeding wound. But the trace of the witness given, the sincerity of glory, is not effaced even in the said. (OTB 151).

We make a grave mistake if we think that the testimony of the witness, the index, leads a clear path to the event that she saw, the indicated. And we make an equally grave mistake if we think that the witness, by testifying to the event, has any choice in the matter, can make rational decisions about what to tell and what to omit; about how best to make clear the object or event witnessed; about whether what she says will be mistaken for the truth or will be seen as nonsense. To bear witness—to write "to the memory"—is to bring yourself as close to the event, and to the person you're speaking to, as you can (see "God and Philosophy 73). But to do this—to say "here I am" and to say what you've seen—is to force yourself into that bifurcated position (in which "A does not, as in identity, return to A, but retreats to the hither side of its point of departure"; in which "I" is "an exasperated contracting," an "identity in breaking up the limits of identity" [OTB 114]) and to produce, to write or to say, something beyond what you wanted to say, to write or speak a memory that both speaks to what you saw and indicates the event that has been lost, but which can't represent it at all. It's a witnessing that involves forgetting more than memory: it presumes

> an identity in diastasis, where coinciding is wanting. I am a self in the iden-
> tifying recurrence in which I find myself cast back to the hither side of my
> point of departure! This self is out of phase with itself, forgetful of itself, for-
> getful in biting in upon itself. . . . (OTB 115)

To witness is to forget yourself; it's being in the position of forgetting who "I" am, because to say "here I am" is to cast yourself out of phase with yourself, to make the speaking self noncoincident with its own language—with testi-mony—and with the position from which it sepeaks—the event, the "here." It becomes inevitable that testimony is the result of the act of witnessing—seeing compels speaking; but it's also inevitable that the testimony of the wit-ness will bear a trace of the moment of witnessing—the moment of saying or, in Blanchot's terms, writing—and so (potentially) foil the secondhand wit-ness's attempt to equate the saying with the said, the testimony with the event, and the memory with what happened.

MEMORY AND FORGETTING

The void of memory—memory's kernel—inheres *in* memory, like the saying that inheres in the said, and the trace of the traumatic act of witnessing—"here I am"—that inheres in testimony. The event that has been lost makes itself present in memory, though memory itself fails to represent it. And yet as soon as that which inheres in the memory makes itself present—as soon as one calls to mind the closest among the six million by name—that kernel is subsumed by representation, and the risk of conflation begins again: those named become the name; the destruction of the Shoah becomes "the Shoah." Memory functions as "a unicity that has no site, without the ideal identity a being derives from the kerygma that identifies the innumerable aspects of its manifestation, without the identity of the ego that coincides with itself, a unicity withdrawing from essence" (OTB 8). Though saying and said—forgetful memory and testimonial memory—are inherent and correlative, testimony itself takes place in time. Memory, like language, is made present in moments of lived life that are affected by it, and like language it carries with it a trace of the moment of utterance or occurrence that disrupts and disunifies the present (see Wyschogrod 146–8). Like the relation of saying to said, the forgetfulness that inheres in memory is oriented to others. As testimony, it implicates the listener, inflicts itself upon her like a trauma, and turns her inside out in much the same way as the event, as it presents itself as an experience on the one who was there, impresses itself upon the witness. What is said and offered as testimony is both memorial (as a name) and immemorial (as corrupted by language).

Each utterance carries with it what Levinas calls the "surplus of responsibility," an "incommensurability with consciousness" that "becomes a trace of the *who knows where*" (100). Through time the incommensurability of saying and said—event as seen and the recollection of the event in testimony—becomes visible, and through which the trace of the event offered to the other is produced. It "takes refuge or is exiled in its own fullness, to the point of explosion or fission, in view of its own reconstitution in the form of an identity identified in the said" (OTB 104). Testimony is a recurrence, what Levinas calls "more past than any rememberable past, any past convertible into a present" (105), a repetition of the event, but one that returns out of phase with itself. Because testimony contains a break that can't be reintegrated into the narrative utterance that attempts to represent it, "A" returns as "A," but with a difference. To say "this happened," to speak a memory of what occurred, is to bring your listener's attention to the utterance rather than the event it indicates, and to its discursive order or pattern (or lack of it) rather than to the event that resides behind it.

So memory offers itself, not as a representation, but as echo. It functions as "a torsion and a restlessness, irreducible to the function of the oneself" that would rather not remember aspects of a past that can't be reduced to narrative. It is as though the atomic unity of the subject were exposed outside by ". . . continually splitting up" (107). The writing of testimony, as torsion, involves both risk and, inevitably, loss. It involves risk because the others, the individuals, to whom you offer it will inevitably misunderstand it; and it involves loss because the moment you commit the event to testimony, aspects of the event are lost to discourse. This is partly what Levinas means when he says that to testify—to act as a witness and to speak memory—is a sacrifice, an "uncovering itself, that is, denuding itself of its skin, sensibility on the surface of the skin, at the edge of the nerves, offering itself even in suffering" (OTB 15). Finally, speaking memory is a tremendous responsibility. To say "here I am" (*hineni*), to offer the occurrence as it makes itself apparent to the witness, is to "divest [him]self, under the traumatic effect of persecution, of [his] freedom as a constituted, willful, imperialist subject" (*OTB* 112); it is to be responsible for what happens as the result of the testimony, and that result is often not a happy one.

How, then, does this harrowing account of memory-as-immemorial, and the risks associated with it, function in relation to an ethics, let alone a post-Holocaust ethics? Levinas tries to answer this question in a section of *Otherwise than Being* entitled "Questioning and Being: Time and Reminiscence." Here he goes some way to suggesting how the risks of testimony and the failure inherent in memory might be seen as the beginnings of moving "to the memory" of those closest among the six million. It is here where he most clearly indicates the stakes involved in replacing ontology with ethics as first philosophy. Without describing the position of the observer and taking seriously how that position impinges upon what she is able to say or see, "inflexions of forgotten voices resound" but the philosopher either doesn't hear them, or mistakes them for noise. But what are these forgotten voices, and where do they come from? And do those voices belong to those of blessed memory, those who, among the six million, are close enough to be heard either as traces or as audible expressions of an immemorial past that makes itself apparent when we'd rather it did not? If nothing else, Levinas suggests here that the "dispersion of duration" (27), the scattered moments that comprise our experience but that precede its organization as experience, is itself comprised of past acts, past events, some of them mundane and some of them—in Edith Wyschogrod's terms, heterogenous—resistant to knowledge, and intransigent to ordering logic. Those heterogenous moments, resistant to memory, open up and present the opportunity for memory (and, in Wyschogrod's formulation, the historian) to speak. What happens, and what one sees happen, becomes dispersed, and lost to memory while—in spite of ourselves—we strive to remember.

For Levinas (as for Wyschogrod), the paradigmatic utterance of the witness—"hineni" ("here I am")—works against memory-as-recuperation ("rediscovery, reminiscence, reuniting under the unity of apperception" [*OTB* 29]) because it focuses the speaker's and listener's attention upon the moment of speaking. That moment disrupts the narrative's tendency to refer backwards to some point of origin, and insists on its presentness as an indication of the moment of utterance rather than on the moment of seeing. Such a testimonial account, as a presentation of memory, presents the observer with a moment that may not be temporally or causally (that is, reasonably) connected with the "event" that would presumably form its core, but that is shot through with heterogenous moments of time (the present and the past, the inflexions of forgotten voices or moments long past) that come crashing down into the present. Hineni is the indication of the immemorial kernel of the event. The memory of the past as narrative "comes unstuck or parts with itself, undoes itself into this and that, no longer covers itself" (*OTB* 30) and becomes denuded, exposed, turned inside out.

Any testimony designed to reflect the event will inevitably fail, but testimony is, ironically (and troublingly) the only vehicle in which that moment can be conveyed. Hineni makes apparent the radical discontinuity of the self with the utterance of self, of seeing with the memory of what was seen. Every moment is a potential opening to future action, and every human action is taken in the presence of (and impinges upon and affects) others. Any utterance, founded in "saying," is founded in an immemorial past, a forgetful memory, and each utterance, as a said, carries with it an aspect of noncoincidence, which affects others. "Immemorial, unrepresentable, invisible, the past that bypasses the present, the pluperfect past, falls into a past that is a gratuitous lapse. The past cannot be recuperated by reminiscence, not because of its remoteness, but because of its incommensurability with the present" (*OTB* 11). It's this incommensurability—the noncoincidence of what is remembered and the moment that compels both memory and testimony— that founds ethics: "All the negative attributes which state what is beyond the essence become positive in responsibility, a respsonse answering to a nonthematizable provocation. . . . Th[is] positivity of the infinite [made evident in noncoincidence] is the conversion of the response to the infinite," of the said to the saying embedded in it, of the immemorial kernel at the heart of memory, "into responsibility, into approach of the other" (12).

This is where ethics, founded in forgetful memory, turns and orients itself not toward the past—toward history, or the act witnessed, or the collective memory of events as they become known in a language with which we have become familiar—but toward the future. The immemorial past propels itself, like Benjamin's reading of the Angelus Novus which is blown ever forward on the winds of the disaster but with eyes fixed on the destruction,"into the future to which his back is turned," but into a future of the trace, the "who knows where" (Levinas, *OTB* 100). In his discussion of the *differend*, Lyotard makes clear just what sort of future-oriented memory this is. In the section of *The Differend* entitled "The Referent, the Name," he claims that "reality does not result from an experience," but rather from the palpability of utterances, assertions about the real (46). But the real is not the same as what happened; what is currently the case (and the utterances that bring the case to others) and what can be established as a prior case (history) are built differently in language. Expressions about what is currently the case, he goes on, aren't expressed like *x is such*, but by a phrase like *x is such and not such* (45), in which "the thing one sees has a backside which is no longer or not yet seen and which might yet be seen." So any statement about what we see is "simultaneously an allusion to what is not the case," a statement whose inconsistency must always allow for the possible, for what we cannot imagine at the moment but which may be the case but just out of the line of sight. The one who sees—the witness—can never see all aspects of an event; and as a result cannot testify to all its aspects. Even if the witness could see all aspects of the event—not just what can be called to mind but that which, in Yerushalmi's words, falls by the wayside—the language we have at our disposal could not bear it.

We traditionally think of history as a "fairly stable complex of nominatives," terms that make reference to states of affairs, to events and objects, that we can all agree happened, or existed, or have a certain durability through historical artefacts, documents, and other material detritus of the event itself. These are not traces in Levinas's sense but the bearers of the historical trace. The witness testifying to what she saw doesn't simply make a statement about those states of affairs which she and she alone saw, but makes those utterances in the context of history, and of collective memory, of what is known and said about a past that is hardly immemorial: it happened, and we know that it happened. "It suffices that something be shown and named (and thus can be shown as often as desired because it is fixed within nominal networks, which are independent of deictic) and that this something be acccepted as proof until there is further information" (53). But the simple distinction between historical reality and the real—between the stability of history and knowledge and the need to account for the possible or unsayable in memory—breaks down, because the complex of nominatives on which history and collective memory is built can itself be said to contain a trace of the possible.

"Reality is not a matter of the absolute eyewitness, but a matter of the future" (53). All possible senses of the object or event need to be accounted for and projected into the future; what happed matters less than what one allows the other to see, what effect the eyewitness has upon the listener in order to produce the moment—the ethical moment—in which what happened (prior to memory or to the event-as-experience) emerges in the present as something altogether new and unprecedented as knowledge. "For [the event] to become real, it is necessary to be able to name and show referents that do not falsify the accepted definition," but in the case of disasters such as the Holocaust (which is Lyotard's point of departure) the stable complex of reality has been destroyed. This destruction prevents memory from being tested against the stable complex—history—and requires from memory an eruption of the immemorial.

> The impossibility of quantitatively measuring [the event] does not prohibit, but rather inspires, in the minds of survivors the idea of a very great seismic force. The scholar can claim to know nothing about it, but the common person has a complex feeling, the one aroused by the negative presentation of the indeterminate. *Mutatis mutandis,* the silence that the crime of Auschwitz imposes upon the historian is a sign for the common person. (56)

Auschwitz, for Lyotard, is the limit case—the case of the disaster—in which "the testimonies which bore the traces of the *here*'s and *now*'s, the documents which indicated the sense or senses of facts," have been destroyed. The witness, as much as the historian, is charged with "breaking the monopoly over history granted to the cognitive regimen of phrases"—in Levinas's terms, ontology—and must lend an ear "to what is not presentable under the rules of knowledge" (57) those inflexions of forgotten voices that are barely audible but nonetheless present over the din of knowledge and history. It requires, to put it another way, a writing that allows the immemorial to impress itself upon the written, a saying that impresses itself upon the said; and it may require a language other than that of history or the narrative of memory to do obey this injunction. The beginning of ethics—to press together Levinas and Lyotard here—is the utterance of a word that brushes against history, that in its most radical sense worries less about the facticity of history (which is anyway exceedingly difficult to establish in the case of the Holocaust, in which the witnesses are either dead or sentenced to testifying to a world that takes language for the event itself) and attempts instead to write the impossible, to write that "which [may have not] yet taken place" so far as history and the narrative of memory is concerned (Lyotard 47).

THE MEMORY OF THE HOLOCAUST

It is the obligation to "speak memory immemorially" that characterizes the orientation of Jews (like Levinas) after the Holocaust. In an essay on Paul Claudel, Levinas wonders about the relation of Jews to Christians, the relation of Jews to the Arabs who live in the occupied territories captured by Israel in 1967, and about the responsibility Jews owe to the Palestinians. He ends the essay with a question: "Is it for a Jew to say?" His answer is yes, because "*every survivor of the Hitlerian massacres—whether or not a Jew—is Other in relation to martyrs. He is consequently responsible and unable to remain silent*" ("Poetry and the Impossible" 132; original italics). Events of history, including the Holocaust, are both part of Jewish collective memory and of the immemorial; but it is the immemorial that obliges us (Jew and non-Jew) to bear witness to events, to speak their memory, and to write that which has not yet taken place. It does not require us to speak against anti-semitism, though there is certainly a need for it; and it does not oblige us to "remember" Auschwitz, if by memory we mean a recuperation of the event. It does, however, require us to shoulder the responsibility of acting and speaking ethically, to do so in the recognition of the openness of the present, its ethically limitless (and often dangerous) possibilities, and the immemorial past, as a trauma, that makes itself apparent in the present through the act of the witness. The Holocaust witness and the testimonies of the survivors should not be sanctified (*kiddush ha-shem*) but should be seen as radically separate, unredeemable, and irreplaceable (*kadosh*). They can't be spoken for; they can only be spoken. In this way memory resists the status it often has in the canon of Holocaust writing as icon, as the image of dead.

One of the essays in which Levinas most explicitly deals with the memory of the Holocaust is "Loving the Torah More than God." There he examines a "memoir" written during the final hours of the uprising in the Warsaw ghetto published in a Parisian Zionist journal. In fact, that memoir—published as *Yossel Rakover Talks to God*—was written by Zvi Kolitz, a refugee who in 1940 settled in Palestine and in the closing years of the war heard second hand about the destruction of Warsaw and the Jewish communities in his native Lithuania. Though "he witnessed nothing," "he *knew* more than any of the fighters in the ghetto the true extent of the Holocaust" (Kolitz 51, 52). As such, Levinas writes, the account is "true as only fiction can be" (*Difficult Freedom* 142). What is it, then, that Levinas, and other survivors, sees in this memoir which is not a memory? How could the "writer" of the memoir, Yossel ben Yossel, have experienced events similar to those experienced by Levinas's family members during the war, since its author was in Palestine for the war's duration?

It's these questions, and Levinas's resistance to making an icon of Warsaw or Auschwitz, that lies at the heart of the ambivalence in his treatment of the story. "I shall not recount the whole story," *Yossel ben Yossel Rakover from Tarnopol, who Speaks to God*—or does he mean the story of the Shoah?—because to do so would turn "the Passion of Passions into a spectacle, or these inhuman cries into the vanity of an author or director" (142–3). To do so would claim the memories and the inflexions of voices heard in the story—and "the thought they express"—as his own, and to make an equation of Levinas and Yossel and of their experiences, without acknowledging that there may be some difference that falls out of the equation that troubles them both. Yossel's direct address to God in this story functions as an act of witness: it is less a request than it is a response, because in it Yossel tells us less about the last hours of the ghetto uprising than he does about the burden of witness. He is a latter-day Abraham, saying in response to God's request, "hineni," here I am; he opens himself up to the suffering that comes with seeing. Levinas calls this suffering an "intimacy." But it isn't an intimacy with God or with suffering but with the saying that makes itself present in the said. The said may easily be understood in this case as "the Warsaw ghetto" or "the Holocaust," but it far exceeds both and leaves a trace of what resides behind or before the name—a kernel of the historical real, perhaps, but more likely what Blanchot calls the immemorial, the event as it precedes our ability to bring it under an historical concept. Yossel ben Yossel, in his conversation with God, focuses not on what he sees—God, the destruction of the ghetto, the events both mundane and terrifying that make up Yossel's reality but which Yossel him-self can only gingerly narrate—but on the conundrum of how to present the immemorial as a memory.

To love Torah more than God is to acknowledge the impossibility of sep-arating the saying from the said, or the immemorial from the memory. Though one might say that God is the origin of the Torah and of history, we have no way to know that origin except through the Torah and through his-tory. Though the immemorial event is the origin of memory, we have no way to know the immemorial except through the language of memory. It is only through the word that one is most clearly able to remember. What Yossel is taught in the Torah more than by God is the responsibility that comes with opening oneself up to another as a witness. For Yossel to say that "God is real and concrete not through incarnation but through Law" is to acknowledge that the closeness and unbearable responsibility of witness is available only through writing. It's a writing that orients itself to the future, a writing that will be read, that has an influence over others, and that allows them to bear witness—to see—in their turn. Such a writing listens "to what is not pre-sentable under the rules of knowledge" (Lyotard 57), not to the past but the moment of writing. It's a writing that disrupts our ability to recreate the object of memory-as-past, and yet produces a memory in which a trace of the object, as surplus or excess (as what can't be reclaimed for history), presses itself in upon us. It's a writing from which God (or the object of history) has withdrawn to make room for saying, for the "other" of the event. This is the void at the heart of memory: what is recalled is the loss of knowledge and the indication of what precedes it. It's a recognition of the name and what the name, as a memorial, indicates in the immemorial.

The dedication in the opening pages of *Otherwise than Being*, then, can be seen as something like the inscription of the impasse between memory as collective and understood (mneme), and memory as radically individual and resistant to knowledge (anamnesis). The dedications at the beginning of Lev-inas's book could be said to inscribe a memory that is not a memory but an aspect of memory—the trace of a face—that haunts the book, and that haunts its author and its reader, casting over them a shadow that they can't seem to get out from under. The first dedication, written in French, "To the memory of those who were closest among the six million," is effectively pub-lic and collective. It recalls the six million in a way that is clearly recogniz-able to readers in France in 1974 and the United States in the last twenty years since its English publication: its invocation of names—"National Socialism," "antisemitism," "six million"—provides a universal language, a language of the known, a historical knowledge that has, since 1945, become such a "stable complex of nominatives" as to be nearly unshakable and insus-ceptible to revision. The first dedication is a mnemonic that stands for and replaces the memories themselves, memories that most readers simply do not have but which can be called to mind as tropes. That first dedication also poses a question: whose memory is this. Levinas's? The reader's? "To" whom is the writing of this memory intended? Given what we have said about Levinas's understanding of memory and its relation to ethics, one plausible answer is that the memory belongs to no one. The book is as an attempt to render in a language of philosophy that resists essences and "knowledge" as such and instead brushes knowledge against itself showing its seams and the traces of what it can't quite contain. But it is also an attempt to approach the reader and the closest among the six million and to open both the reader and the writer to see, although to see what is an open question still. The first dedication, in other words, is the opening up of a very public act of naming to the proximity of others, to the inflexions of voices not generally heard by such invocations.

The second dedication is different: it names names, but it names individuals—Yehiel, son of Avraham Halevi, Levinas's father; Deborah, daughter of Moshe, his mother; two brothers and his in-laws—who are "remembered" only by the author himself. These memories aren't available to the reader of the first dedication, who so clearly understands the historical metonyms, except as other kinds of metonymic substitutions for the names of their own parents, brothers, family members, family members who may or may not have been "assassinated by the National Socialists" and who may be alive still today. These individuals, invoked by the names called out by Levinas, may be recalled to us, but in their *nonidentity* with the names in the dedication. These memories are not memories-as-content, but memories as ruptures of the narrative invoked by the first dedication, and they indicate the impossible equation of the reader's father with Levinas's, and of the events that comprise the life (and death) of the one and of the other. They also resist memory in the language of their inscription: Hebrew not French (or English). This is a distinctly Jewish memory in a decidedly secular book, a Jewish form of remembrance that is common and readable by Hebrew readers or by Jews but unavailable (and "other") and so unfamiliar to non-Jews. This second dedication, the second memory, complicates the immediacy and the closeness invoked in the first. The names invoked here are also memories—words standing in for the object or the person named—but the mnemonic here functions in tandem with the first: here are those closest to Levinas, and yet what memories, what events are brought to mind? Their lives? Their deaths? The commonplace events that fall by the wayside of memory except during yizkor or the kaddish? The imagined terrors of the Holocaust? In fact, Levinas did not know what became of his family in Russia; he only knew that they were killed as a result of "the National Socialists," "the same antisemitism."

So, though there is a metonymic relation of word to word (a displacement) in this second invocation, and between the dedications, there is also something produced between them as surplus, something beyond the names, and the memories, that are familiar to the reader and those that are not. Both events, the Holocaust and the deaths of the six named family members, are gone. They have receded into the no-place of history, the who-knows-where, for good. But both names function each against (or in relation with) the other, and between them comes the trace, evidence of something beyond memory. This is not the event, for which event, really, would it call to mind? It may be a trace of the event, that kernel that resides at the center of memory. But it's a trace made present by the word, by the names that don't name so much as they make present that which is impossible—the deaths of six million whom we never knew, and the lives of these six whom Levinas knew only aspects of. And what follows from the memory is writing, a writing that doesn't attempt to render the known but which attempts to cast into the future an aspect of the known that resists knowledge. In Lyotard's terms, the memories that introduce the reader to the work call up both silence and speech, both block the memories of the reader—for these memories are not the reader's, anymore than the ethics implied in the book will be familiar or easy for him—and provoke a profusion of words, of speech, and of saying. They signal a silence for the historian but a sign for the common person, a sign of what has not yet taken place, or an aspect of the past, an immemorial aspect of the past, that requires a witness (see Wyschogrod 207). If Yosef Yerushalmi is right, and the memory of the Holocaust is better rendered by a writer like Zvi Kolitz than by historians (94), then Levinas seems to imply that the memory inscribed by writing needs to attend less to the details of the experiences of the survivors and the victims that have been inscribed as a memory and written, and more to the voices that haunt that writing's margins.

PART II

Writing and the Disaster

THREE

"If I forget thee, O Jerusalem"

The Poetry of Forgetful Memory in Palestine

YOSEF YERUSHALMI CLAIMED that if history and memory were to meet in the years after the *Shoah*, the discursive field in which they might intersect would be not history but fiction (and, one could add, poetry). He makes this claim in part because the violence wrought on history will have an effect upon the language of history itself, and in part because the aesthetic effect of poetic or fictional language more closely approximates the effect of memory and its counterpart, forgetting, on both history's agent and upon the reader of history. What is perhaps most important about Yerushalmi's claim is that it recognizes that memory and forgetfulness are not opposites but counterparts in the historical, and by consequence the narrative, project: forgetfulness is not the absence of, but rather an integral element of memory; and all memory is shot through with moments of forgetfulness, moments that are constitutive of what we can remember, and remember as history, at all.

If forgetfulness is what David Krell has called memory's abyss or "verge," then one could argue that for those living in contemporary Palestine—the nation of Israel and its current and former Arab residents living both in and around the nation—the abyss's correlative historical events are the destruction of the European Jews during the Shoah and its displacement of the survivors; and the founding of the state of Israel and the dispersal of its Arab residents. This relation between memory and forgetfulness is akin to the connection—particularly in the context of Palestine and Israel—between exile and the disaster. There are two ways of looking at this relation. The first is that the historical case of the disaster—war, genocide, natural catastrophe—is the proximate cause of an equally material, but also conceptually complex, state of exile, in which the destruction of home, nation, or culture leads to an absence that must be filled with some other means to identify one-self as a subject (either "national" or ethical). The second permutation of the relation between exile and disaster is that exile is the human instantiation of disaster: the post-war polity and economy are marked by dislocations (of cap-ital, of humans, of nationalities and cultures) that are in Blanchot's sense "disastrous." Those historical dislocations mark, perhaps as in no other moment, an equally profound epistemological dislocation, in which our abil-ity to create order and a point of origin from which to create it is thwarted by language's correlative displacement. Common to both these senses of the relation between disaster and exile is the sense of continuity: that historical disasters and exiles are epiphenomena of broader conceptual dislocations.

Forgetful memory is intimately related to exile and disaster in the sense that it is constitutive of the terms. If exile and disaster are historical instances of broader conceptual dislocations that can be seen as in some sense tran-shistorical, memory and forgetfulness are inherently material, marking the language of individuals attempting to deal with the exilic remnant of the dis-aster. Memory and forgetfulness might best be seen as the instruments of cat-astrophe and exile, particularly since 1945 when not only historical memory but individual memories were marked by the revelation of the events of the Shoah, events that might arguably have their severest repercussions in Israel and Palestine. In this chapter, I will describe how the work of two writers pro-foundly affected by the violence of the *Shoah* and the *nakbah*—Mahmoud Darwish (primarily in *Memory for Forgetfulness*) and Yehuda Amichai (pri-marily in his last volume of poetry, *Open, Closed, Open*)—inscribes the events not in a language of memory and forgetting, but through what I'd call the language of "forgetful memory." In doing so, these poets attempt to ren-der what is on the verge of history—the events that collective and cultural memory, let alone history, can't bring themselves to say—and each, in his own way, makes clear the impossible position of the exile: one who is dis-tanced not (or not only) from one's origins, but from one's ability to recollect them without falling into the void of forgetfulness.

The complexity of memory is made especially complicated by the fabric of events with which both Darwish and Amichai are working. Both writers were displaced by the second World War and its aftermath—Amichai was born in 1924 in Bavaria, and emigrated to Palestine with his family in 1935 when it was still possible for German Jews to leave the country; Darwish was born in 1942 in the village of Birwe in northern Palestine, and escaped to Lebanon with his family in 1948, only to return to find that his village had been destroyed in the war for Israeli independence. Both Amichai and Darwish have to contend with memories—which aren't their own memories so much as they are collective invocations—of places forcibly abandoned (Germany, Palestine) and the ways in which the narrative of memory confounds the language with which each poet attempts to come to terms with his present. Both events—the Shoah and the destruction of Jewish life in Europe leading to a diaspora (or a return) to the land of Israel; the nakbah and the destruction of Arab rural life in what would become Israel and the Palestinian diaspora—involve not just a geographical displacement but also a memorial one, in which their attempts to connect an identity with a location are undermined by an absence, and a forgetfulness, of what has been irretrievably lost.

But it remains to be seen how the geographical displacement and the displacement of memory in forgetfulness inscribe distinct memorial positions. Amichai's poetry—particularly the poems in *Open, Closed, Open* (2000)—is not unlike Darwish's writing in *Memory for Forgetfulness* (1982): both, in the words of Munir Akash, are sensitive in their "lyric responsiveness to the contemporary history of the region" (Darwish, *Unfortunately, It was Paradise* xviii). More accurately, both Amichai and Darwish work to undo a sentimental memorial attachment to the land—to Israel or to Palestine—by focusing their attention on the quotidian elements of location rather than on the familiar images of either the *sabra* of Israel or the martyr of Palestinian nationalism. For Darwish, in *Memory for Forgetfulness*, the siege of Beirut registers at least as forcefully upon the poet in the distressing lack of coffee on the morning of 6 August 1982, as it does in the knowledge that the siege will force the PLO to abandon the city for Tunis; for Amichai, the metaphor that pulls the poems in *Open, Closed, Open* together like a string is not Jerusalem but a fragment of a gravestone, inscribed with the word "Amen," that the writer keeps on his desk. For both poets, it is the personal memory as it displaces the collective, and the effect of that displacement, that is central in their understanding of identity, of location, and of origin.

Conceptually, what connect Darwish and Amichai are their concerns with the problem of place, the peculiarities of the particular locations of Beirut and Jerusalem, the impossibility of return, and the dissociation of memory from history. For Darwish, the memory of Palestine is complicated because Palestine no longer exists: Birweh has been destroyed, along with four hundred other Palestinian villages, and Beirut—which is home to displaced Palestinians, and to the PLO up until the early 1980s—doesn't want the Palestinians to remain. Darwish's book is written as a series of memorial tableaux set during a particularly violent day during the Israeli siege of Beirut of 1982. It doesn't follow a plot so much as it circles around a number of interrelated themes: how to define oneself as a Palestinian, how one contends with exile, how to establish an ethical course of action when factional politics is all one can see, and how to survive as a humane individual when you're trying to be killed as a part of an imagined collectivity. While the book is most often seen as a memoir of the siege or as a rumination on what it means to be Palestinian, *Memory for Forgetfulness* seems to me to be at least as much about the role memory—and what can't be remembered—plays in the attempt to survive the disaster of exile. In an imagined conversation that runs throughout the book, Darwish explains:

> "You're aliens here," they say to them *there*.
> "You're aliens here," they say to them *here*.
>
> And between *here* and *there* they stretched their bodies like a vibrating bow until death celebrated itself through them. Their parents were driven out of there to become guests here, temporary guests, to clear civilians from the battlegrounds of the homeland and to allow the regular armies to purge Arab land and honor of shame and disgrace. (13)

Elsewhere, Darwish responds in frustration to his Israeli lover, who cannot understand his love for Lebanon (he has just told her that he loves the song "I Love You, O Lebanon"), because it isn't his "home" as far as she is concerned, nor why he won't emigrate back to Palestine. By way of explanation he says, "For us to go back there, we must be somewhere; because he who goes back—if he does go back—doesn't start from nowhere" (40). The problem for Darwish is that Beirut is not his home, though he finds it beautiful; and "Palestine has been transformed from a homeland into a slogan" (49). Fouad Ajami, professor of Middle East Studies at Johns Hopkins and widely-published writer on the predicament of the Palestinians, has said in another context that "The idea of Palestine [is] far grander than the squalor of Gaza" (267); the squalor of Beirut, unmentioned in Darwish's memoir, remains in effect invisible. The name "Lebanon" is not so much a place as a song, and the place "Palestine" has likewise been transformed into a name or, at best, an idea. Both Palestine and Beirut themselves are voids, canceling each other out—though as we'll see, it's not quite this simple.

This same dynamic is visible in much of Yehuda Amichai's *Open, Closed, Open*, the last volume of poetry published before the poet's death in 2000. The book is something like a recapitulation of the history of Israel, seen through the eyes of someone who sees in the country's landscape not just the sins and hopes of its founders but the hopes and fears of its grand-children. But it's more than just a set of poems about the place of the poet in Israel (as it has been most commonly received); it speaks to a great ambivalence about the land and who can and cannot live on it. In the poem entitled "Jewish Travel: Change is God and Death is his Prophet," the metaphor of travel is used to explore just this Jewish ambivalence toward the land. Like Moses wandering in the desert, or like an imaged Abraham bringing his sons every year to Mount Moriah to recall another sort of exile, Jews are on an "endless journey," "between self and heart, to and fro, to without fro, fro without to" (117). Jews

Call their God *Makom*, "Place."
And now that they have returned to their place, the Lord
    has taken up
wandering to different places, and His name will no longer
    be Place
but Places. (118)

The conundrum Amichai describes is the one in which the memories and the
names of the places—of those in Israel through which Moses and the Jews
traveled; of those in Jerusalem named for the Palmach; of those in Germany
associated with Amichai's childhood—have become more real than the
object or event named, and in which the object has atrophied from memory
altogether. It is as if in extending the dynamic of yad vashem, the place and
the name, the name has replaced the actual event. The political circumstances of Amichai's lament for stability are quite different from Darwish's:
the place in which God and the Palestinians no longer reside is for Amichai
the Jewish, and not the Arab, homeland. Nonetheless, the dialectic of here
and there is never resolved, except perhaps in the chiasmatic abyss of the language of the poetry itself.

For Amichai, although the tension between memory and forgetting—
mneme and anamnesis—is never quite resolved, it is nevertheless arrested by
the instantaneity of individual moments: moments in time and moments in
the language of individual poems. But unlike David Roskies, who sees a kind
of stability in the collective memory of Jewish loss and annihilation—the
"symbolic constructs and ritual acts" both "blur the specificity and the
implacable contradictions of the event" but also, and for that reason, keep
those memories alive (*Against the Apocalypse* 4)—forgetful memory here in
fact makes such a blurring virtually impossible, and ruptures any collective
attempt to preserve a memory of loss. It's not possible, Amichai, suggests, to
return to a past that wasn't your own—"I've never been in those places where
I've never been," he writes with reference to the injunction to remember the
Holocaust. In "I wasn't one of the six million," one of the poems in the first
few pages of the volume, the last stanza reads like a credo:

I believe with perfect faith that at this very moment
millions of human beings are standing at crossroads
and intersections, in jungles and deserts,
showing each other where to turn, what the right way is,
which direction. They explain exactly where to go,
what is the quickest way to get there, when to stop
and ask again. There, over there. . . .
I believe with perfect faith that at this very moment. (7–8)

The problem with such a view of instantaneity, which annihilates both memory and forgetting, is that it is constantly deferred, and it continually subsumes

memory—any memory—to the present. If "every person is a dam between present and future," as Amichai writes in "In My Life, On My Life," then that dam consistently moves, from now to now, from there to there, leaving no trace of origins. In the same poem, Amichai writes "Life is called life as the west wind is called / west, though it blows toward the east," "as the past leads to the future / though it's called the past" (111). There is no origin to which to return. Memory here gives way altogether to forgetting and to the abyss, and one is left not with the now but with nothing at all, the subjectless sentence that ends "at this very moment."

Much as "the Holocaust" is for Amichai the past to which he is to be returned even though it may not be his past, in Darwish the return to the land is equally vexing. With no "here" and no "there," the myth of return is as impossible as it is tempting. Throughout his memoir of the siege of Beirut, Darwish uses the metaphor of the sea, and its waves returning to the shore, as the correlative political conundrum. He writes,

> A wave from the sea. I used to follow it with my eyes from this balcony as it broke against the Raouche rock, famous for lovers' suicides
>
> A wave that carries a few last letters and returns to the blue northwest and azure southwest. It returns to its shores, embroidering itself with puffs of white cotton as it breaks.
>
> A wave from the sea. I recognize it and follow it with longing. I see it tiring before it reaches Haifa or Andalusia. It tires and rests on the shores of the island of Cyprus.
>
> A wave from the sea. It won't be me. And I, I won't be a wave from the sea. (70)

The wave, however, does not return to the shores from whence it came; it returns, instead, to different shores; not to Andalusia or to Haifa, but to Cyprus; it returns, but not as the same. Like the memory of the place of origin, or the object we associate with a figure of speech, it doesn't return as itself, but as an other, its double. Darwish's negation is figuratively doubled: neither the wave returns, nor does he ("It won't be me"). Whereas Amichai's hope resides in moments of time in which past and future return in the present, in moments of lived life vouchsafed by the doubling of name and place, here Darwish's hope of return is elusive: name and place are not doubled—Haifa is not Cyprus; Beirut is not Jerusalem—and there is no memorial geography, no shore, on which to rest.

Both the vexed geography from which Amichai and Darwish are exiled (Europe and Palestine) and the places where they find themselves at the moment they write (Jerusalem and Beirut) are interior geographies. Their memories of place are convoluted, turned in upon themselves, as if both Beirut and Jerusalem aren't found so much written on a map as inscribed in the writers themselves. The most significant difference between the writers is that for Amichai, Jerusalem functions as locus and as an origin: he has lived there for decades, and his poetry of the place—in two volumes (*Songs of Jerusalem and Myself* [1973] and *Poems of Jerusalem* [1987])—is the poetry of local geographies and individual memories, not so much of the myth of independence. In *Memory for Forgetfulness*, though Beirut is the place where Darwish lives, it functions only as a sanctuary, one among many—which also include Haifa, Moscow, Cairo, Paris, Amman, and Ramallah—in which he has spent the years since his village was erased from the map. And yet for both writers, while cultural memories of "homelands" drive their language, it's the impossible, individual memories that render those homelands both interior and divided.

Darwish calls Beirut "a meeting place of contraries. " It has been, he continues,

> turned into an obscure naming, or a lung which a mixture of people, killers and victims among them, could use to breathe. This is what made of Beirut a song celebrating the singular and distinctive, where not many lovers asked whether they were really living in Beirut or in their dreams. (92–3)

Like the meeting place of memory and forgetfulness, each resident's vision of the place, and their visions of the places they have left to find what's missing here, cancels that of each other's, producing not a void, but "a song celebrating the singular," like a strange memorial excess. The problem with this song, as with excess itself, is that it cannot be named, or—if it is named—it is misnamed. Darwish recognizes the problem, and this section of his rumination ends with the song: "the transformation had begun, that the shell of regionalism had been broken and the pearl, the essence, had shown itself. So it seemed to me then. So it seemed to me" (94). Later on, Beirut—the idea—collapses of its own weight, "accomodat[ing] the chaos that for every exile resolved the complex of being an exile" (135). As disorder, the excess produced by the meeting place of contraries works, like forgetfulness, against collectivities, against history, against identity, and against reason. If there is hopefulness in such an interior geography, it's because it is so radically particular that it can't be attached to an earthly geography: Darwish writes in *Hadarim* that "the geography within history is stronger than the history within geography. . . . I am referring to a place that is stronger than what has gone on in it throughout the course of history" (194).

While Darwish is physically distanced from his home in Birweh, and from the part of his identity that is Palestinian, Amichai (while dislocated from Germany) feels at home in Israel. Amichai resides in Jerusalem, a city whose geography and history mutually reinforce one another. For him the city is less "home" than it is a "shelter," and a divided one at that. His poem "The Bible is You" establishes a connection between contemporary Jerusalem and the Jerusalem of David, the "singer of the Song of Songs," and the

prophets. Unlike Darwish, for whom such a correlation is politically dangerous at best, and dishonest at worst, in Amichai's Jerusalem it is altogether
possible—the city is familiar and just a little run down. Still, Amichai's city,
like Darwish's Beirut, is also divided. In his imaginings, the singer of the
Song of Songs wanders about contemporary Jerusalem; sometimes "he even
got as far as our home with its broken roof on the border between Jerusalem
and Jerusalem" (28). This is a border between the past and the present,
memory and a contemporary life of broken roof tiles; but it is also a border
between life and life, the moment between the present that has already
plunged into the past and the present that just a moment ago was the
unknown future. Though Jerusalem is Amichai's place of residence, it is a
dangerous and chaotic place. "Jerusalem is forever changing her ways," he
writes; those who live there, in spite of mannequin-like "frozen gestures,"
would prefer to "go wild in the dark storerooms with untrammeled joy / as in
the Garden of Eden."

> [T]he saints who ascended on high in the distant past
> . . . [seemed to be] running away from her to heaven.
> For compared to Jerusalem, even the outer space of infinity
> is safe and protected, like a true home.
> ("Jerusalem, Jerusalem, Why Jerusalem?" 135)

The vertigo associated with Jerusalem here is partly the result of a quotidian
inconstancy—changes in light, changes in season, and changes in its contemporary political fortunes—but it also has much to do with its vexed history. While for Amichai that history is predominantly its Jewish history, what
lies buried beneath that history, beneath its "sea of memory," is something
that Amichai can't quite bring himself to discuss except in terms of alternate
geographies, such as New York, Mexico City, Petrograd—namely, the "sea of
forgetting." There is, in Amichai's poem, a history in the geography, at least
as much as there is geography in the history, and yet that historical weight is
such a burden to memory that it remains unspoken, and becomes visible only
in moments when the poet himself seems to be looking away: Jerusalem, as a
woman, is adorned with "jewels," houses of prayer, in the "English, Italian,
Russian, Greek, Arab styles," as if those styles, as adornment, carried with
them no history at all. In fact, what is "between Jerusalem and Jerusalem"
seems to be the void of forgetting, the unspoken (and unspeakable) historical events that left their traces in the geographical and architectural chaos of
the city; and it's this, the place's very presence—and not the place's absence,
as is the case with Darwish—that keeps it from providing Amichai, or perhaps anyone else, a home.

   As Jerusalem and Beirut fail to provide the stability of geography on
which the writers might finally stand, so do the histories of the writers also
fail to help them identify, once and for all, a narrative of temporality that

might help them make sense of the timelessness in which they find themselves. What Amichai and Darwish bear out in their writing, in fact, is that
Yerushalmi was right: history and memory are irrevocably divided, and
though they interanimate one another, that interanimation is vexed. In a
passage in *Memory for Forgetfulness*, Darwish recalls listening to Beirut radio
during the siege, particularly the song "I love you, O Lebanon!," which had
become something of an anthem for Palestinians living there. He says of the
song that it was "a declaration not heeded by a Beirut preoccupied with its
blasted streets, now compressed into three streets only." He goes on:

> And the sung beauty, the object of worship, has moved away to a memory
> now joining battle against the fangs of forgetfulness made of steel. Memory
> doesn't remember but receives the history raining down on it. Is it in this
> way beauty, past beauty come back to life in a song not suited to the con-
> text of the hour, becomes tragic? A homeland, branded and collapsing in
> the dialogue of human will against steel; a homeland, rising with a voice
> that looks down on us from the sky . . . (146)

There are two memories here, the collective and the individual. The collective memory, mneme, is the memory that the song invokes, the Lebanon
of song and of national identity that, so far as it goes, produces a kind of filial loyalty to a homeland that isn't quite a homeland (the "object of wor-
ship") but will do for now. If the song invokes history, it is a collective history
whose narrative is as fictional as the song is beautiful. Individual memory,
that produced one listener at a time, renders the song tragic, in which the
preoccupation with its ruined geography is commingled with the longing for
an earlier time, an earlier place. What is notable here, however, is that both
these memories are cut across by another history, one that "rains down" on it
in the form of destruction: the siege, experienced not in collective memory,
and certainly not in song, is nonetheless in this passage a "steel wolf," more
real than the collective reality of the song; it is a historical real that risks dec-
imating not only the song but also memory, rendering it not forgetful but
absent altogether. It's as if both mneme and anamnesis are divided, finally, by
history's real: the siege sticks a wedge between them, and produces nothing
but a void, both geographical and historical.

Amichai is likewise troubled by the divide between memory and history:
in "Once I Wrote *Now and in Other Days*," Amichai imagines himself resid-
ing in his former future—now his present—and seems to measure the latter
against the former in memory. He writes, "Once I wrote 'Now and in Other
Days. / Now I have arrived at those other days.' When I wrote it, they were
at the end of the century; / now they are in the past, in the middle of the century" (31), in which the "otherness" of those days are both interchangeable
and unique to the circumstances of the writing. In those other days, Amichai
believed, as most Israelis did, that the Huleh in the north was a swamp to be

drained; now, those other days are those in which the wetland was lost and now must be reclaimed. Along the continuum of history, each event bears a causal relation to the other: the swamps were drained, the wetlands were lost, and they are now being reclaimed. But in the realm of memory, each action is distinct and yet "other," each has an imaginative power all its own—as is true for the volume of poetry *Now and in Other Days* as well the more recent *Open, Closed, Open*—that involve both memory and forgetting. The swamp is forgotten in favor of the wetland; the reclamation project is remembered as a mistake. In *Open, Closed, Open*'s next poem ("Gods Change, Prayers are Here to Stay"), as if responding to this conundrum, Amichai writes of the Rosh Hashana prayers,

> To the confession 'We have sinned, we have betrayed' I would add
> the words 'We have forgotten, we have remembered'—two sins
> that cannot be atoned for. They ought to cancel each other out
> but instead they reinforce one another. (45)

If it's a sin both to remember and to forget, that sin involves the problem of naming: Huleh as swamp, Huleh as wetland, or for Darwish, Lebanon as homeland, Lebanon as devastation and exile. What's left, then, is the immediacy of now, in which neither memory nor forgetfulness reside. Or in Amichai's terms, describing *kashrut*, there is now only a cleft between the past and the future, which "gives me the strength to stand it all" (45). For both Amichai and for Darwish, history and memory come into contact briefly, but between them is a cleft, an abyss, that can only be indicated as a moment occurring in and through poetic language.

The year 1945 serves as a historical and conceptual watershed. It marks the end of the second World War (and the Shoah), the beginning of the final push toward Israeli independence, and the beginning of what would become the Cold War, with its proxy conflicts in the middle east and elsewhere. But as a watershed, the year is (and the events that follow from it are) as much forgotten as remembered. After 1945, survivors of the Shoah leave the DP camps for the US, Palestine and elsewhere; people in the colonies of the victorious Allies begin working for independence while also moving to France, Britain, and Germany; Jews attempt to redefine their relation with the non-Jewish world as both exiles and as (potential) members of a national entity—in short, memories are replaced (and displaced) as individuals become displaced. The results of this displacement in mandatory Palestine include the creation of Israel, the destruction of Arab culture in the new Jewish nation, and the invention—sometimes out of whole cloth—of an Israeli history and culture that is both part of and wholly disparate from the diaspora culture it seeks to replace. History and memory since 1945 are up for grabs, and what Amichai and Darwish attempt to do in their work is both to recuperate something irretrievably lost, but also to note how—in the language of their poetry and sometimes at that language's interstices—displacement and exile are constitutive of the positions from which they write. While there is no evidence to suggest that Darwish and Amichai took note of one another's work, what they hold in common is an uncanny sense that even in the poetic imaginary, the best they can do is grapple with what has dropped out of their memories of their cultural, national, and ethical locations.

What's left to describe at this point is what divides the two writers—the Israeli and Jew from the Palestinian and Arab—or, perhaps more accurately, what is particular in each of their circumstances that accounts for their preoccupation with memory and forgetfulness, and with what can and cannot be called to mind (what cannot be witnessed) and what cannot be written (or given as testimony). Most obviously, the historical fact of the partition of Palestine in 1948 and what Meron Benvenisti and Benny Morris—notable among Israeli historians for their "revisionist" assessments of the founding Israeli national myth, in which the empty land was converted into a new Eden—have called a program of expulsion (one that bordered on ethnic cleansing) of resident Arabs, account for the loss of the land and of memory on which Darwish founds the language of loss and through which Amichai, far less explicitly, describes his ambivalence toward deep cultural memory and his preference for an avoidance of memory in the infinite regress of the present. What is most interesting, however, is the way in which the loss of the land—of home and of origin—in the political and historical reality of the second World War's aftermath in Palestine becomes submerged (and one could say forgotten) in the poetry and prose of both Amichai and Darwish.

Darwish tells Halit Yeshurun of the Israeli journal *Hadarim* that "no one can return to the place he imagines or to the man he once was." Moving beyond the obvious problem of nostalgia, he makes clear that this is an historical and political problem: "Al-Birwa [Birweh] no longer exists" (175), having been bulldozed in the immediate aftermath of the war of 1948; when Darwish's family returned from a brief exile in Lebanon, they had to settle in another village. But how to rectify the situation becomes more troubled as the poet goes on: "Palestine is not a memory but an existing entity. . . . The return is a mythic idea, whereas the reality of going [to Palestine] is realized through revolutionary activity. . . . [The poet's job is to] repeatedly reconnect [with the past by] going back and forth between the mythical and the mundane" (185). The poet lives between the actual Palestine and the mythical one, and his work—presumably a version of the "revolutionary activity" he cites—must rush between them. But as Ajami has so bluntly put it, Palestine actually exists in Ramallah, Jericho, and Gaza, where much of existence is defined by its squalor. There is, in Darwish's poetry, the reconnection of the present and the past through memories of the details of everyday life; in "Until My End, Until its End," a son responds to his father's question about finding his way back to his village, now in Israel, by citing familiar landmarks from memory: "East of the carob tree on the main road / a short path with a *sabra* bush narrowing its beginning / and afterward it breaks free / and broadens toward the well, and finally opens out / onto the vineyard of Uncle Jamil. . . ." This isn't the mythical Palestine, but it isn't the real one either: this set of landmarks, with its carob trees and its vineyards, is likely now a *moshav* or *kibbutz*, or even more likely part of an Israeli village which has paved over the local vegetation altogether.

Darwish wonders, in *Memory for Forgetfulness*, why Palestinians living in Beirut would be asked to forget their history, and their lands, in order to survive in exile. "Why should so much amnesia be expected of them?" (15). The answer, provided by Darwish himself later on in the memoir, is that even "memory doesn't remember[,] but receives the history raining down on it" (146), the history that includes the siege, destruction, and absence. The history raining down on memory, that which seeds the poet's remembrance with forgetting and enjoins those in exile to do the same, is Ajami's squalor, which is also part of memory, but one that memory resists. It is "in this way that beauty, past beauty come back to life in a song not suited to the context of the hour, becomes tragic" (146). That tragedy, chillingly like the tragedy of the Jews slated for destruction by the Nazi Final Solution, is the tragedy of subjectlessness. "For the first time in our history," Darwish writes referring to the agreement of the Palestinians to leave Beirut, "our absence is conditional on our total presence. Present to make oneself absent" (149). To be present in Beirut is to be absent from Palestine, and it's this absence that predicates another absence. Ajami's squalor and Darwish's absence are, like the Jew in central Europe fifty years earlier, signs of nonexistence written on history as that which is unspeakable, unrecognizable, and left at the margins of memory.

And it's this same marginality, written differently but founded upon the same historical forgetting, that so vexes Amichai and his Jerusalem. In "What Has Always Been," he writes starkly, "Nineteen forty-eight—that was the year. / Now everything is different here" (66), though primarily what Amichai refers to is the Israeli myth of the rebirth of the land. More problematically, in the same poem, he writes that "two generations of forgetting have passed / and the first generation of remembering has come. Woe to us / that we have already come to remember / because memories are the hard shell over an empty heart" (63). The earlier generations—those who came of age after the Holocaust and the declaration of the state, and those who came of age between the 1967 and 1973 wars—have forgotten. They have forgotten both because they were actively creating the historical reality that would be transformed into myth for the current generation, and because that creation rested on the decimation—the active forgetting—of the cultural memory of Palestine. The generation of remembering is the one that rests secure inside the borders of an expanded national entity, one contiguous with the borders of Palestine in the mandatory period just prior to independence, a generation that remembers only the national myth, and the land's continuity with Biblical ancestors and its mundane details (the missing tiles on a Jerusalem roof).

What is marginal to those memories, what has been forgotten, is the everyday lived lives of those who, like Darwish, simply (and perhaps conveniently) disappeared. They turn up, in Amichai's poems, not as people but as ghostly images. In the poem immediately following the one cited above, entitled "Israeli Travel," there is the following description:

> A picture in color of plowman and horse from the turn of
>   the century
> in one of those early settlements in Palestine
> hanging on the wall of a summer home in a land far across
>   the sea.
> And outside, a luxurious lawn
> surrounded by flowers, and on the lawn an empty chair.
> And I said to myself: Sit down in this chair, sit here and
>   remember,
> sit here and judge—if not, someone else will sit in this
>   chair
> to remember and judge. What took place an hour ago
> had its place, and what took place on that farm at the turn
>   of the century
> had its place, and there were trees whose leaves blustered
>   in the wind
> and trees that stood by in silence. And the wind
> the same wind. In the trees, the bluster and the silence.
> And what was and what might have been are as if they never
>   were.
> But the wind is the same wind,
> the chair is the same chair for remembering and judging,
> and the plowman in the picture goes on plowing
> what has always been, and sowing
> what never will be. (70)

This photo, or the one of a clock-tower in Jaffa from the same period, or the poet's memories of the draining of the Huleh swamp, or a brief stop to admire a crusader fortress, all seem here to be continuous with the present— "and the wind the same wind"—and with the poet's insistence on stopping the clock in favor of forgetting rather than (as in the current, impoverished generation) remembering.

But this forgetting is indeed forgetful of those other events and objects associated with those photographs and those other moments. Like Ajami's squalor, whose reality must be forgotten along with the idea of Palestine, what is forgotten here is the possibility of just who this plowman is. Which village, Arab or Jewish, do we see in the distance, and whose land is being plowed? Was it the Arab owner of an orange grove, (and the owners were almost exclusively Arab) who looked up at that clock-tower in Jaffa? And what of the farmers in the Huleh, the breeders of water buffalo who lived in Arab villages whose landscape was destroyed by the draining of what the newly-arrived Israelis called a swamp? And was it really a crusader fortress that Amichai stopped to admire on his way back to Jerusalem, or a remarkable instance of Arab village architecture, which itself may have been superimposed upon the foundations of a crusader-era building? All of these historical details—chronicled so well by historians like Benvenisti, Morris, and others but forgotten in the poetic memory of Yehuda Amichai—are an integral part of the forgetful memory inscribed perhaps unknowingly so by the poet of Jerusalem. It is these images, which lie outside the margins of memory but which return unbidden to the poet and reader alike, that indicate a history of devastation, of loss, and of erasure that bind Amichai to Mahmoud Darwish as national citizens and also as poets.

Implicit in the notion of forgetful memory are two theses. The first is that historical consciousness and collective memory play against one another, and that between history and collective memory fall moments of individual memory related to witnessing or seeing, moments that are themselves a structural part of memory, but that give evidence precisely of the loss of the event rather than of its recuperation. There is perhaps no neat distinction between mneme and anamnesis; in fact, if there is a distinction at all it is supplied by a third term—or perhaps a null term—that represents what lies between them: the crux or void of memory, the presence of events that are irrecuperable because they did not, for our purposes, occur as "experience" at all. They precede our ability to know them, though we see them, and they register on us and result in what the literary theorist Shoshana Felman calls a "relentless talking" or precocious testimony that is so maddeningly difficult to map onto history (see her essay, "Education in Crisis").

A second thesis is that historical writing, while it "cannot replace [the] eroded group memory" (Yerushalmi 94) after the destructions of the Shoah and the nakbah, doesn't have to. In fact, writing of a different sort—the writing of poetry, or narrative, or memory—registers a disjunction between mneme and anamnesis that produces the uncanny reaction, moments of disastrous or forgetful memory that act as a crux, a no-place, and produce moments of seeing in the reader that are structurally similar to, but do not replicate, those moments in the witness. Such writing is neither collective nor historical but indicative, producing what Moshe Idel, in his studies of the

Kabbala, calls "cairological" or apodictic effects that let the memory—the loss of the event—"shine through." It presents moments of seeing that are more memorial—though immemorial, in that they indicate loss as much as they indicate presence—than the collective memory we'd build to forge a community of faith or of suffering.

FOUR

Memory and the Image in
Visual Representations of the Holocaust

IMAGES AND COLLECTIVE MEMORY

IN DESCRIBING PHOTOGRAPHS of the liberation of the camps at the end of the second World War, Barbie Zelizer suggests that the trope of witnessing was valuable in the war effort: depictions of allied soldiers, townspeople that lived near the camps, German camp personnel, and others made clear that these atrocities should be imprinted upon the world's memory. Her point here, and the point of her book, is to make clear that photos are important instruments of memory, and yet like all such instruments they fall prey to the context in which they are used, and may have as much to do with a domestication of their object—in this case, the atrocity of the Holocaust and other subsequent atrocities—as with a memorialization of it. And then Zelizer comes across a photo that seems out of place in her narrative: a young boy, well fed and well dressed in a sweater and short pants, walks down a road whose curve exits a forest. His attention is focused on something outside the frame, to his right; behind him, barely visible and a good hundred paces away, are two women rapt in conversation. The road is dusty and the sky is clear. What makes the photo horrifying is that just to his left, strewn along the road's embankment and in the woods just beyond, are over a hundred corpses, anonymous bodies dressed not in rags or blankets but in ordinary clothes. Zelizer includes this in a genre of photographs of German children who refuse to bear witness to atrocity; the photo's caption—it's unclear whether it was written by the photographer himself or the magazine (*Life*) for which it was taken—explains that this is a Jewish boy outside the concentration camp at Bergen-Belsen. The boy is identified by the curators of the German Historical Museum, where the photo now resides, as a Belgian Jew, Sieg Mandaag, "[who] survived the dying after the liberation of the camp by the British Army" (Honnef and Brenmeyer 202).

What do we make of this photo, and what part does it play in the construction of memory, particularly memories of the Holocaust? Zelizer's thesis in *Remembering to Forget* is that memories of the Holocaust, particularly for those in the second and third generation who were not there on the spot, are built through the compilation of historical documents, testimonies, and images, and that as they are mediated by historians, the media, and other family and cultural narratives, they come down to us—individuals—already well-wrought. "A memory," she writes, "can invoke a particular representation of the past for some while taking on a universal significance for others: the word Auschwitz has certain meanings for Holocaust survivors' children that are not necessarily shared by contemporary genocide scholars. This follows from the rather basic fact that everyone participates in the production of memory, though not equally" (4). The event itself disappears, and it is only through the significance it has accreted, and the images by which it is invoked, that the witness and those to whom she recollects the memory decides what gets put aside and what takes the place of the lost event. The relation between the image and recollection is particularly powerful, but especially vexed: the repetition of the image, especially those of the atrocities in Belsen, Majdanek, and other locations on the terrain of the Final Solution, though they force the viewer to see, as if she were there, the bodies and the crematoria and the starvation, they also are mute and require a stabilizing context for the viewer to integrate what would otherwise be beyond the pale of knowledge. For Zelizer, this is the double-edge of the medium: while they force the viewer to bear witness—which "constitutes a specific form of collective remembering" (10)—the captioning and the context in which the photo is seen determines to a large extent the object of witness. So, while "one did not need to be at the camps [since] the power of the image made everyone who saw the photos into a witness" (14), the question remains: just what was it that the viewer saw? Photos, for Zelizer, are indexes of collective memory which serves for us, as we pay attention to ethnic cleansing disasters of our own making, as a background.

The photo of Sieg Mandaag, though, seems to tell another story. While it may be integrated as part of a narrative of witness, and placed alongside other archival photos of witnessing, refusals to bear witness, to the atrocities in the camps and the ghettos, to do so would be to place it into a collective memory that we have already learned to accomodate. As Zelizer and others have made abundantly clear, these photos—taken as an index of a collective memory—are also the medium of a collective amnesia. Sieg Mandaag stands in for us: we've seen these images again and again, as the young Belgian child must have seen corpse after corpse; and that accomodation, like the child's, allows our attention to be diverted from the memory of atrocity (which is, after all, not our own) and so from the atrocity much closer to home. No wonder, then, that Zelizer's book concludes with the suggestion that it is our memories of the Holocaust that prevent us from being traumatized—shaken out of our moral torpor—by images of destruction in our own back yard. But that photo of the boy at Belsen still has the potential to shock: whether the boy is German or Belgian, Jewish or non-Jewish, his glance and his appearance defy the destruction all around him, and it is this horrifying incommensurability (of the normal and the abnormal, of the left-hand side of the photo and the right) indicates, if only fleetingly, something that escapes the memory of the Holocaust. We've seen the bodies and the camps, in both color and in black and white; we've seen them in file footage of the liberations, and we've seen the locations of the events, decrepit and overgrown, in films like *Night and Fog* and *Shoah*. And of these images we've constructed a knowledge of the Holocaust, and when we see more images—either in last week's *New Yorker* magazine or in *Schindler's List*—we remember. But there is, in the image of this child, something that exceeds this recollection, this memory we have built for ourselves of the Holocaust, and it is just as much the product of a memory, though a different sort of memory, as the edifice of atrocity built by the repetitive images of destruction.

What Zelizer has failed to include in her discussion of memory and the image is memory's underside—though not its opposite—which cuts against the grain and troubles the neat though troubling memory we have constructed of the disaster of the Holocaust. It is this facet of memory—what I'm calling "forgetful memory"—that is a byproduct of what we see in photographs like the one of the child at Belsen, and what we see in other images (both photographic and artistic) that take as their subject the Shoah. If collective memory consists of our reconstructions of past events through their receptions and mediations between the event's occurrence and the present, "forgetful memory" is the interruption of the fabric of memory by the trace or effect of the event that it can't contain. Forgetful memory can be distinguished from "absent memory," what Henri Raczymow calls *mémoire trouée*, literally "breached memory;" whereas absent memory is a "lack of memory" of the event filled with voids, blanks, and silences, accompanied by a "sense of regret for not having been *there*" (Fine 187), forgetful memory makes itself felt as a presence, though a terrifying one, that is characterized not so much by loss as by physical trauma. Forgetful memory, too, makes itself apparent as a disruption or a gap in the narratives of memory we construct of events, and the events are therefore inaccessible either to the one who was there or to the one who wasn't; but whereas the second-generation witness experiences regret at this inaccessibility in absent memory, there's no such regret in forgetful memory. In fact, the witness—the viewer of the photograph, the one who listens or views a testimony—is overtaken by a sense of the event, as though it came unbidden. While forgetful memory cannot retrieve the event irretrievably lost, the instrument of memory produces what might be called a memory effect, a sense of displacement that disrupts the viewer's ability to construct a narrative of, or to sympathize with, the object of the image. Though it is not quite the same thing, either, as Marianne Hirsch's notion of "postmemory," which is an effect of the repetition of images as they are "adopted" by the second and third generations, it shares with postmemory the notion that the image, like the image of the boy in flight from Belsen, has a traumatic effect upon the viewer that disrupts rather than conforms to collective memory or knowledge of the object depicted.

My task in this chapter is two-fold. First, I want to lay out a notion of forgetful memory that contrasts with a more orthodox notion of remembrance that is commonly associated with the Holocaust and the foul trove of photographic images associated with it. Forgetful memory destroys knowledge, and like Maurice Blanchot's disaster, "ruins everything" while leaving what we remember nevertheless intact. Second, I want to spend some time describing how photographs with which we have become familiar, and even more photos with which we have not, may invoke just such a forgetful memory. The photographs I refer to here are not photos of atrocity as such—there few corpses or burned synagogues. These are not photos taken by the liberators, but by the captors and, in some instances, by the victims themselves. Through these images I want to suggest briefly how their use in photography and, even more briefly in artistic invocations of photographic images, provides a space of forgetfulness that may be more effective—though ironically are potentially destructive of the certainties accompanying history—in making plain a trace of the event.

What we've seen in our investigations of forgetful memory so far is that all individual memories are constrained by reality, that which is "beyond the modes of narrative, the mythopoetic intensity of the narrator, the intervening subconsciousness and superego," and which "escapes our control, [and] forces itself upon us whether or not we welcome it," but it is also "that which we make relevant, construct, manipulate" (Krell 68–9). Memory, as anamnesis, is an instance whereby that which is beyond the modes of narrative ("the event," reality as it impinges upon us and our conventions of thought and language) is an instance of just this facet of the real. And though it impinges upon us, it may or may not be narratable, though it is most certainly visible as it works its way against the grain of the narrative of collective memory.

FORGETFULNESS AND THE IMAGE

The question now before us is this: how do images from the Shoah both fix a memory, as Zelizer suggests, and at the same time work against that memory's grain through the indication of another, forgetful memory? How do photographic and artistic images force on the secondary witness the displacement

Marianne Hirsch associates with a memory that imprints itself on the witness as a trauma that is associated, but only associated, with the irrecuperable event that forms its source? In working through collections of photographs and other images of the Shoah, what strikes me is the difference between those collected by Barbie Zelizer for her work on atrocity photos and those countless other photographs that were taken before and during the second World War. Zelizer's book focuses on the images that were collected immediately before and during the liberation of the camps in the east but mainly in greater Germany, photos that were collected by photojournalists travelling with the Allied Armies (mostly the British and Americans, though some images collected by the Soviet army are also accounted for). But there are countless archives and collections of photographs that were taken surreptitiously by anti-Nazis, by members of the sonderkommandos in the camps, officially by those responsible for the Final Solution as a way to catalogue the liquidation of Jewish civilization in Europe and unofficially by individual soldiers who were either curious, proud, or disgusted by what was taking place at their hands. Two such collections are the Bilderarchiv Preussischer Kulturbesitz (the Photo Archive of the Prussian Cultural Trust), which was opened in what was then West Berlin in 1966 and to which have been added over seven times its initial number of photos (now over seven million); and the collection of photographs of Jewish children deported to the east from France between the summers of 1942 and 1944, a collection compiled by Serge Klarsfeld between 1993 and 1996 from the US Holocaust Memorial Museum, Yad Vashem, and survivors' and relatives' albums. These two collections, in particular, contained photographs whose images at times do not speak directly to the disaster, and whose contexts—particularly in the case of Klarsfeld's collection—only partly account for the disruptive capacity of the images. They, it would seem, would provide a test case for whether photographic images might indicate a forgetful memory that cuts across the broader contours of a historical or cultural memory of the Holocaust.[1]

In effect, the photographs from the Prussian Photo Archive would seem to be the most susceptible to being "stripped of their referential power," their connection to a specific time and place, because the captions that would connect them to that context are so thin. Zelizer makes the point that it was common during the liberation of the camps for photos used in newspaper and magazine accounts of the atrocities rarely to be linked to the specific camps or to the photographers who served as witnesses. Instead, they were able to stand in for the larger atrocity—"the Holocaust"—and for that reason were able to serve as markers for the larger cultural significance of the atrocity and metonymically substituted the memory that was constructed by the photos for the witnesses' presence (or, in the case of most American readers, absence) in the midsts of the event. And it is true that, in large measure, the photos in the Prussian Archive depicting life in the Warsaw ghetto, or the liquidation of the Jews of the Russian pale of settlement, are familiar to most of us, and may well serve as a memory-by-proxy of the Holocaust. There are also photographs that, whithout caption or the context of their place in an archive that documents the destruction associated with the Final Solution, would not seem out of place in a chest full of photos from the old country: men sitting together at a table with the *Megilla* on Purim, with the reader wearing a *tallis* and *kippah* while the men, most in fedoras and suits, tolerate the younster at the edge of the photo making noise with a *grogger*. There are no yellow stars, or swastikas outside an uncurtained window, to give the game away. Photos such as these would seem to indicate nothing of the disaster at all; it is only their location in the archive itself that gives them a double life as a marker of destruction.

The photos I want to pay attention to, however, are those that indicate a disaster—though the particularities of time and place can only be indicated by their captions—but that also carry with them signs of some other event. These are photos that, to our second- or third-generation eyes, create a knowledge and a memory of the events in Europe in the years between 1933 and 1945, memories that bear the weight of history and comprise a tapestry of destruction that is all too familiar to us. And yet these photos also indicate—at their margins, or in what cannot be captured by the camera but which is just off to one side, or just prior to, the frame of the plate or the instant the shutter closes—what has been lost, forgotten, and yet which troubles the memory conjured by them.

In a photograph taken in what the caption tells us is late 1940, in Warsaw, the center of the frame is taken up by an open door in a nondescript gray building. It's one of those doors that is somewhere near twelve feet tall, and is of carved wood, and it marks the entrace to one of those buildings whose institutional use is well known to Europeans: built in the very late part of the nineteenth century, they are made of sandstone and are, like the one pictured, pillared. On either side of the door stand three men, each in military-style peaked cap, one in a dark uniform, and two others, to the door's left, in light coats. As the caption on the photo also tells us that this is the Jewish Council office, we can surmise that these two men, in ill-fitting uniforms and, in one case anyway, badly-made shoes, are Jewish police, and they seem to be each looking at the individuals who are coming out of the door of the office. Just inside the open door stands a man in bowler hat, buttoning his coat, who cannot be more than five feet tall. He is following a couple, a man in full-length coat and a woman beside him in a frock coat, a leather purse slung over one arm, a lovely hat on her head and—is it possible?—stockings. The man seems to be saying something to her, and her left hand, reaching for her head, seems to be in gesticulation, perhaps in response. Under her right arm is either a book or a set of documents.

Out of the line of sight of any of the pictured individuals, but very much in the viewer's, is a man to the photo's lower left. Sitting on the second of the

FIGURE 1. Entrance to the Jewish Council office with Jewish police at the door. Warsaw, late 1940. Copyright Bildarchiv Preussischer Kulturbesitz, Berlin.

two-step entryway to the office, and either asleep, passed out from hunger or dead, is a man in rumpled dark coat and some type of hat. His head is bent sideways, and is just barely propped up on the elbow of his left arm; he legs are sprawled out in front of him in no particular direction, and as he lies there, his mouth hangs open. Unlike the others in the photo, the shadows of his face are hollow: he is not well fed, or well dressed, and he is, more like the man just leaving the building, much more so than the police to the sides of the door or the couple exiting just before him, unable to return a glance, unfocused upon the scene around him. On the margins of the photo in more ways than one, he is neither engaged in the drama of departure from the building, nor is he a central figure in the structure of the photo.

This is no image of atrocity but, in the context provided by the Prussian Archive, simply one of several hundred photos of "Poland under German Conquest," and is more tightly contextualized as one of a number of images of ghetto "street scenes" taken in 1940 and 1941, before the terrible privations of the later years of liquidation and transportation. It accompanies other photographs of life on the streets of Warsaw: women engaged in conversation in front of a kiosk, a couple—man in peaked cap and a woman, perhaps his wife, in fur coat, knit hat and purse in front of a door through which bearded men and others enter and exit quickly, judging from the blur—caught looking behind them at the photographer, three women walking arm-in-arm down the center of a street. The bustle of activity in front of the door of the building, like the bustle of activity in each of the street scenes from these years, does not so much engage us in the creation of a memory of the Final Solution, with its images of gas chambers and of skeletal corpses, which form the center of "the Holocaust"; instead, these images seem to build a memory connected to a collective sense of a European past, a fast-paced urban engagement with bureaucracy and barely-concealed commerce whose inhabitants apparently express the full range of human emotions we might expect. Barely visible—if visible at all—in many of these images are the armbands on which appear the mandatory sign of expulsion, the Star of David that identifies them as Jews, and therefore as Other.

And yet, just at the margins of the photo of the police office, lies this man: not quite a corpse perhaps, but certainly not able to make his way through the door, either as an entrace or an exit. Starkly visible in this particular photo is an image and a memory of the bureaucracy of the Final Solution: its bizarre cast of characters comprised of Jewish men who become instruments of the concentration of the Jews of Europe, who look no less Jewish than any of the other individuals in the frame (and, in this photograph, perhaps more, as the police officer just to the right of the door looks like an unshaven Leon Trotsky); former inhabitants of Warsaw, now crammed inside its ghetto, who look like they've lived in a city all their lives and who refuse to walk to the office of the police in anything but smart clothes; and the nondescript building. Just as visible here, but just to the edges of the frame, is the one who undermines this well-wrought narrative, and this well-founded memory, of the urban bureaucracy of the ghetto: who is this man, and how did he come to be here? More importantly, what calamity is it that no one, not a single person pictured here, seems to notice that he's here? (Or, is it not calamity at all, but simply the callousness that comes of living in a crowded city, one that allows us to step over those who don't have a place in our, or anyone else's commerce? Or is this memory my own displaced sense of a turn of the twentieth century urban ethos?) This one man, without a clearly-marked role and without an identity at all inside the frame of the photo, troubles the image whose caption seems to provide it a coherence in the context of the officialdom of the Final Solution, and opens the door to what will be painfully evident less than a year later, when the starving, anonymous, and barely visible inhabitants of the ghetto move from the margins of the photographs into their center. It works against the memory that would allow us to keep the date and place of the photo—"Warsaw, late 1940"—sealed from the dates and places and memories of atrocity we know too well— "Auschwitz, late summer 1944;" "Dachau, spring 1945." In other words, this marginal image intervenes in the memory that we would otherwise be allowed to construct, and like memory's double (like a flash of anamnesis in the midsts of the narrative provided by recollection, mneme), calls to mind if only fleetingly that which is otherwise forgotten, stands in the way of the name of the image, and forces the viewer to acknowledge that which would otherwise fall out of memory altogether.

Included in the Prussian Arvhives are countless photos of children and families, some during the early years of the ghettos, and some—heartbreaking photos—that document the toll the concentration took in the months just before liquidation in 1942 and 1943. By far, the most wrenching images are from the ghetto in Warsaw, images that include families sitting together on curbs, mothers emaciated and nearly dead with their children—perhaps fed from her ration of food, alive and clearly aware of the situation at her side; and of five- and six-year old boys, looking like little old men with hollow eyes, begging for handouts. But one image in particular, this one from the Lodz ghetto, seems much less explicitly about the tragedy of the ghetto. Captioned "boy feeding younger child, Lodz ghetto, 1942," the photo captures a boy of between ten and fourteen, crouched or sitting against a wall, holding a can of what might be soup in his left hand and holding a spoon in his right. With his right hand he is lifting the spoon into the mouth of a toddler, a child of perhaps two years old and which could easily be his sister, who stands at his side, clutching the lapels of her coat with both hands. Neither child suffers from the hollow cheeks or the fatigue that comes with starvation; though dirty, neither child is dressed in rags as many of the children pictured from the Warsaw ghetto in those same years. What is striking about the photo is

FIGURE 2. Boy feeding younger child, Lodz Ghetto, 1942. Copyright Bildarchiv Preussischer Kulturbesitz, Berlin.

the determination in the visage of the older child, whose lips are pursed either in imitation and sympathy with the younger child's eating, or in what might be brotherly impatience with a younger sibling. Equally striking is the younger child's appearance: slightly grimacing either because the soup is hot or, more likely, because she is hungry, she seems to be watching something outside the photo, but not the photographer, as she stands slightly pigeon-toed in her sandals. Remarkably, there is what appears to be a ribbon in her hair.

What is striking about the photo, in other words, is what cannot be explained. The image is indicative of an object with which we are familiar, and even without the caption we could take some fair guesses about the memory it wishes to invoke. The boy's cap, the grainy background, the absence of adults, all speak to that vague but very well-defined image of the events in eastern Europe that took place in and outside the major urban areas of Warsaw, Lodz, Riga, and Kracow. But it indicates beyond what it contains, and invokes an absence, a space at the center of the photographic and memorial image, that evades the cultural memory of which it is a part. That absence— the relationship between the two individuals pictured, what has occurred just before and just after the photo was taken, where (and who) the children's parents are, and who put that impossible bow in the little girl's hair—bothers the image. Potentially drawing the viewer's attention away from the object of memory, the destruction by attrition of the ghetto in Lodz before its liquidation in 1943, it evokes other memories, individual memories, that cannot be contained by the photo's frame: which viewers are reminded of a cousin, or a child, or a incident, of their own, an incident that occurred well outside of the context of Lodz, of 1942, and of the desperation of rationing, but which is nonetheless invoked by this photo that apparently means to focus attention on something else? There are at least two memories here. There is the one forged, in conjunction with the caption, of the events that occurred in Poland, in the major cities that included Lodz, a memory of the Final Solution. But there are also forged, apart from and in the midsts of that broader memory, myriad other memories that flash before the eyes of the viewer and tear at the fabric of the collective, and of what we think we can know about the events at the center of the frame.

Serge Klarsfeld's attention is likewise focused on children, but outside the contexts of their destruction. If the Prussian Archive focuses its attention on the calamity of the Shoah by forming a mosaic of images—street scenes, images of liquidation, photos of National Socialist propaganda, news images of the camps' liberations and of the resettlement and the trials after the war— in a metaphorical association, Klarsfeld's photos of children transported from detention camps in France to death camps in Poland are largely repetitive, metonymic, and with few exceptions simply full-on shots of individual children. Klarsfeld's aim is made clear at the beginning of his book: after putting together a huge book that simply listed the names, dates and places of birth,

nationalities, and the convoys on which 76,000 Jews were transported from
France to Auschwitz, he became "gripped with an obsession . . . to know their
faces," particularly the faces of the children (xi). The heart of the book is
essentially a photo album, comprised of single photographs—many of them
posed formal and informal snapshots of the children well outside the context
of destruction—that captures the children as they might have appeared in
well-worn pages of albums that they themselves might have kept for their
children as remembrances, had they survived. Klarsfeld, in other words, is
consciously building a memorial, a collective memory of a generation of
French Jewish children that has been lost. But what interests me here is that
which escapes memory in some of these photos, and how the photos themselves seem to invoke it.

Of the posed photographs, the sittings of Aline Korenbajzer are among
the most striking. Most obviously, Aline is a beautiful child, with the fine features we have come to associate—in its own complicated way—with the tiny
beauty pageant competitors like Jon Benet Ramsey. One photo is of head and
shoulders, and the child appears to be looking directly at the camera: her
blond hair is quite long for a child of two or three, and it is pulled away from
her shoulders to reveal only a necklace, while the child's arms are crossed to
prop her up. A second photo, which in Klarsfeld's book is on the recto page
facing the first photo, has the child standing in a photographer's studio in
front of an arras and small chair, on which is seated a nude porcelain doll.
Aline has a hand on the seat of the chair, and is facing forward and just to
the right of center; she has on a striped dress, and has on knee socks and
white ankle-height shoes, and has tiny bracelets on each wrist. Her chin is
just barely tucked into her collar, and it looks as though she's either posing
awkwardly or is slightly dubious about the photographer.

Like many of Klarsfeld's photos, this one was likely chosen from among
several that were donated by surviving family members or borrowed from the
archives of Yad Vashem and the US Holocaust Museum, which came into the
possession of thousands upon thousands of photos that were left behind in
families' belongings as the members themselves were killed. Like many of the
photos in the book, it shows the child absent any sign that she would be
exterminated less than a year after the photos were taken. Even with the caption, we know know only about where the child lived and the name of her
mother, along with the roundup and the convoy that sealed her fate. We are
clearly meant to forge a memory of this child as she was and as she might have
been, had she escaped the destruction of occupied France. And yet like many
if not most of Klarsfeld's photos, this one—in particular, this one—poses as
many problems for Klarsfeld's aim as it does provide a context and a narrative
for it. This child, blond and blue-eyed, with bracelets and necklace, and
whose mother took such care to have her photographed as though she were
a much older child, both stands in for the countless other images of children

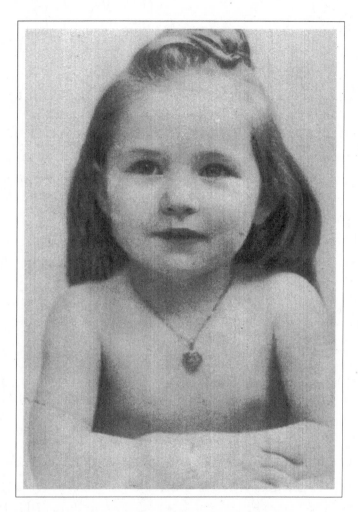

FIGURE 3. Alina Korenbajzer. Serge Klarsfeld Collection.

lost, and works against them. If it is the repetitive series of images that may be substituted, in Klarsfeld's memorial, for a collective memory of the loss of France's Jewish children, this one image (perhaps unlike any of the other images) arrests the series, and inserts some other image—and some other memory, perhaps—into it. Just what this image attests to is anyone's guess, and in fact it is consistent with a notion of forgetful memory that the image attests to no memory at all but to an aspect of the event that is unavailable to the viewer at all except as a blank, an empty kernel, or a breach. If we are meant, in Klarsfeld's book, to forge a memory of loss, what we have instead is a memory comprised of an endless series of children's faces, in which one could substitute for any other, which is not so much a memory as it is a representation of a memory, a representation that functions almost mechanically, as the images spun, one by one on the reel of a moving picture seem to acquire, through their repetition, a life of their own. And yet this one image of the child Aline Korenbajzer stops the reel.

But this photo may not do it for you; it may be that other photos in Klarsfeld's litany arrest the series more effectively. It may be the photo of Irene Simon, standing casually in a clearing in a park, who smiles into the camera while she holds the hand of an unseen individual who lies outside the photo's frame. It takes a minute—particularly if you focus on her hand—for you to recognize that the blotch on her dress, just over her heart, is the yellow star embazoned with the word "juif." Or it may be the photos of the Rozenblum family, set into an oval that contains head-and-shoulders shots of the unnamed mother's four children. The oval is set inside a grave marker, whose partial Hebrew is unreadable outside the frame of the photo but for the word for "in memory," l'zakhor, inscribed just above the oval, and whose French is partly readable just below, "memoire de ma chere," in memory of my dear ones. Or it may be the occasional photos of children, perhaps the only ones that survive, that are stapled unceremoniously to identification cards, photos that were taken for bureaucratic reasons on the spot (and we can tell because the children's hair is rarely combed, and they each hold a small slate on which is written a number that corresponds to the number of the card). Perhaps is is that rare identity card, like Samuel Gutman's, that was created before it was necessary to stamp the word "Juive" on each one, and which includes not a photo taken on the spot but a posed sitting in which the crudely painted balcony scene—with a church steeple in poor perspective—is visible behind him. The point is that regardless of which photo arrests the series, and produces a glimpse of that which escapes memory, each such moment is unmappable, unforseeable, and destructive of the narrative that the photos—in Klarsfeld's telos or anyone else's—desperately try to forge. Outside the series—taking each photo on its own—it is equally true that the photos, taken as substitutes for a memory that cannot possibly be ours, may be inserted into a collective memory whose images include face upon face of

FIGURE 4. Irene Simon. Serge Klarsfeld Collection.

individuals destroyed by the Final Solution that attempted to eradicate individuals in the name of the collective. But even as they form a part of that series, there is at the margins of each photo an unspoken and immemorial past. Perhaps it's only that past invoked by the opening and closing of the shutter of the camera, the moments in whose midsts the image is taken and which are lost except as traces that reside in the curious faces of the children; perhaps it's the past marked by the names of detention camps stamped across the faces of the children in identity cards, places and names (yad vashem) whose histories seem incongruous with the histories of children that appear so happy. Perhaps it is the moment at which kaddish is said by a distant relative at the unveiling of a monument on whose face is inscribed the image of children, arrested (photographically and politically) for the viewer. These incongruities of time and place, of a collective memory and memories lost and marginal to the greater narrative, that interrupt Klarsfeld's memorial.

CONCLUSION:
"FIGURES OF MEMORY AND FORGETTING"

In her discussion of the displacement involved in the second and third generation after the event, Marianne Hirsch sees post-memory as the traumatic memory effect produced by photographs and other images created during and immediately following the Holocaust. Moreso than with the first-generation, the photographic images is not connected to the viewer's experience of the past, but that experience is "created" through "figures of memory and forgetting" (222), and so the repetitive litany of images has the effect of a trauma by invoking that which is not available in the image or the mnemonic recollection. More to the point, it's not so much that these images create a representation of the event, but rather they impress upon the viewer a trace of the event as it is lost—as it occurs prior to its integration into the viewer's experience and, hence, knowledge—that is made palpable in the medium's failure to contain its object. "[T]he image shows that time cannot be frozen: in the case of Holocaust photos . . . the impossibility of stopping time, or of averting death is already announced by the shrinking of the ghetto, the roundup, the footprints pointing toward the site of execution" (224); the photo, in other words, undoes the tidy narrative provided by memory.

It is just this memory effect—the effect of the forgotten and immemorial event—that Bracha Lichtenberg Ettinger attempts to render in her mixed media works. If it's true that the margins of the photographs in collections like the Prussian Photo Archive and Klarsfeld's memorial undo the collective memory of what is at the center of the photo, Ettinger's paintings, which cite rather than represent images from photographs taken during the Shoah, seem

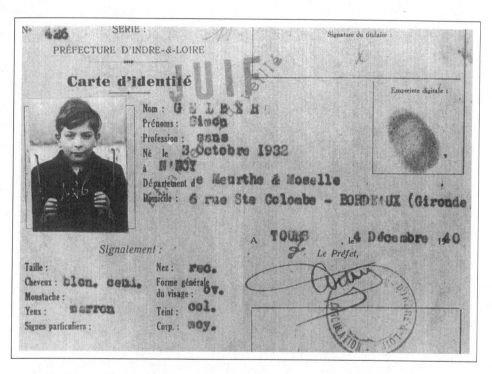

FIGURE 5. Simon Gelber. Serge Klarsfeld Collection.

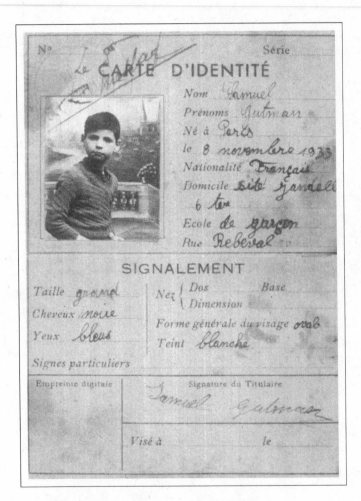

FIGURE 6. Samuel Gutman. Serge Klarsfeld Collection.

to focus their attention on that very margin. Her paintings, in a manner that seems much more self-conscious than those intimated by the photographs taken of the ghetto and at least as self-consciously as Klarsfeld's choices of snapshots used in his album of implied atrocity, speak as much about the trauma of what lingers at the back of memory as a trace than they do about the bludgeon of atrocity itself. Her collection of collage-paintings, entitled *Autiswork* (connoting, vaguely, a sort of autistic inner space of the mind that inhabits neither the "here" of the image's origin nor the conscious representation of the image in word or narrative or visual representation),[2] include realistic images, text, what Alain Kleinmann calls the "annulled image" (in which the object of representation is scratched out or disfigured by the artist in such a way that the blot itself becomes the object of memory [Feinstein 233–6]), and vaguely recognizable photographs seen through a pointillist or impressionist screen of paints and washes.

Born in Tel Aviv and educated in psychology and psychotherapy in Jerusalem and Paris, Ettinger has created paintings that are quite explicitly about the aftereffects of the Shoah. The child of survivors, she says that "My parents are proud of their silence. . . . But in this silence all was transmitted except the narrative. In silence nothing can be changed in the narrative which hides itself" (Ettinger 137); it's as if in her paintings, she wants to indicate the silence which transmitted itself silently. Like Hirsch's trope of memory and forgetting, the work seems to work against the narrative closure that would be reproduced easily in the second and third generation as narrative. Several of the images Ettinger uses in her paintings are from collections widely available, including one or two from the Prussian Arvhives and Klarsfeld's book. Eerily similar to the couple making its way out of the Jewish Police office in Warsaw described earlier, one of the images used over and over again in Ettinger's work is of a couple walking briskly down a street accompanied by a third man. The setting could as easily be Paris as it could be Warsaw, and because of the poor focus of the camera it's difficult to tell whether the whitish blotch on the left-hand lapel on the man's coat is a magen-David-shaped patch. The photo, like others included on the walls of an entranceway to a portion of the exhibit of Ettinger's work in Villeurbane in 1992, includes casual photos, street scenes, that are integrated into the impressionist-like images recast in the paintings as ghostly afterimages that reside just out of reach of collective memory.

Another image repeated again and again is less easy to see, and in reviewing the literature surrounding Ettinger's shows, I cannot find that the original image was hung as correlative to the paintings in which it appears. Those paintings, the most striking of which is a single oil that you might imagine is superimposed upon the photographic image, is entitled "Autiswork No.1," and it depicts four figures, probably female, in purples, blues, and whites. One of the women is clearly cradling what appears to be a child, and

FIGURE 7. Bracha L. Ettinger, "Autiswork No. 1" (1993).

even in the context of the exhibition, which includes images of women and, in the literature accompanying the show, questions the possibility of the female subject position as fixed by the history of painting, it seems to suggest something beyond what it portrays: the child, it seems, is being clutched not cradled. In fact, this image is a repetition of one of the photos in the Prussian Archive, one that has been reproduced in the US Holocaust Museum's permanent exhibit as part of its narrative of the *einsatzgruppen* but which in fact depicts events in Poland in 1943: two dozen women, naked and huddled together in a line, stand at the bottom of a low grassy rise. In front of them, partly occluded from view, are two uniformed soldiers, and just beyond are strewn the clothes the women have just been ordered to remove. In the line are also two children: one of perhaps four in one woman's arms, and the smaller child that appears in Ettinger's image, of perhaps two. The caption tells us that the women are lined up for execution in Mizocz in 1943.

Speaking of other images of execution, Marianne Hirsch says that photos like these don't allow us to see a point before and a point after the photo was taken in which we might imagine another life, another existence, other possibilities. Rather, these women "were already killed by the murderous Nazi gaze that condemned them without even looking at them. This lethal gaze reflects back on images of European Jews that precede the war, removing from them the loss and nostalgia, the irony and longing that structure such photographs from a bygone era" (235). There is no narrative of before and after that we can imagine and to which we can tie the images of destruction; rather, the image speaks to an event we simply cannot know: the annihilation that has been predetermined, and that we know can't escape from under Barthes' punctum, the point of life before which and after which we have to construct narratives of memory and which are only understandable from the perspective of the death of one depicted. Rather, there is something uncanny about the image because the punctum is unmoored: not only are they now dead, whereas in the picture they live; in fact they are already dead at the point when the picture is taken, deprived of self under the Nuremburg laws and stripped of their dignity as they stand naked at the bottom of a hill. Such a punctum, one dead on arrival, is unavailable to us, and it is unavailable to Ettinger as she cites the photo in "Autiswork No.1." But because it is unmoored from memory— Ettinger, born a good ten years after the event and a child of silence—its reproduction as an image can't "desensitize us to the 'cut' of recollection"; it instead has the effect "of cutting and shocking in the ways that fragmented and congealed traumatic memory reenacts the traumatic encounter" (Hirsch 237). It is a figure not of memory but of forgetting, of what escapes the image and the narrative that might tell us what we're seeing.

It may well be true that, as Barbie Zelizer has told us, the repetition of the image, if it works to produce a collective memory of atrocity unconnected to *yad vashem*, the place and the name, the particularity of the disaster is emptied

FIGURE 8. Naked Jewish women line up for execution, Mizocz, 1943. Copyright Bildarchiv Preussischer Kulturbesitz, Berlin.

out of the image and we are left only with a shell: this, we think, is the Holocaust, and Rwanda and Bosnia and Sudan are simply reinstantiations of "the
Holocaust." As part of the collective memory, it is simply that—and there's no
way to break out of the similacrum of horror presented time and time again to
our eyes. "Our memory bank of atrocities . . . works backward in time—using
the past to stand in for the present" (210), and the endless substitution has no
anchor in the event itself. But Zelizer fails to account, I think, for the problem
inherent in figures of repetition—that though they repeat the same, each
instance of the sign is not identical to the one just before or just after it, and
it is this nonidentity, Levinas' encounter with the other, that eventually makes
itself apparent and shatters the collective memory that has no point of origin
in the atrocity itself. Speaking of the image we began with, of Sieg Mandaag
as he makes his way past the corpses outside Bergen Belsen, Edith Wyschogrod
says that regardless of questions historians might ask about this child, or these
corpses, or any other reality depicted by the photo, "so long as the boy in his
uncanny flight is permitted to break into the narrative of what is depicted, the
child's face becomes the escape route for an unsayability that seeps into the
visual image and contests any narrative articulation of what the camera captures" (142). This way of seeing the image, or any of the images discussed here,
doesn't give us knowledge of the events whose object is apparently depicted in
a photograph, or painting, or narrative. It does, however, give us a sense of the
contours of memory, of what lies at its margins, and how the marginal disrupts
our knowledge of the event at the same time it provides a point of entrance—
or departure—for its trace as an effect of what cannot be remembered at all.

FIVE

"Thou Shalt Not Bear False Witness"

Witness and Testimony in the Fragments *Controversy*

━━━━━━━━━━

Then the Lord said to Moses: "Write this in a document as a
memory, and read it aloud to Joshua: I will utterly erase [blot out]
the memory of Amalek from under heaven!"
                        —Exodus 17:14; translation Sarna

It is upon losing what we have to say that we speak—upon an
imminent and immemorial disaster. . . . We speak suggesting that
something not being said is speaking: the loss of what we were to
say; weeping when tears have long since gone dry. . . .
                        —Blanchot, *The Writing of the Disaster*

DOMINICK LA CAPRA has written extensively on what he calls the "exceptionally vexed" relationship between history and memory after Auschwitz:
history and memory cannot be conflated, and in resisting this conflation we
trouble the relation between witness and testimony, as well as the relation
among what happened, what we recognize as occurrences, and what we can
say about those occurrences.[1] "Memory is both more and less than history,
and vice versa," he says (*History and Memory* 20); "with respect to trauma,
memory is always secondary since what occurs is not integrated into experience or directly remembered" at all (21). Cathy Caruth goes even further:
"the victim of [trauma] was never fully conscious during the [event] itself"
(187) and so any testimony of the event will bear at best an oblique relation
with it, since we can only say what we know as experience. Though we live

in what Shoshana Felman aptly calls an era of testimony, testimony's relation to the events of history—to what the witness saw—has become a tenuous one (16–17). We cannot view testimony as a window on the past; at its
most extreme—in cases of memories of trauma—testimony marks the
absence of events, since they didn't register on, let alone become integrated
into, the consciousness of the victim. A testimony may be effective, and it
may allow a reader to catch a glimpse of a trauma (though perhaps not the
one that purportedly lies at its source). But it alone does not provide evidence of that event.

It is this vexed relationship of memory, witness and testimony that I
want to examine through the lens of Binjamin Wilkomirksi's *Fragments*, a
"memoir" whose main character survived the Holocaust as a child. The book
was originally published in Germany in 1995; by 1996 it had been translated
into a dozen languages and become an international sensation, in part
because it was a lucid, excruciating tale that registered upon—traumatized—
its readers.[2] In late 1998, Daniel Ganzfried, whose investigation of
Wilkomirski appeared in the Swiss weekly *Weltwoche*, shocked those who'd
lauded the book: he found documents to suggest that Binjamin Wilkomirski
is a fabrication of a Swiss-born clarinet-maker named Bruno Doesseker, that
Doesseker had never been to a concentration camp "except as a tourist," and
that if *Fragments* is a memoir, it's comprised of other people's memories.

It seems clear now that the events depicted in *Fragments* and the events
of the author's life as found in the historical record don't coincide. But for
many the matter is not settled: even for some of the its detractors, *Fragments*
stands as a powerful testimony to events which are unavailable to those who
were not there, and which are available as open wounds to those who were.
Israel Gutman, a survivor with serious doubts about the historical veracity of
the book, says nonetheless that "Wilkomirski has written a story which he
has experienced deeply, that's for sure" (Lappin 61). If La Capra is right, and
the traumatic occurrence isn't "integrated into experience or directly remembered," then testimonies involve both a remembering and a forgetting—the
suppression of the event and its articulation as narrative; a blotting out and a
writing down—and the authentication of testimonies of events like the
Shoah becomes difficult at best, at least in part because corroborating testimonies and other evidence has been lost. What I want to suggest in this
chapter is that in the case of the Wilkomirski memoir, our ability establish its
authenticity on historical grounds is complicated by its ability to compel
readers to "see" the events about which that the author writes, though they
may not have been experienced by the author at all. This characteristic seems
to fly in the face of history, where the veracity or coherence of eyewitness testimony—the testimony's ability to render or represent a series of events in
terms that are plausible or verifiable—is one of the pillars on which the historical reality or truth of events rests. But it suggests that a testimony's

authority, the extent to which we might say that the speaker or writer provides an opportunity for the reader to bear witness to an event, is relatively autonomous from history; it suggests that there is a marked difference between history as what happens to people (the events that lie beyond or behind historical accounts) and history as what we know about what happened (and for which there is evidence); and it suggests (*pace* Lyotard) that to write what happened we need to be attentive to and find ways to express "what is not presentable under the rules of knowledge" (57) or history.

The central question is how a memoir like *Fragments* can be at once a "false testimony," and still produce an effect upon readers that induces them to witness. To answer this question, I will consider three problems inherent in the structure of memory, particularly traumatic memory, as it has been developed in the work of Cathy Caruth, Shoshana Felman, and others over the last ten years or so.[3] The first is testimony's relative autonomy, or independence, from history. If it's true that the traumatic incident is repressed at the moment of occurrence or deformed in the process of testimony, then testimony cannot easily be elided with the act of witnessing. But if this is the case, then—as a second, correlative problem—we also need to consider whether utterances or texts that are not tied directly to the historical events that are purportedly their object (like *Fragments*, but also like, say, *Life is Beautiful*) should be considered testimonies. Third, we need to consider how testimonies—as relatively autonomous from the event itself—shape a witnessing in the reader or viewer, and whether this "transference" of trauma takes place at the level of content or of structure. Finally, I'll consider at the end of this chapter the risks involved in a theory of trauma and testimony that result from what I take to be the inescapable relation of memory and forgetting that lie at their foundation.

L'AFFAIRE WILKOMIRSKI
AND THE STATUS OF THE TEXT

In early 1994, Eva Koralnik, a literary agent in Zurich, received a copy of the Wilkomirski manuscript through the mail; it made such an impact upon her, and upon members of the press she sent it to, Suhrkamp Verlag in Frankfurt, that it was sold within six months and in production by February 1995. The story was presented as a memoir told from the perspective of a child who, at the beginning of an ordeal that "escap[ed] the laws of logic" (4), was presumably no more than four or five years old. The story takes place in the years between the German occupation of the Baltic countries and the immediate aftermath of the war through the early 1950s, and alternates between two main narrative strands: the author's experiences in two camps (Majdanek and an unnamed camp that was identified later as Auschwitz), and his later life in orphanages immediately after the war. In the afterword to his book he writes that he had at that time "received a new identity, another name, another date and place of birth," but that none of it has to do "with either the history of this century or my personal history" (154). The book seemed to attest to the radical disjunction between history and memory, between the fragmentary but indelible images of a past the author couldn't shake and the historical circumstances into which those images were fit.

It was the disjunction between memory and the historical record that most bothered Daniel Ganzfried, an Israeli-born Swiss writer whose own novel is based on his father's experiences as an Auschwitz survivor. Ganzfried began a process of investigation that would, he hoped, uncover just who the author was and to learn about the contours of his memory. What he found was what most of the people who are familiar with this story already know:[4] that Fragments was written by Bruno Doesseker, a clarinet-maker whose adoption papers record his birth in early 1941 to Yvonne Grosjean, an unmarried woman who was herself, along with her brother, separated from impoverished parents. He was placed with foster parents, Kurt and Martha Doesseker, in 1945 and was eventually adopted by them legally in late 1957. Up until that time, the boy's father paid toward the cost of his son's care. In 1981, Bruno Doesseker inherited a small sum from the modest estate of Yvonne Grosjean, who he calls his "so-called natural mother." The writer's house is full of archival material, including oral testimonies, films, photographs, and historical accounts of the events that comprised the Final Solution and its aftermath. Ganzfried was convinced that this archive forms the core of the Wilkomirski memoir, and that inconsistencies in the account—for example, a female camp warden would not have worn a formal uniform out on patrol in the Polish countryside, as Wilkomirski "remembers"—are the result of the autodidact's scattershot approach to a history of the Holocaust. (Doesseker claims that the research helped to place into context the flashes of memory that result from a child's perspective on events, and that it offered "the calming 'possibility' of finding 'the historical center' of [my] own past" [Gourevitch 56–7].) Ganzfried asked Wilkomirski whether he was circumcised, a "natural question to ask of a Jewish man," to which the latter answered yes. When asked, Doesseker's former girlfriends responded that he was not. Ganzfried claims that no child so young could have survived not just one camp but two, and this claim has been bolstered by Raul Hilberg, who believes it all but impossible for a child to have been hidden for three years. And yet Israel Gutman, a survivor of Majdanek though not during the time Wilkomirski claims to have been there, says that though very few children survived, there were an extraordinary few who did: "Look . . . we know that during the Holocaust extraordinary things happened, which did not correspond to the general rules. . . . I don't know whether one should look at every-

thing [Wilkomirski] said under a microscope" (Lappin 46). Ganzfried is especially wary that Doesseker is far too emotional about the stories he tells and
the reactions he gets from readers of his work: "He cries a lot—and always at
the right moment," he says, and both Lappin and Gourevitch report that they
were equally taken aback. Doesseker's companion, Verena Piller, and a psy-
chiatrist with whom he has travelled and spoken at conferences, Elitsur Bern-
stein, both said that his emotional condition and physical infirmities are consistent with a man who has suffered a severe trauma or set of traumatic
experiences. Lappin suggests that as a child Bruno Doesseker constantly tin-
kered with the story of his origins—one friend recalls that "'he used to say
that his adoptive parents wanted him as a medical experiment,'" and a couple says he told them in the 1960s that "'he had been in the Warsaw ghetto
and was saved from the Holocaust by a Swiss nanny'"—as a way of dealing
with the trauma of a forcible separation from his mother, Yvonne Grosjean.
She found that Doesseker's mother was separated from her parents as *verd-
ingkind* ("earning child") under a seventeenth-century system of child welfare, which was not abolished until the 1950s, in which poor or unmarried
parents sent their children away to work for other families in exchange for
food and shelter. "Beatings and sexual abuse were often part of their childhood"; Bruno himself may have been separated from his mother under similar circumstances (Lappin 63).[5]

The most straightforward interpretation of these contradictions is that
Fragments is a fabrication, a hoax, or a delusion. But regardless of whether or
not there is a traumatic kernel that lies at the heart of the book, it may well
function as a vehicle for witnessing even though it does not qualify as a testimony. And this raises an interesting question: does fiction serve equally well
as a vehicle for memory? One warrant for an affirmative answer can be found
in a rhetorical tradition that pays attention to what resides behind the language of a discourse rather than in the speaker's integrity or the degree to
which the discourse can be squared with a state of affairs. The extent to
which a discourse has authority depends on the its ability to move an audience to "see" an issue or an event that exceeds language's ability to narrate it.
A text's authority finds its source in its ability to indicate (though perhaps
not produce) knowledge of what lies beyond what can be logically understood, or that "makes sense."[6] But in the case of the Shoah, regardless of a testimony's ability to make sense, can't it be called into question if we impeach
the character or the veracity of a speaker? How can what they say be possible, we might ask? Any testimony would have to agree with or at least corroborate a good deal of other eyewitness testimony of the Holocaust in order
to tell a certain truth. It would have to represent a reality to which other witnesses have testified and which is internally coherent (see Ginzburg, "Just
One Witness"; Jay, "Of Plots".) Yet Holocaust testimony is often both extrinsically incredible—the events to which the witness testifies seem impossible,

unreal—and intrinsically incoherent, exhibiting gaps, silences, and disjunc-tions. It is also true that potentiallly corroborating eyewitnesses and other documentary evidence have been destroyed. The relation between truth as content and what lies beyond truth—what might be called, in psychoanalytic terms the "real"—is the matter at issue in the debate, late in the *Phaedrus*, on the value of writing. Ammon charges that writing is not a drug for memory, but for reminding (275a): writing cannot bring the object of knowledge to the reader, though writing does *remind* the reader of it (making it "truly writ-ten on the soul" [278a]). In fact, the conundrum is whether writing/rhetoric produces truth or an image of truth, and most readers of the *Phaedrus* suggest that the best it can do is the latter. What writing, and ideally rhetoric, can do, however, is indicate what lies at the source of language—what lies at its point of origin but to which language does not provide unfettered access.

Lyotard, in *The Differend*, makes a similar point: particularly in the case of limit events like Adorno's "Auschwitz," it isn't enough for an eyewitness to testify to the reality of an event to give the event authenticity or establish its veracity. "Reality is not a matter of the absolute eyewitness, but a matter of the future" (53). To project an occurrence into the reader's or viewer's future, "it is necessary to be able to name and show referents that do not falsify the accepted definitions" but also to name the event in different instances so that it "obey[s] heterogenous regimens and/or genres" (55). Literary language (fic-tion) qualifies as such a projection; to qualify as testimony, literature must also to be mapped onto "the signification that learning establishes"—the tapestry of historical evidence, other testimonies that verify and corroborate the witness's—while it "lends an ear to what is not presentable under the rules of knowledge" (57). Yet Lyotard is unclear about the relation of what this kind of language allows the reader to see to the historical events that lie at its heart. Whether the horror of Auschwitz is what the reader of testimo-nial accounts of it sees can't be answered easily; whether what he sees is his-torical, and meets the demands of "accepted definitions" is less difficult if there are other accounts whose historical details match it. *Life is Beautiful* may allow readers to catch a glimpse of events beyond what the film itself can represent; but *Life is Beautiful* is not historically accurate unless it meets not just an indicative criterion but also an intrinsic or extrinsic one. The same is true of *Fragments*: it may function as testimony; but what the reader sees may not match what's in the narrative, let alone what Bruno Doesseker saw.

WITNESS AND TESTIMONY

In the late winter and early spring of 1997, a pair of interviews were con-ducted with a Holocaust survivor, Mary R., who lives in St. Louis and acts as a docent in that city's Holocaust Museum. In part Mary's job is to testify to the events that she witnessed during her childhood in Lodz and later in the women's barracks in Auschwitz. Listening to her interview, it is clear that she has become accustomed to providing a narrative of the events of the Holocaust as she herself was connected to them. But the testimony she provides is an imperfect vehicle that fails to contain what she saw. As she puts it, her work at the Museum is not easy because what she says day after day "may be similar, [but] it's not learned by heart stuff; after all I can only tell my particular story, I can't tell you anything else . . ." (Stanovick 1997, 2). In fact, her particular story of the events to which she bears witness *is* something else, something other than the testimony she provides. Whatever she manages to get across can only pale in comparison to the horrors of watching her mother die in the ghetto, or of four years in Displaced Persons camps. But in this case Mary herself cannot recall those experiences because as they are witnessed, they are not conceptualized *as* experiences.

As they make their way through the St. Louis museum during their first meeting, the interviewer asks some initial questions, and as she points to a railway car she asks about Mary's transport from Lodz.

INTERVIEWER: You were there with your mother and father?

MARY R.: Just my father. My mother died in the ghetto.

I: Of starvation?

M: [hesitation] She became sick. [Hesitation] And that combination, I guess. . . . [Silence]

I: Was she living with you?

M: Oh, of course, we were in that one little room together, but she had hepatitis and she had pneumonia, there weren't enough medications, she was a fragile person. [Silence]

I: How was taking care of her?

M: Very difficult. I don't even like to think about it. In all, eleven million civilian people killed in the concentration camps and otherwise by Germans. Out of that were six million Jewish people, and out of that were a million and a half children. (Stanovick 1997, 1–2)

The silences and hesitations that appear throughout this section of Mary R.'s interview mark spaces in which the experience of her mother's death cannot be narrated at all, but which haunt her. Cathy Caruth would say that the gaps mark a separation between the survivor's witnessing of the traumatic occurrence before it is processed as "experience" and its return as a departure in the narrative of the testimony. The mother's death returns in the context of the death of eleven million during the Shoah—the particular act of witnessing

becomes embedded in another, more generalizable and historically understood event that can (though problematically so) be conceptualized at the
universal level. "Very difficult. I don't even like to think about it. In all
eleven million civilian people killed." The act of witness makes itself apparent only in the gap between the particular event and the conceptual, historical narrative of the Shoah, a testimony that is so troubled by the traumatic
occurrence that it falls apart before our eyes. The witness makes available an
absence that so disrupts her present that presence and absence become
absolutely inseparable, so much so that Mary R.'s language becomes submerged by her gestures, and while she cannot provide a testimony to the
interviewer that describes the death of her mother in the ghetto, the interviewer may see something else in the rupture of that testimony: "eleven million . . . six million . . . one and a half million."

Caruth's point in "Unclaimed Experience" and in her book of the same
title is that history and trauma bear an indissoluble connection with one
another. We consider history as that which can be preserved as a memory and
written, but the event that serves as the object of history, that which happens,
is erased or blotted out. Blanchot's argument about the "immemorial" nature
of the disaster suggests that once an experience occurs, it is forever lost; it is at
this point—"upon losing what we have to say" (Blanchot 21), the point of forgetfulness—that writing begins. Forgetfulness is the source of memory. The
"victim of [trauma] was never fully conscious during the [event] itself: the person gets away, Freud says, 'apparently unharmed'" (Caruth 187). The witness
saw, but *only* saw, the deed or the circumstance that presented itself as trauma;
the traumatic circumstance was never fully known—and hence could not be
remembered—at all, and what follows is a profusion of language. What we
read in survivor testimonies like Mary R.'s is the displacement of the traumatic
event—the historical event, lost to memory—by the language of the testimony, the sometimes broken, sometimes contradictory stories of the camps, or
of hiding, or of the aftermath. But it is a language that is disrupted by that
event, the language of repetition, in which the event is narrated over and over
again but in language that may not be clearly associated with the event at all.

Wilkomirski's book is comprised of such language. It is not a narrative
that reconciles two lives and languages so much as it is a series of tableaux,
in which one set of experiences of orphanages, homes, and schools is connected to another set of experiences of the camps. One such pair of images
involves the young Binjamin hiding near a pile of corpses, one of which—a
woman's—begins to move. As its belly bulges and writhes, Binjamin watches
in horror as a rat emerges, slick and blood-covered, and he wonders what this
birth-scene suggests of his own origins. Then:

> Many years later, I went with my wife for the birth of our first son. . . . The
> first thing that slowly became visible was the half-round of the baby's head.

As a first-time father, I didn't know how much dark hair a newborn baby can have. I wasn't ready for this little half-head of hair. All I could do was stand still and stare at it, once again, like an echo from before, I heard the ringing and crackling noise in my chest. (88)

In Langer's terms (following Charlotte Delbo's), there are two irreconcilable selves, or narrative memories, at work here doing battle for control over the story, and over control of the writer's ability to understand the relation between images that—if we take him at his word—indicated memories separated by thirty years (Langer 47). The two selves "interact and intersect continually" (7) throughout the narrative of *Fragments*. But there is no history—a knowledge of what happened—available to either the witness or to the viewer/reader of the testimony, that can be gleaned from the passage above. Between the horrible memory of the corpse that Binjamin can't seem to shake and the image of his son's birth into which that memory intrudes unbidden is something unavailable to knowledge. Whatever it is, either in the narrative of *Fragments* or in Mary R.'s testimony of her mother's death, it can't be presented as a narrative. Whatever it is, it is seen but not recognized by Bruno Doesseker and—in different terms, but seen nonetheless—by the witness to the text: the reader. But whatever it is, it is lost "to what we were to say" (Blanchot 21).

What cannot be placed into the narrative—what the boy Doesseker saw that became coded in the language of the Holocaust and that makes its way to the surface of the text as Binjamin Wilkomirski's memory—finds no place in the language of narrative, but it does have a place, of sorts, in testimony. "There are no feelings left. . . . I'm just an eye, taking in what it sees, giving nothing back" (87). The moment of witness is here: in losing what he has to say, the testimony begins, a testimony that refers to what has been blotted out as much as to what has been fixed as a memory. Here, in the no-place of the narrative, is the gaping, open wound, the trauma experienced by the writer (who may or may not be the boy Binjamin; we may never know) and that is witnessed only in terms of the absence of Doesseker's own place in the historical circumstances he narrates. In Langer's terms, the self caught up in the time during the killing wins the battle over the present.

Testimonial narratives don't disclose history; instead they disclose— where the narrative most clearly shows its seams—the effect of events upon witnesses. As a memoir, *Fragments* functions in the same way: its language doesn't easily follow the patterns that correspond to the general rules of historical narratives—"very difficult; I don't even like to think about it; in all eleven million were killed"—and by itself doesn't give us a way to adjudicate the competing claims of Bruno Doesseker and Daniel Ganzfried. As for the narrative itself, and its depiction of events that bore it, its gaps cannot be said simply to represent inaccuracies; rather—as Caruth suggests, speaking of

Freud—they represent and "preserve history precisely within this gap in his text" (190). Each encounter with memory repeats the initial trauma, but by other means—narrative means—that are constantly interrupted by a "gap" of both memory and of experience.

SECOND-HAND WITNESSING

This doesn't mean that *Fragments* (like testimonies, written memoirs, or fictions) can't be disproved as an inaccurate account of the events it purports to narrate. It means that whatever the book's significance, it can't be attributed to its worth as history, but must be connected to events unrecorded (or unwritable) as history (or, as one reader of a draft of this chapter has aptly put it, apart from history). But Shoshana Felman's work goes further, suggesting that the effectiveness of the work may not be the result of any correspondence between what it represents and the object of representation, but of a kind of "transference" effect. The effect of testimony, in Doesseker's case coded in the language of the Shoah and structured by a language that displaces the reader's sense of the normal (or of history), opens a moment in which the reader of the testimony himself becomes a second-hand witness, and sees not the experience described but something that stands beyond or before it, not history but history's real (Vidal-Naquet, qtd. in Ginzburg 86).

Felman's understanding of trauma parallels Caruth's: as in Freud's case of the accident from which the victim has apparently escaped, the traumatic event remains unknown. What follows in the absence of the name but in the full awareness that something horrible has taken place is a compulsive speaking "in advance of the control of consciousness, [in which] testimony is delivered in 'breathless gasps'" (29). It is a *"precocious testimony . . . that speak[s] beyond its means,"* that testifies to the event "whose origin cannot be precisely located but whose repercussions, in their very uncontrollable and unanticipated nature, still continue to evolve even in the very process of testimony" (Felman 29, 30). One of the problems inherent in the historical testimony of the event of the Shoah, then, is that—as people like James Young and Saul Friedlander have warned—the memory of the event, particularly the traumatic one, "evolves" in the process of the telling, and that its language is uncontrollable and cannot be anticipated. Pursued by the obligation to speak, the witness is not necessarily pursued by the obligation to provide an historically accurate accounting of the event, because the event as such has disappeared.

What complicates matters is that, for Felman, the trauma that pursues the witness also pursues witnesses to the witnessing. In her seminar at Yale, students experienced what she calls a "crisis" of witnessing, in which—after reading poetry and narratives of witness, and after viewing several video-taped testimonies from the Fortunoff Archive—they became profoundly ill at ease with what they were seeing, and broke into an "endless and relent-less talking." The accident—the disaster—"had *passed through* the class" (52, Felman's emphasis). The trace or abyss of the event that made itself evident in the "stuttering" of the texts—their silences, their incommensu-rabilities, their figural displacements—produced an anxiety in Felman's stu-dents. The Wilkomirski book, marked by the stutters, breaks, and impossi-ble juxtapositions of images relies, like all written and oral testimonies, upon metonymic substitutions, in which one term displaces another, where the terms bear a resemblance to one another and whose association is pre-sumably provided by the larger text. For Hayden White, the importance of metonymy is that the extrinsic relation—the order of reality outside the discursive situation that provides the context in which these terms may be related—allows the reader to understand more clearly the aspects of the reality the metonymic figure is meant to distinguish (see *Metahistory* 34–6). But this focus needs to be paired with another, critical dimension of the nature of displacement: the distance between the effect of metonymy or of metaphor and its (absent) cause. Metonymy, as a contiguous chain of signi-fication, a word-to-word exchange, presumes the context in which terms make sense, and the *displacement* of one term by another defers understand-ing (or closure of the historical hermeneutic). But it also forces a disjunc-tion between a term and its substitute: the displacement of metonymy, because it does not allow a reader outside the chain of signification (because it presumes the context inside of which the substitution takes place), is potentially disruptive of that context. In Françoise Meltzer's terms, "in spite of its apparent difference of meaning in each case, each sig-nifier in this chain has in fact the same meaning as the one before it: the lack which spells desire" (160), forcing the reader's attention not on that which appears familiar—the different aspects of the same—but upon the impossible relation between all of the different attributes of the object or event and the singular, palpable sense of the object or event itself.

In a different context, Saul Friedlander makes the connection between the repetitive nature of metonym, which reduces the object of discourse to something inanimate, and the uncanny. Through repetition "we are con-fronted with [an uncertainty brought on by the representation] of human beings of the most ordinary kind approaching the state of automata by elim-inating any feelings of humanness and of moral sense. . . . Our sense of *unheimlichkeit* is indeed triggered by this deep uncertainty as to the 'true nature'" of the referent of the narrative itself (Friedlander 30). Wilkomirski's narrative is a catalogue of metonymy: German soldiers are referred to as "the gray uniform," "the black uniform," "bull-neck," and, as their Swiss counter-parts, civilians, "fat faces, strong arms, terrible hands." The writer refers to himself as "skin" or "the voice." These repetitions become a sign that what we had once recognized as the homely or familiar is actually made up of the shards of its attributes, but that they are attributes that cannot possibly be the sum total of the familiar. This does not mean that the point of origin of the metonymic chain—history as "what happened" to Doesseker—is identical in both the writer and the reader. The disruptive capacity and displacement of metonymy is here related to that experienced by the reader, but they are not comparable, let alone interchangeable. Whatever originated the writing—whatever it was that brought Doesseker to write *Fragments*—is lost to memory, and is only available in the historical record; what the reader sees through the anxiety, the unheimlichkeit, resulting from the repetitive language of the book, is likewise lost at the moment she tries to regularize it as knowledge. The best we can say is that the moments are related structurally; whatever would hold them together in a homologous relation is lost.

Felman argues that the uncertainty brought on by a repetition of figure or image in combinations—like the uncanny—defy our capacity to link them or provide a context that makes sense of them. What remains is the resulting talk—the testimony of the second-hand witness—and the need to "work through" the resulting chaos by producing a narrative that orders the precocious and puts it in its proper place (see Felman 54–7; see also La Capra, *Representing*, especially 205–23). One of Felman's students, "caught between two contradictory wishes at once, to speak or not to speak," says " I can only stammer," and turns, as a result, to literature, and "read[s] as if for life" (58). Clearly the crisis that passed through the class and the irretrievable event—the initial trauma—are not commensurate events. To say that the events of the Shoah that form the kernel of Mary R.'s testimony and the crisis of witnessing are the same is absurd. But structurally, they are intimately related: in both cases the language of testimony is a locus of witnessing, marking both the loss of the event and the cause of writing.

Philip Gourevitch reports that while he was interviewing Bruno Doesseker for his *New Yorker* essay, he read an essay on memory by Alan Baddeley. Baddeley reports that memories can be "coded" differently depending upon the context in which one does the remembering (66). Gourevitch goes on to suggest, as Lappin did earlier, that Doesseker's attempts to address the forgotten events of his own life with a narrative were biased by the reaction he received as he "encoded" them with the context of the Holocaust. As the public reception of the Holocaust changed gradually from shameful taboo too hallowed icon, the reaction to the stories Doesseker told about his own experiences as a "survivor" changed as well.

When [Doesseker] said "nightmare" and [the reaction] came back "Holocaust," he could both resist and creep up on the possibility, in a hypnotic, semiconscious manner, which not only seemed like memory but felt like it, too. . . . Wilkomirski [said], "By the time I started my historical research I slowly got used to the idea that a part of my memory is in a part of Auschwitz." (Gourevitch 66).

Whatever Doesseker's motives, it's no surprise that, if his aim was to produce a document through which readers would experience the shock, if not the traumatic instance, of the horrors of the Shoah, then his research (which involved looking at photographs of the camps and of their destruction of Jewish central Europe) would have provided a vocabulary of the unhemilichkeit with which to do so. And if Doesseker himself was shocked, if not traumatized, by what he read and saw in his research, then it's perfectly plausible that he would have experienced an uncanniness similar to that which Felman's students did. The relentless need to bridge the abyss of memory brought on by the recurrence of trauma as it impinges upon one's ability to write or to speak may be filled with images and language one has already come upon. If Elena Lappin is right, and Bruno Doesseker was forcibly separated from his mother and was subject to experiences to which he still cannot put a name and which have had a hold on his imagination since that time, we should not be surprised that he testifies to those experiences through the language of the most significant horror of the twentieth century, whose effect upon individuals and upon a culture is unspeakable and altogether unknowable as a whole may well take the place of and (mis-) name the events to which he does not have access. As Elena Lappin has said, "Wilkomirski often refers to his memories as being film-like. They are, I believe, more than that: they are, I believe, derived from films. . . . I cannot believe that *Fragments* is anything other than fiction. And yet, . . . anguish like [his] seemed impossible to fabricate" (Lappin 61). Whether the events and the story bear any direct relation to one another is—given what we know about the dynamic relation between forgetfulness and memory—an open question.

CONCLUSION

I want to conclude by indicating some of the ethical implications of the preceding discussion of testimony, implications that trouble some of the assumptions we hold about Holocaust remembrance that are associated with the injunctions like "never forget," and "never again." If a witness's participation in the events of history—particularly traumatic events—are irrecuperable except through the fragmented and troubled narratives that fail to contain them, then the connection between the event and the resulting testimony is more tenuous than we'd like to think. These narratives may well serve as evidence of the events comprising the day-to-day litany of destruction; and the historical circumstances of these written accounts—some of which were found buried amidst the rubble of ghettos, some of which are corroborated detail by detail in other accounts—would seem to bear out and confirm their status as evidence. But when those historical circumstances—corroborating witnesses, documents, place names recollected—cannot be recovered, the best we can do is to rely upon the effect of the diary itself. Hayden White would argue that its status as evidence depends in part upon its effect, and that effect—produced metonymically either by design or by circumstance—is, in the case of the Wilkomirski book, a profoundly disturbing one.

But this case puts a great deal of pressure on the relation between the effects of a testimony and its source. Such a conclusion is disturbing—Wilkomirski may be a liar, after all; no one would say the same of Mary R.—and it is all the more profoundly so if it leads, as Philip Blom has suggested, to an "ero[sion of] the very ground on which remembrance can be built" and leads eventually to "a new revisionism that no longer attacks the truth of the Holocaust but only individual claims of survival" (Blom). He is right to be concerned, if he means to say that if we can undermine the authority of the writer of a Holocaust testimony, and say with certainty that he was never there and that he did not see what he claims to have seen, we have eliminated one piece of evidence that we can use to argue that the atrocities of the Shoah occurred. Such testimonies—in the form of eyewitness accounts, documentary evidence, trial transcripts, and diaries—taken together form the tapestry of suffering that we have inherited as the narrative of the Holocaust. But such testimonies, as accounts of horrible events that are as inaccessible to the memories of those who survived as they are to those who claim to have done so or those who read their accounts, function in similar ways and have similar effects: they indicate an event as it occurs prior to her ability to speak it, not so much in their accordance with the facts of history (facts which are accessible only through narrative) but in they way they disrupt the narrative of history and force the reader, or the interviewer, to see something horrible, perhaps a trace of the traumatic event itself. These effects are *only* available one witness, one reader, at a time. In the case of the Wilkomirski "memoir" we may well be able to undermine the authority of the writer if we take him to be trying to establish a narrative of the circumstances of the Holocaust that will settle the matter, either of history or of biography. The converse is also true: a lack of credibility seems to throw open to question the veracity of testimonies of other survivors. But this is not to say that it lessens the disastrous effect of the testimony, or the testimony's ability to indicate something about the nature of the event, though that disaster may not be the historical object whose "content" we take to be coequal with the narrative's shape. Elena Lappin suggests that the author of *Fragments* may have suffered some shocking accident in the events surrounding his separation from his mother, or the years in which he lived in orphanages or foster care or in the care of adoptive parents. Such an event renders the uncanny effect of the book's metonymic language as an indication of an event that is not only inaccessible to its readers but inaccessible to its author as well.

This is a troubling place to be left, given the stakes. I am reminded of how high they are this year by my eleven-year old's question about the armed police officer stationed outside the door of our synagogue as we entered to recite the Kol Nidre, by the violence in Jerusalem, and by the cries of "death to Jews" that have been heard coming out of the mouths of stone-throwing men in Ramallah and those of demonstrators here at home. As some have said of the Wilkomirski affair, to suggest that false testimony may nonetheless be an effective instrument through which we may bear witness to the Shoah is to provide Holocaust deniers with one more way to doubt all testimonial evidence about what happened in Europe between 1933 and 1945. So to conclude that there is, in the Wilkomirski "fraud," a traumatic kernel that may be connected somehow to the horrors inflicted on the victims of the Final Solution would seem to fly in the face not only of good taste but of human decency as well. Our jobs, as teachers and as righteous people, should be to honor the memories of the dead and to ensure that we recognize the destroyer Amalek in whatever guise he might return—Hitler, czar, antisemite, demagogue—and blot him from memory; in short (though this may not be the same thing) to destroy him.

And yet this is precisely the problem: how do we do this? Let me recall two stories. The first is that of Amalek found in the portion of the Torah in Exodus called Beshallach. In it, the Jews, who've left Egypt and seen the Pharaoh's army destroyed by the hand of God, begin to complain: they don't know where they're going, they're hungry, and they're beginning to grow impatient with Moses. To make matters worse, their flank is attacked by the Amalekites, who pick off the elderly, the young, and the weak. At the end of the portion, the Amalekites are defeated, and the Lord says to Moses: "'Inscribe this in a document as a memorial, and read it aloud to Joshua: I will utterly blot out the memory of Amalek from under heaven.' . . . The Lord will be at war with Amalek throughout the ages." On a traditional reading, this passage is understood to be God's imperative to Israel that they should always bear in mind what Amalek did to them so that they may with God's help blot him out in whatever incarnation and in whatever age. But the language of the passage is not quite so clear; in fact, it inscribes an ambivalent relation between memory and forgetfulness. In the command to Moses to inscribe as a memory in writing and then blot the memory of Amalek out, the same root—to remember—is used both to command memory, writing, and its blotting out. In his commentary the Torah scholar Kornelis Houtman notes that the Hebrew for "blot out," means quite literally to erase, to un-write. So what is commanded is literally to remember to unremember, to create and inscribe a memory that at the same time blots out or unwrites what lies at the very core of the memory itself. This is precisely the point Cathy Caruth makes about the relation of traumatic memory to testimony: the event itself is blotted out, making testimony's relation to the event troubled at best and altogether tenuous at worst. So Amalek doesn't stand as a warning to be ever vigilant to recognize Amalek again; this injunction warns about the impossibility of such recognition.

The second story was told to me by Sydney, my father-in law, several years ago. As an infantryman in Europe during the second World War, he was shipped overseas quite late and he, along with his outfit, slowly travelled through the ruins of western Europe toward Germany. In one little village, he was out on patrol when he came across a couple who immediately identified him as Jewish (he never said why), explained to him that they, too, were Jewish and had remained alive by hiding from the Germans. My father-in-law, panicked, turned and tried to get away as quickly as he could. He finished the story by saying that he is mortified by his reaction, and that he wouldn't have recalled the incident at all had I not asked him, oddly enough, about *Schindler's List*. I'm struck by two things. His reaction to that couple, not unlike the reactions of many Americans and particularly American Jews to the Holocaust, was simply to avoid it. On finishing the story Syd told me that what bothers him most about the public reception to *Schindler's List* is that many people believe that, through watching that film, they understand what the Holocaust was like. That reaction is the polar opposite of avoidance: give the event a name, or a face—make it recognizable, like something you know (noir, horror, suspense, bittersweet but happy ending)—and cover over the horror of the event that you'd rather not confront. And yet this strategy, like avoidance, prevents us from confronting the abyss of the events themselves by filling it in with a knowledge—with what we already know. We'll know Amalek when we see him coming because we've so thoroughly coded horror (or antisemitism, or trauma) as "Holocaust." Both forms of avoidance rest upon prior knowledge: the first keeps what one knows unchallenged by refusing to encounter the difference; the second refuses the difference by simply calling it something that makes it familiar. As was the case with my father-in-law, the horror itself (what was seen but not contained by language or knowledge) remains disruptive and leaves a mark.

At the heart of any memory is a forgetting, the loss of the event that forms its core and that loss's destructive force upon any subsequent testimony; this is all the more true in the case of traumatic memory. And it is this loss that complicates the project of recuperating the fact of the Holocaust through the memories of those who were there, and it lies at the heart of the problem of those testimonies that may not bear witness to the Shoah but provide evidence of some other trauma. This is why Wilkomirski's "memoir" is so problematic: there may be some traumatic kernel wrapped inside the narrative of destruction, but it's one to which neither we nor the writer have access. That the elusiveness of this kernel should give succor to the deniers is a terrible result, but it is an unavoidable one. So instead of trying to avoid this problem, we should recognize it and in so doing find other and perhaps firmer ground on which to take issue with the deniers' lies. It is the void at the heart of memory that makes the tasks—of writing, of speaking, about the Shoah— at once so urgent and so fraught. It means that while we desperately wish to anticipate the next Amalek so we can blot him out, there exists the likelihood that we will be mistaken, and be outflanked by the actual disaster. But it also means that our jobs involve understanding the ways in which our writing is indicative of aspects of our language and of our being that are both much less and a great deal more than what we would readily acknowledge.

Common sense tells us that testimony undoubtedly bears some causal relation with the events it depicts, and once we find divergent accounts of those events, we generally think of the testimony as erroneous, flawed, or patently false. But if much of the contemporary work on trauma is right, and the horrible events witnessed by the survivor never registered consciously at all and instead produce a void in memory that triggers a torrent of language whose "precocity" we cannot predict, then testimony may also (or may instead) bear a relation to an event to which even the witness himself may not have access. Such an event is not distinct from history, if we think of history as what happened. But the event lies outside of, or precedes, history if we think of history as what Louis Mink calls what is *"there* with a determinateness beyond and over against [the historian's or witness's] partial reconstructions" (Mink 93). As in the testimony of Mary R., whose response to the question of her mother's death in the ghetto is a rote answer about the numbers of children who died at the hands of the Nazis, what was seen and what one can say both have their source in the events of history; the effect of the seen, however, gets in the way of the fabric of testimony, leaving the witness to find some other language to stand in the breach. Witness is the moment of forgetting, the moment of seeing without knowing that indelibly marks the source of history as an abyss. It is the moment of the disaster; and it is that moment, the moment of forgetting, that demands that the memory be inscribed, though it is a memory—a testimony—whose historical circumstances and whose discursive control are simply not available to subsequent witnesses. And what we experience as readers of such testimonies is just as susceptible to rewriting, and to misrecognition, as the memories of Bruno Doesseker or of Mary R., and as soon as we testify to the event, work through it in such a way that we find a name for it, we inevitably misname it. Such a conclusion doesn't seem preferable to the alternative, which is that testimonies proven false can be banished from what one writer has called the "Holocaust archive" so as not to taint what remains. But it's a conclusion we have to contend with given the structure of memory, witness, and testimony that has been laid out over the last several years. If nothing else, it requires us to recast our thinking about testimony's relation to witness and to history in order to be on guard against the "new revisionism" that Blom is rightly concerned with. Blanchot is right: the disaster ruins everything": writing, memory, the certainty of knowledge. But if it also forestalls turning the Shoah into a certainty to be filed (or argued) away or made sacred and untouchable, perhaps this kind of "ruin"—though it doesn't give us access to its historical correlative—may be preferable, as it provides access to the complexity of witness itself.

PART III

Memory and the Event

SIX

Denials of Memory

HISTORY CAN BE DEFINED as both what happened and a description of what happened. The description is pieced together from testimonies, artefacts, and other bits of the detritus of events, material that is itself partial and in need of interpretation (though in some cases ultimately uninterpretable). Short of having been there oneself, what is available of an event is—as they say about the phenomena that science takes as its object—at best an approximation, the best explanatory narrative available at the time. The more aspects of the event that narrative can account for, the better the narrative; but no narrative can account for every bit of detritus, and every narrative is missing those aspects of events that aren't attached to material detritus: individual suffering, moments of elation, the small everyday events that are lost forever to memory.

Memory thus has two historical aspects. The first is what we consider to be related to the real, but whose effect—the effect of the real—is disruptive and fragmentary. This facet of memory is what we have been calling *anamnesis*, that which cuts across cultural memory and disrupts the narrative of the past, and of our identities as we place them in the context of the past and present, and stands in the way of the language of the ready-to-hand. The second is what we have been calling *mneme*, what we consider to be narratable or what is available through representation, and which—for better or for worse—we consider to be what we know about the past. This first aspect of memory is indexical, or forgetful, since what intrudes upon the witness's consciousness isn't a representation of the event, but a disturbance in whatever representation she is capable of producing, and at best gives her a sense of what happened, and produces a memory effect rather than a memory as such (see Stoekl). The second is mimetic and rational: the representation of the event—either in discourse or in some other medium—is substituted for the event itself, and remembered as the event. Memory as mimesis—mneme—

provides access to the past by producing representations that are coherent if not necessarily rational; memory as index—anamnesis—provides access to absent events by pointing precisely to that absence, the void of memory, which disrupts knowledge and representation.

This becomes all the more complicated, as I've tried to suggest, when dealing with the void of the Shoah. Of course the Shoah occurred, and in its sweep and in the overwhelming numbers, the events that comprise it seem to have produced so much evidence—so much material detritus—that failures of memory or the contradictory testimonies of eyewitnesses would pale in the face of the mountains of shoes or the fingernail scratches on the walls of the gas chambers. Yet it's this very complexity that is the focus of Holocaust deniers: because of the missing document, we cannot say for certain that the Final Solution was the systematic will of National Socialist Germany; because of the missing caption on a blueprint, we can't say that the gas chambers were used for human extermination; because of disagreements about numbers and the causes of death, we can't be certain that six million—or even six hundred thousand—were killed. Holocaust deniers—and there are many of them with many motives—see the complexity of history and memory (and particularly memory's void) as the justification they need to make their case against the very historians whose job it is to make sure that, in Amos Funkenstein's words, "'reality,' whatever its definition, 'shine[s] through [the narrative].'"

In effect, deniers play each of these aspects of historical memory against the others. The fact of indexical memory—the fleeting interruption of memory that stands in the way of knowledge and yet provides a glimpse of what happened by other means—undermines the authority of mimetic memory, by suggesting that what cannot be represented did not happen; and the fact of mimetic memory—the apparently orderly marshalling of evidence and the construction of a coherent narrative of events—is taken by the deniers as either a fabrication (its coherence betrays an author) or as a backdrop against which any inconsistency (including those produced by indexical memory) as a lie.

Those who deny the Holocaust come in many stripes, and while their insistence is virulent their knowledge of the events and their willingness to deny all or part of it varies a good deal. David Irving, for example, has wavered between taking the Final Solution's link to National Socialist policy—and to individuals in the highest ranks of the party—for granted, and denying that there was any link at all. (He insists, for example, that the word "ausrotten" found in document after document means "stamp out" rather than the more commonly accepted "exterminate," though he himself insists on the latter meaning in much of his published work.) Mark Weber, one of the most active (and knowledgeable) members of the Institute for Historical Review—the deniers' pseudohistorical professional organization—and Irving both seem unhappy to be associated with the lunatic fringe of the denial movement that seems more comfortable in white robes and jackboots than on a dais at academic conferences. And yet they all have in common a method and a project. The project is to dismantle, piece by piece if necessary, what they call the myth of the Holocaust, the narrative they believe has been concocted by "world Jewry" and its allies, a narrative that wins Jews the world's sympathy and functions as a cover for their plan for world domination. Their method is to see complexity as fallacy, to see contradictions in testimony as lies or bad faith, and to see the community of historians' insistence on peer review as the clubby exclusion of pathbreakers and outsiders.

The task of those confronting Holocaust denial take as their aim to collect in a single argument the historical facts—Funkenstein's "reality"—that may once and for all silence the deniers and show their lies for what they are; and to provide an account that explains who these deniers are and what their motives might be. In other words, it is to produce rock-solid, coherent narratives on the one hand, and to marshal so much evidence that even the outlying and inconsistent fact can be accounted for. But the problems with these approaches are well illustrated in an exchange on the *Donahue* show, taped in 1994, during which the Holocaust deniers David Cole and Bradley Smith share a stage with David Shermer, a historian, and a camp survivor named Judith Berg. At one point, the producers show the audience a film clip of the concentration camp at Dachau, and in what Shermer hopes is a rational discussion of the relation of what we know about the Holocaust to what we have heard, he refers to the claim (now known to be, in all likelihood, untrue) that soap was mass produced from the remains of dead Jewish inmates. Berg, insists, "It was true. They made lampshades and they cooked soap. It's true" (Shermer 113). In response Shermer tries to explain the difference between reassessment of facts and the wholesale denial of history, but Smith quickly accuses the survivor of lying. From this point things get ugly, and Berg shouts, "I was seven months there. If you are blind someone else can see it. I was seven months there—," to which Smith replies "What does that have to do with soap? No soap, no lampshades. The professor [Shermer] says you're wrong, that's all." The eyewitness's very real suffering, and her confusion of her own memories and others', become conflated: it doesn't matter at all that she was there, and that what she has to offer by way of evidence is both heartfelt and unquestionably verifiable. Her "mistake" is enough for Smith to discount her testimony altogether, regardless of the event that the testimony clearly indicates (though perhaps fails to represent clearly), and the historian's explanation is seen as the hair-splitting of the base casuist.

Denial is insidious because, though many of the deniers are not sophisticated historians (or thinkers of any kind at all), they prey on the void of memory that is inevitable in the event of the Shoah. Even the most coherent narrative representation of the Holocaust—at the USHMM, or in photographic images, or in historical texts—runs the risk of becoming a simulation, of being substituted for the event itself with the result that the event is lost to memory in even its indexical sense (see Lisus and Ericson). And even the most robust accounting of the facts, and for even the best collector of evidence (and, as Raul Hilberg once called himself, of footnotes), risks creating of the past a monolith, making any defense of history in the name of its facts something like the creation of a taboo, which fences the Holocaust off from history alto-gether, something all the more plausible now that those whose memories are cut across by anamnesis become fewer and fewer as the years go by.[1] My task in this chapter is to examine the relations among memory, forgetfulness, and Holocaust denial in two recent cases in which what happened, and what peo-ple remember (and have forgotten), part company. The first—the controversy surrounding the publication of Jan Gross's *Neighbors*—isn't an instance of denial as such, though some of Gross's severest critics, particularly in Poland, use the deniers' language and tactics. The second—David Irving's lawsuit against the historian Deborah Lipstadt and the debates about free speech that it promulgated—is a more obvious instance of denial, but presents a far more troubling case of failure on the part of the deniers' critics. Finally I'll suggest some of the consequences, some of them troubling, inherent in the arguments over memory, history, and forgetfulness.

NEIGHBORS AND DENIAL

On the 10th of July 1941, not far from the village square in Jedwabne, Poland, several townspeople forced most of their Jewish fellow residents into Bronislaw Szlezinski's barn, and burned it to the ground. This act preceded the brutality of the Final Solution, but was part of the dynamic of anti-semi-tism and xenophobia that existed in much of Poland during the war years. The killing is all the more horrifying in part because it was an act of neigh-bor against neighbor. And it was an act that, like many during those years, was witnessed by many whose testimonies are troubled by doubt, by forget-fulness, the inevitable passage of years and of regimes, and by the calcifica-tion of what we now know as "the Holocaust." The monument put up to commemorate the pogrom memorialized the over one thousand killed simply as Polish victims of Nazi brutality. In May 2000, Jan Gross' book *Neighbors* was published. Like earlier accounts of the killing in Jedwabne, it presented eyewitness testimony and other documents to make clear that "the Polish half of [the] town's population murder[ed] its Jewish half." Since that time, and particularly since the book's translation into English, the memory of the events in Jedwabne, if not the events themselves, have raised charges of bad faith, shoddy historical work, and—in their most extreme form—Holocaust denial. The book's veracity has been called into doubt, and this in turn has led to charges that the book is an instance, if not a useful tool, of denial. At issue in Gross's book is the possibility that the evidence available, and the eyewitness testimonies of the survivors and perpetrators, can't be understood simply, and that in fact that evidence doesn't provide "history" at all but only its raw materials. The book and the charges against it are an example of the predicament of historical writing in the face of the absence of the event: when confronted with the incredible, witnesses and readers alike reduce the events to what *is* credible, what *is* narratable, and what *is* manageable. Those aspects of the event that seem to resist logic, or that—when put into words— seem outrageous or just plain wrong, are often either left to the side or are seen as irreconcilable details best chalked up to failures of memory or bad record-keeping. And Gross's account of the Jedwabne killings seems to have an aspect of the incredible to it.

The outlines of the story are as follows: between the signing of the nonaggression pact between the Soviet Union and Germany in 1939 and the German invasion of the Soviet Union in 1941, a swath of Poland changed hands three times. For the years between the conclusion of the first World War and 1939, it had been in independent Poland; between September of 1939 and June of 1941, it was occupied by the Red Army; and from 1941 until the last year of the war it was occupied by the Nazis. Jedwabne, a town in that swath of Polish land, had been on the map for a couple of hundred years by 1941, and had—like many small towns in the "pale of Jewish settle-ment"—always included a fairly large number of Jewish residents, numbering about 1400 in that year. It was a rural town, in which a majority of landown-ers were non-Jewish, and a majority of shopkeepers and other merchants were Jewish (again, much like many small towns in the Polish pale). It had a *cheder*—a Jewish day school—and many residents belonged to Jewish reli-gious and social organizations, including the socialist Bund. While the non-Jewish and Jewish residents of the town generally got along with one another, there was also mutual suspicion and envy, particularly after the signing of the nonaggression pact that placed Jedwabne in the Soviet sphere of influence. Because Jewish residents were rightfully suspicious about the Germans' inten-tions toward the Jews after 1933, and because some residents were politically sympathetic to socialism, the pact was welcomed by some Jewish residents; some of the more active socialists among them celebrated the erection of a bust of Lenin in the town not long afterward, and one or two Jewish residents were put into positions in the town's governance.

After the Nazi invasion in June 1941 events turned badly very quickly. Within a day of the invasion, witnesses reported a car-load of German soldiers riding into town, though the numbers of soldiers in the car (or truck) differ depending upon which witness's testimony you read. Included in this number were officers, and a group of them spoke with members of the Jedwabne town council—non-Jews, by this time, since the town government had rid itself of Soviet "sympathizers" before the arrival of the Germans. Almost immediately, a number of non-Jewish townspeople began to take action against several of their Jewish neighbors, in some cases invading their homes and, in one event noted by a large number of eyewitnesses, several Jewish men were forced to topple the statue of Lenin and to carry it out of town while being whipped and struck and forced to sing socialist marching songs. In towns neighboring Jedwabne, similar events were taking place; a number of Jews who managed to escape those towns made their way to Jedwabne to report that the entire Jewish population of the places were being killed, some by German soldiers and some by non-Jewish residents. By the beginning of the second week of German occupation, a plan had been hatched by a number of residents. Together, they drove the majority of Jews into the square and from there into a barn. The doors to the barn were closed and locked, and gasoline was poured onto its walls. A fire was lit in the barn, and while townspeople looked on—some with shovels and hoes to beat to death anyone who tried to escape—the barn, with hundreds of people inside, burned to the ground. Those who stayed in their homes, afraid to come out, reported hearing the screams of their neighbors and smelling the burning bodies from miles away.

This is the story Jan Gross, professor at New York University, tells in *Neighbors*. He tells it with the aid of testimonies taken from trials of perpetrators held in the decade after the conclusion of the war, from records found in the town's archives (both formal and informal), in Germany, and from *memoribuchen* or *yizkor* books, written remembrances of Jewish townspeople who either escaped or who retell stories they themselves had heard from relatives and friends. In some instances, the testimonies provided at trial and those taken in the years during which Gross conducted his research differed quite a bit. Recent excavations in Jedwabne since the publication of Gross's book have unearthed physical evidence that at once contradicts Gross's account and supports it, depending upon how one reads it. And records left by the German military of its actions in Jedwabne and surrounding towns sheds little light—or no light at all—upon whether the Germans instigated or plotted the murders, or stood by and watched while non-Jewish Poles did it on their own. And the entire episode—both what happened in Jedwabne and what happened after the publication of *Neighbors*—is vastly complicated by the history of Poland just before and during the war and the even more vexed history of Jewish relations with non-Jews in Poland after the war's end. A good deal has been written about the years between 1939 and 1941, during which some non-Jewish citizens had very mixed feelings toward Poland's Jews. They were often seen as aliens, transients, communist-sympathizers, plutocrats, often all at the same time. Non-Jewish Poles in Jedwabne and elsewhere became concerned in 1939 when invading Soviet troops were welcomed by some of their Jewish neighbors, and took minor positions in the soviet bureaucracy.

The four central points of disagreement over the historical "accuracy" of Gross's account (or, maybe more accurately, the historical authenticity of that account) are its use of the evidence found in archives and on the Jedwabne site itself, the "context" in which that evidence can best be understood, the reliability of the memory of those individuals involved in the events, and the "emplotment" of the narrative provided by Gross. In the years since Gross wrote his study, the vicious disagreements over its veracity—mainly in Poland, but also in the United States—have hinged on precisely these questions, and not long after the publication of *Neighbors*, the Polish Institute of National Memory (IPN) undertook what it claimed was an exhaustive study of the massacre in order to settle the matter. That the IPN study upheld, in most matters of substance, Gross's narrative of event seems not to have settled anything at all for those who see Gross's version of events, like Goldhagen's attempt to tar all Germans as anti-semites, as a kind of cultural smear campaign. What all this suggests is that though matters of history may be settled, matters of history's narrative may never be settled at all.

The evidence in the Jedwabne case falls into two main categories. The physical evidence, in the form of documents and of the detritus of the massacres, forms the first category. The documents on which Gross relies are transcripts taken immediately after the war from survivors across Poland and housed in the Polish National Archives; transcripts of trials of several of the main actors in Jedwabne taken in 1952 and 1953; and German documents, dated 1941, that record the movements of the Einsatzkommados in the Bialystok region of Poland (in which Jedwabne is located). The physical evidence, mostly brought to light in the IPN investigation, includes the remains—mostly ashes—of those murdered in Szlezinski's barn, and bullets found inside the barn among the remains, presumably from German carbines. The second category of evidence is the eyewitness testimonies, along with those found in the trial transcripts, of those who were present in Jedwabne on 10 July 1941.

Gross reports that the 1500 Jews in Jedwabne—those that survived the first few days of anti-semitic violence immediately after the German occupation—were killed together in the barn. The physical evidence uncovered in the barn, however, suggests that maybe a quarter of that number were burned to death there. Several writers, Norman Finkelstein and Tomasz Strzembosz the most vocal among them, note that this grave error on the part of Gross throws his entire study into question.[2] But the fact remains that there are still three-quarters of the Jews of Jedwabne left unaccounted for: there is no evidence whatsoever that they survived either the massacres in July or the remainder of the war. This means that they were either driven out of the town, left of their own accord having seen what their non-Jewish neighbors would do or had done already, or were killed by other means. The matter of the bullets found in the remains of the barn are also seen as evidence that

Gross's argument—that the Germans in the town had nothing to do with the massacres except perhaps its planning—fails to account for the Germans' part in the massacre. Strzembosz and others suggest that the presence of two German bullets is evidence that soldiers or police must have prevented the Jews from exiting the barn, and that some of those Germans must have shot into the barn, thereby actively taking part in the massacre. That these bullets may have been in the barn before the burning, or that they may have been fired by residents of Jedwabne, or that they were fired after the massacre at either terribly burned survivors of the fire or at non-Jewish Polish looters by German soldiers, is not accounted for by Gross's antagonists.

Eyewitness testimony given by perpetrators has also been disputed. Gross estimates—by doing the demographic math—that in a town with under a thousand non-Jewish residents, the total non-Jewish adult male population was around 225, and that this number is the baseline from which the number of perpetrators would have to be calculated; Gross eventually puts the number of active perpetrators at 92. The investigation concluded by the IPN put the number of active perpetrators at 40, a number that does not include the possibility of German soldiers or gendarmes. Many of those who dispute Gross's findings argue that his initial number, 225, so inflates the number of potential non-Jewish perpetrators (by a factor of nearly six) is evidence that Gross must have an anti-Polish bias; in fact, though the actual number determined to have been active in Jedwabne is more than double Gross's number, it is hardly evidence of an insidious agenda. Moreover, both Gross's book and the IPN report that a crowd of residents actively took part in rounding up the town's Jews, taunted them as they were driven into the town square, and eventually herded into the barn at the point of shovels, axes, and clubs. Steve Paulsson, arguing against Finkelstein recently, writes "So we have a crowd, which is standing around, while 40 (or maybe 92) people are taunting and tormenting the Jews, driving them towards the barn, forcing them inside, dousing it with gasoline, and setting it on fire. It doesn't seem that any of them did anything to try to stop the perpetrators or help the victims" (email, 17 July 2002).

Finally, on the point of the German presence in Jedwabne, the documentary evidence is contradictory. German archive documents suggest that Einsatzkommandos had already passed Jedwabne by the time of the massacre; other documents suggest, however, that a Gestapo detachment, following the Einsatzkommand, had established a presence in Jedwabne in early July. Eyewitnesses in Jedwabne remember two or three "taxis" arriving before the massacres, dispatching a lightly-armed group of German police, the officers which met with the town council and, according to some, helped plan the massacre. The same eyewitnesses recall some of these Germans taking photographs—none of which, apparently, have survived the war—of the burning of the barn, but that none of them actually participated in either rounding up the Jews that day or driving them into the barn. (They did, however, have a part in forcing several Jews to take down the Lenin statue and be humiliated in the process).

The problem of historical context also complicates matters. While it is impossible to make blanket statements about Jewish and non-Jewish allegiances during those years, some Jewish and Catholic Poles in Jedwabne were often highly suspicious of one anothers' motives. Writing a few months after the publication of Gross's book, Tomasz Strzembosz argues that any Catholic reprisals against the Jewish residents of Jedwabne are perfectly understandable: "Roman Sadowski . . . wrote me on November 10, 2000: 'During the Soviet occupation Jews were the "masters" of this region. They entirely cooperated with the Soviet authorities. According to the accounts of my wife's cousins, it was Jews together with the NKVD [the Russian secret police] that compiled lists of those to be interned (deported)'" (Strzembosz 232). Strzembosz goes on to say that one of the participants in an action against collaborationists "called for settling scores with the Bolsheviks and Jews, saying: '. . . [T]he time to settle accounts has come, down with communists; we'll butcher every last Jew'" (234). Surely the actions of the Jedwabne residents might be understandable when read against a background of Jewish-Bolshevik complicity, he suggests.

Adam Michnik, writing in *The New Republic* not long after the publication of Gross's book, cites an example from 1942 of what he calls "the paradox of Polish attitudes toward Jews": "Our feelings toward the Jews haven't changed. We still consider them the political, economic, and ideological enemies of Poland. . . . [But] the knowledge of these feelings doesn't relieve us of the duty of condemning the crime." In response, Leon Wieseltier demands a reassessment of the notion of collective responsibility. In fact, Gross's book is an argument for working *against* a collective memory that risks reducing the events of the Shoah to a well-wrought narrative.

> When considering survivors' testimonies, we would be well advised to change the starting premise in appraisal of their evidentiary contribution from a priori critical to in principle affirmative. By accepting what we read in a particular account as fact until we find persuasive arguments to the contrary, we would avoid more mistakes than we are likely to commit by adopting the opposite approach, which calls for cautious skepticism toward any testimony until an independent confirmation of its content has been found. . . . All I am arguing for is the suspension of our incredulity. (22)

It's incredulity that leads a writer in 2001 to take the virulent anti-semitism of 1942 as the paradigm in which to witness the Jedwabne massacres. But it's that same incredulity that leads Israel Gutman, a survivor and Yad Vashem historian, to say that "Strzembosz's rumors and generalized accusations . . . are the products of fantasy and are not worth discussing. Although he does not say so clearly, these words suggest a certain tit for tat approach to Jedwabne—'you hurt us, so now we'll hurt you!' It is difficult to hold a conversation" in the midsts of hostile anti-semitism.

Each eyewitness—those of the current generation, like Strzembosz, Wieseltier, and Michnik, who weren't there; or those, like Jakov Piekarz or Szmul Wasersztajn, who were there in Jedwabne—can only remember what has been called to mind *as* a memory. Whether it is the burning of their neighbors and family members alive in a barn, or the horrifying narrative account of it that disturbs their sense of history, or membership in the collective "we" of Polish identity, or simply their own memories, those events have had the effect as of staring into the sun. They've been blotted out from the narrative that would integrate them into history. To bear witness to the possibility that those whom you know might for whatever motive herd you into a barn and set it afire is to look directly into the sun. Antoni Niebrzydowski issued kerosene to his brothers at his warehouse and then they "brought the eight liters of kerosene that I had just issued to them and doused the barn filled with Jews and lit it up; what followed I do not know." Perhaps he doesn't; but he saw. It would be easy to deny what he saw because it is simply too horrible to remember. In fact, what Antoni Niebrzydowski saw may be lost to knowledge altogether, though his testimony ("what followed I do not know") can be corroborated by others who were there and thus be called a lie. But his testimony is not inauthentic. If we, like the witness himself, were to "suspend incredulity," we could only be horrified by what glimpse we catch of the event. Is he denying history or the Holocaust by refusing to see?

This is the crux of the problem: the impasse between what the witness saw and what he can tell us. How firm is the connection between the testimony and the events that are its object? It is a question about the relation between the memory of the witness and the immemorial and irretrievable events that the witness saw as much as it's a question of history. To suggest that the testimony is finally incredible, given all of the evidence that can be marshaled against it, is maybe the most rational answer. But by saying so and then ruling out of court evidence of what the witness saw that doesn't accord with the available historical record would also be hugely problematic. In the case of the Jedwabne massacre, in which the testimonies of eyewitnesses disturb the prevailing histories of Poland just before and during the war, Gross's historical narrative provides a glimpse of something that may not be in the end substantiated by other documents or testimonies. But his book forces readers—the next generation of witnesses with no historical link to the events—to confront aspects of the history and collective memory of the Holocaust that aren't easily integrated into the seamless fabric of narrative.

In his book *Selling the Holocaust*, Tim Cole makes a smart point that's relevant here: that Holocaust denial could only happen if the Holocaust itself were so firmly established as to become altogether intransigent as an historical construct. "In many ways, 'Holocaust denial' has emerged only within the context of the emergence of the myth of the 'Holocaust.' It was not until the 'Holocaust' emerged as an iconic event that it was perceived to be an event which was deemed worth denying" (187–8). The collective memory of the event has become ossified, and because there are so few survivors whose own individual recollections of the event, shot through with what might be called the kernel of the real (and which might force us to, in Gross's words, suspend incredulity), there is nothing left to go on but accretions of memory not our own. We believe we know the events of the Holocaust because we have read them over and over again, against the backdrop of national identity (be it ours in the United States or Jan Gross's in Poland) and whatever personal stakes we have in the event. So we read Gross, which troubles that collective memory, or find that the Wilkomirski memoir, which accords so well with it, is a fake, and in both instances we simply want to deny it and its implications. Auschwitz has been turned, in Daniel Ganzfried's terms, into a matter of faith. Though the aim is directly opposite of the aims of the Institute for Historical Review, the structure of denial is quite the same: what doesn't accord with knowledge is seen as non-knowledge, even though we are aware that what the witness saw strains at the boundaries of knowledge and of testimony's ability to contain it. In effect, this kind of denial is an attempt to keep what we see in such testimonies at bay—either the neighbor's ability to kill his neighbor, or the terror of a child separated from his mother so violently that the only language available to him is that which has become attached to the Shoah. The Wilkomirski case shows that it's possible to use others' experiences to keep from having to make good on something beyond our power to conceive (see Ganzfried); and when that which we wish not to see is brought to the field of vision, like Gross's account of the Jedwabne massacres, we simply put it out of sight altogether.[3]

The repetition of testimonial accounts of atrocity, whether by witnesses or through the trope of the eyewitness, work to produce a collective unconnected to yad vashem, the place and the name. But while these testimonies and images of destruction may appear to repeat the same, each is not identical to the one just before or just after it, and it is this nonidentity that eventually makes itself apparent and shatters the collective memory whose that has no point of origin in the atrocity itself. Gross's *Neighbors* is problematic because there may be some traumatic kernel wrapped inside the narrative of destruction, but it's one to which neither we nor the witnesses have access. It can easily be argued that the elusiveness of this kernel will give succor to the deniers. And this is indeed a risk if we make a fetish of history. But the fact is that testimonies, narrative, and photographic images don't give us knowledge of the events whose object is apparently depicted in them. It does, however, give us a sense of the contours of memory, of what lies at its margins, and how the marginal disrupts our knowledge of the event at the same time it provides a point of entrance for its trace as an effect of what cannot be remembered. As I've said, our jobs involve understanding the ways in which our writing is indicative of aspects of our language and of our being that are both much less and a great deal more than what we would readily acknowledge.

IRVING V. LIPSTADT

In 1996, bolstered by the smugness of those on the fringes of the political right (who themselves had been emboldened by Timothy McVeigh, the rise of the militia movement, and the grenade-slinging back-bench Republicans in congress led by Newt Gingrich), David Irving—the intellectual front man for Holocaust denial—sued Deborah Lipstadt, who wrote in her 1993 book *Denying the Holocaust: The Growing Assault on Truth and Memory* that Irving was (in the words of Martin Broszat) a "Hitler partisan wearing blinkers," and who thought of himself as "carrying on Hitler's legacy" (Lipstadt 161). Irving claimed that she had libeled him, ruined his reputation, and distorted the facts. Lipstadt's title suggested that Irving wasn't only a bad historian, but that he—like the Holocaust deniers she catalogs in her book—was chipping away at truth, at the reality of the events of the Shoah. This was too much for Lipstadt, and she launched a strong defense.

For almost a year, during the process of discovery, Lipstadt's lawyers combed through Irving's research, making their way through the archives that he himself had visited during his researches on the calendar of the Final Solution and on Hitler's subordinates' connections to the evolution of that policy. They also went through his travel records to determine whether his association with the Institute for Historical Review, the deniers' pseudo-historical think-tank, also included contacts with obviously anti-semitic groups. Irving served as his own lawyer in spite of court's strenuous objections. He spent much of his time in court outlining Lipstadt's purportedly false statements about him, calling a number of witnesses whose testimony purportedly corroborated his claims, and pointing to the integrity of his research. Much of that research attempted to prove that the gas chambers at Auschwitz were not used for the liquidation of Jews but for the delousing of their clothes, and that the crematoria were designed to dispose of the bodies of those who died by disease and starvation, not systematic execution.

The case for the defense, unlike that of the plaintiff, took several months, and was founded on two premises. First, Irving's work as an historian was not only in error but was knowingly so. Second, the reason his work was shoddy wasn't that he was a bad historian—though at times she seemed to prove that he was—but that he was sympathetic to the anti-semitic groups that lauded his work and that he was very likely anti-semitic himself. She called a number of historians whose work was on subjects parallel to Irving's own. In one case, she called Robert Jan van Pelt, an historian who went so far as to conduct his own research into the question of just what the Auschwitz gas chambers were used for and how they were engineered for the purpose of killing large numbers of people. She called these witnesses to make clear where Irving's work was wrong, sometimes egregiously so, and she confronted Irving with his own statements and calendars to suggest that he had met with members of anti-semitic groups and spoke with and about them and their agenda in favorable terms. In short, Lipstadt's case was based on the idea that not only was Irving an anti-semite, which motivated his research—leading him to "find" in the historical record that which would support his view of the history of the Final Solution—but also that the record of the event left by camp commandants, Nazi officials, and the physical remains of the camps and gas chambers and crematoria, all "shone through" his (fictional) narrative to render it as the lie that it was.

The literary critic Stanley Fish weighed in on the trial and on Holocaust denial more generally, and it's his analysis of the case that I want to examine here, since I think it's indicative of the dual problem inherent in Holocaust denial and its relation to forgetfulness and memory. Part of Fish's argument was that as individuals—as historical actors—we're encumbered by beliefs and ideological positions, so any ground we stand on shifts depending upon the circumstances, making appeals to truth, or to unmediated events of history, illegitimate. Any claim to objectivity—to evidence or to history—is itself just as encumbered. On the matter of Holocaust denial, Fish makes the same point: Deborah Lipstadt's appeals in her defense against Irving to the inherent validity of evidence and the deniers' (as well as historians') appeals to free speech and academic freedom are equally flawed because each rests on a notion that there is such a thing as unmediated reality, and that narrative accounts of it are stronger or weaker depending upon their ability to hew close to that reality. It is indeed difficult, if not impossible, to make a case against Holocaust denial on the grounds of academic freedom or the self-evidentness of evidence. But it's also true that Holocaust deniers have a profound effect not only upon history but upon memory, including those of survivors, of survivors' families, and people of goodwill for whom historical forgetfulness (or the falsification of history) is injurious. What Fish rightly asks is whether utterances like those of Holocaust deniers are really assertions of truth, based upon an array of evidence and upon the memories of those who were there, which are calculated to have a reasonable effect. In part because the deniers themselves understand—however fuzzily—that historical actors themselves create a narrative of the events in which they act in part because the event itself is lost and must be substituted with a representation that serves as a memory, it's hard to argue "the facts" when those facts—as we saw in the case of Jedwabne—are themselves subject to the vagaries of memory. More to the point, if we take Adam Michnik's advice and suspend incredulity in the face of atrocity (atrocities that are seemingly by definition counterrational), we play directly into the denier's hands. It's one thing to say, as several Holocaust deniers have said, that their case is reasonable and their conclusions are based on a consideration of evidence. Whether serious or not, such statements are clothed in the rhetoric of reason and of mneme, whereby evidence is gathered, synthesized, and conclusions are reached; and whereby the most reasonable conclusion is based upon the coherence of memory. It's another thing to start out with the intention, in Lyotard's terms, of producing a damage, and this is precisely what Holocaust deniers seem to have had on their minds. One of the deniers accompanying Frank Collin during their planned march through Skokie, Illinois (a community in which a number of Holocaust survivors live) in 1978 said:

> I hope [the Jewish residents of Skokie] are terrified . . . I hope they're shocked. Because we're coming to get them again. I don't care if someone's mother or father or brother died in the gas chambers. The unfortunate thing is not that there were six million Jews who died. The unfortunate thing is that there were so many Jewish survivors. (qtd. in Fish, *The Trouble with Principle* 80)

This isn't a statement designed to produce a reasonable (if unconstitutional) effect, namely to counter the passing of an ordinance that would prevent the march. It is a calculated attempt to produce a response that would be altogether *unreasonable*, one that has nothing to do with discourse, or rational discussion, or the changing of minds.

It's the *consequences* of both denial and the discourses that are designed to counter it that seem on their face, anyway, to be reasonable discourses, based upon the cultural memories that have been constructed to contain atrocity, and not the counterrational and traumatic memories that cut against the grain of mneme, the known, and the ready-to-hand. Deborah Lipstadt, regardless of her pronouncements in the pages of *Hadassah* magazine, is a trained historian; David Irving, despite his pronouncements in front of an audience of skinheads, is also a well-regarded historian of military history (though clearly not of the Final Solution). Robert Jan van Pelt and Richard Evans, two of the expert witnesses who testified before the court in the *Irving v. Lipstadt* trial, spent a great deal of their time poring over Irving's books and the documents he and others worked with, and wrote sprawling reports on what they found. The work of these historians and scholars would seem, at least on the face of things, to have been "consequential in ways larger than those made available by the discipline" not because they made political pronouncements or called Irving a liar in court (though Evans clearly did just that), but because their work seems to once and for all have put the lid on

David Irving the "historian" if not his anti-semitic and racist followers on the lunatic fringe. The language David Irving uses in his books on Hitler, and the language used by writers for the *Journal of Historical Review* (the "historical" journal published by the Institute of the same name, the organ of the denial movement in the US and Britain) is discipline-specific and clothed in the language of history and memory, but doesn't take into account the difficulties associated with forgetting.

In 1991, president George H. W. Bush lashed out at the UN resolution equating Zionism with racism, saying that the equation "is to twist history and forget the terrible plight of Jews in World War II and indeed throughout history" (qtd. in Fish, *There's No Such Thing* 60). It's just this "forgetting of history" that has allowed the right to make its case against, among other things, affirmative action policies by ignoring the history of segregation, exclusion, and brutality that have produced the need for such policies in the first place. Historical forgetting enables anti-affirmative action proponents to call the policies it disagrees with "reverse racism," and thereby puts "racism" and "affirmative action" on the same historical plane. But such an equation is possible "only if one considers the virus of racism to be morally and medically indistinguishable from the therapy we apply to it" (61). But such a statement only holds up if we grant a clear and palpable distinction between an event (here, those events that are taken, collectively, as racist actions) and a narrative meant to make those events legible to those of us living in history (here, the equation made possible by the forgetting of history and the replacement of the phrase "affirmative action" with "reverse racism").

Fish's argument with new historicism makes the distinction between fact and event clear. He grants, with the new historicists, that history is textual; but he is not willing to grant their corollary point, that the textuality of history means that matters of historical fact cannot be settled.

> The belief that facts are constructed is a general one and is not held with reference to any facts in particular; particular facts are firm or in question insofar as the perspective (of some enterprise or discipline or area of inquiry) within which they emerge is firmly in place, settled; and should that perspective be dislodged (always a possibility) the result will not be an indeterminacy of fact but a new shape of factual firmness underwritten by a newly, if temporarily, settled perspective. (Fish, *There's No Such Thing* 248)

Challenging the coherence of the narrative on which the evidence of history is arranged does not change the evidence itself, nor does it change the facts that are suggested by that evidence. But the challenge does force us to reconsider and perhaps rearrange those facts according to the challenger's narrative.

Two things must be made clear here: first, the work of challenging the coherence of the narrative must be rigorous and must proceed within established procedures and traditions of inquiry; and second, the arbiter of the disagreement will be those engaged in the "enterprise or discipline of an area of inquiry," which—in the case of Holocaust revision and denial—would seem to fall squarely to historians. Facts are facts; paradigms are another matter. Fish ultimately comes down on the side of good old-fashioned historians, against the New Historicists, and tells us that disputes about history aren't epistemological but empirical: they're arguments over "evidence and its significance" (qtd. in Fish, *There's No Such Thing* 253). The challenges to the historical events that comprise the Holocaust are settled in the court of history, and cannot be settled with reference to the events thesmselves; and those challenges may have consequences for how we see history but not, for example, how Jews understand their place in the a Europe that still shows the aftereffects of the Final Solution, or how we remember those events (255).

Fish is disdainful of those who, like Elizabeth Fox-Genovese, see history as not simply a body of texts and a strategy of interpretation (that is, who don't see history as textual), but as "'what did happen in the past—of the social relations and, yes, "events" of which our records offer only imperfect clues'" (qtd. in Fish, *There's No Such Thing* 245). Fox-Genovese's point about history isn't all that distant from Louis Mink, who is convinced that the past is, after all is said and done, *there*, might suggest that Fish's paradox—that history is made and that history happens—cannot be solved but that we "oscillate" between its two irreconcilable poles. Pierre Vidal-Naquet, one of the strongest voices against Holocaust denial on both the left and the right, acknowledges Fish's subjectivist position, but nonetheless insists that "beyond [discourse], or before this, there is something irreducible which, for better or worse, I would still call reality" (qtd. in Ginzburg 86). The difficulty in Fish's position is that there is very little room left in history for those events or aspects of events that seem to defy a narrative accounting of them, and that are nonetheless identifiable, and that have very palpable and sometimes destructive effects upon both the witnesses who see them and those who hear their testimonies. Fish sees history as the work of historians, sees its effects as fairly narrow and well-defined, and sees its discourse as more or less reasonable and rational. The problem with the Holocaust, and with those who—like David Irving and Bradley Smith (the author of the CODOH supplements to campus newspapers)—would revise it into something else or argue (or wish) it out of existence, is that they're not willing to confine themselves to the historical enterprise, nor are they willing to engage in discourse or, if they are, use a discourse that amounts to "fighting words," arousing not rational counterarguments but the irrationality of hostility and anger.

In Fish's essay, "Holocaust Denial and Academic Freedom," he likewise argues that appeals to historical truth, like appeals to academic freedom, are equally flawed because both seem to insist upon some position of authority (verifiable historical reality, the free marketplace of ideas separate from base motives) that simply doesn't exist.[4] To say that Deborah Lipstadt has once and for all quieted the voices of deniers because she's finally proved the events of the Holocaust is just as preposterous a notion as saying that the deniers should have their say because they should be granted academic freedom. "If the standard of validation [of the facts of the Holocaust] is the establishment of a truth that is invulnerable to challenge, no one, including Lipstadt, could meet it" ("Holocaust Denial" 504). Fish argues that there ought to be some other, less severe standard that depends upon the careful, methodologically sound scrutiny of evidence and the narratives inside of which it makes sense. It works just the same way with academic freedom: it isn't the freedom to say or do anything in the name of intellectual pursuit, "allowing 'new ideas' to flourish willy nilly until time and the marketplace separated the wheat from the chaff" (518); academic freedom is just that, *academic* freedom, which is particular to those practices and enterprises recognized as such by the community of academics, and which is not universally valid any more than historical facts, to be recognized as such, have to be universally seen to be so.

Placed together, these arguments serve as a useful antidote to grand claims for history. But they ignore a more nuanced understanding of history, particularly the history of "limit events," that sees history as having broader effects, effects that are far less reasonable and predictable (they are much more radically particular), than Fish would have it. While history and forgetfulness might seem to be at odds—we do ourselves a disservice by forgetting events that, like the Holocaust, we might rather not remember at all—the events of history are *inevitably* lost to memory, and they are lost at precisely the point at which they are witnessed. Historical work produces a narrative that makes sense of the events' detritus, their aftereffects. But historical events affect witnesses and documentary and evidentiary leavings, and those effects aren't always reasonable, rational, or easily subsumed to the narrative that drives them. The revision or denial of history—marches through towns like Skokie, the demonstrations in front of campus newspaper offices that have accepted the CODOH's circulars questioning the occurrence of the Holocaust, or a libel suit like the one David Irving filed against Deborah Lipstadt and her publisher—is itself an event that leaves traces in the historical narratives built to contain it, and that has effects that aren't easily confined to the law courts of the historical archives.

Fish says of the *Irving v. Lipstadt* trial that the books and other accounts written about it all seem to have in common the idea that what was at issue in the trial was "not [. . .] the accuracy of a particular historical account, but the honor of history itself and even the honor of Truth" and that, in a provocative phrase, Irving "is a perpetrator of crimes against epistemology" (499). The problem with Lipstadt's assertions isn't that she's wrong, but that she's right for the wrong reasons. It'd be one thing for her to say that she's right and Irving's wrong because his understanding of the evidence is in error and his arrangement of those facts, because they are in error, lead to unsupportable conclusions. But she doesn't say this, according to Fish. Instead, she begins from the premise that "any argument denying or diminishing the Holocuast is specious and that the so called evidence it invokes is not really evidence at all but strained rationalization and downright fabrication" (500–01).

But in fact Lipstadt's defense against Irving has little to do with making statements on behalf of History or Truth, and has everything to do with the evidence that Irving and other historians have adduced. A good deal of the testimony taken in the *Irving v. Lipstadt* trial establishes not the truth of the account Irving has provided of Hitler, the Final Solution, or even the bombing of Dresden (on which he has also written), but his manipulations of the evidence. In one instance, Lipstadt's lawyer brings Irving's attention to a memo written by Himmler, which Irving says is part of the evidence which exonerates Hitler from any part in the Final Solution. In the memo that records the conversation, Himmler provides notes for a phone conversation with the general in charge of the concentration camp system, and Irving writes that the phone call amounted to an order to prevent Jews from being liquidated in December 1941. The order, according to Irving was, "Jews are to stay where they are" (qtd.in Evans 208–9).[5] But the memo actually reads "the administrative leaders of the SS are to stay where they are." So we do not have an argument, as Fish would have it, over the matter of Historical Truth here; what we have here instead is the manufacture of evidence, evidence that says what it says and around which contexts of whatever nature can be built to provide whatever historically pertinent account of the Final Solution one wants to build. But Irving has tried here, and at countless other points in the trial where he is caught in the same sorts of blatant lies about evidence, to simply make something up out of thin air.

So it's hard to see how one could reach the conclusion about historians, particularly those involved in the trial of Deborah Lipstadt, that "neither party reaches its conclusion by sifting the evidence on the way to determining the truth of the matter; rather, each begins with a firm conviction of what the truth of the matter is, and then from inside the lens of conviction receives and evaluates (the shape of the evaluation is assured) the assertion of contrary truths" ("Holocaust Denial" 501). Not only is this patently unfair to the way most historians work, it is particularly unfair to Lipstadt and her lawyers in her defense against Irving. Fish says of historical evidence that it "doesn't just sit there unadorned and unencumbered asking for your independent evaluation" but rather it exists "in the midsts of a structure (of belief and conviction) that precedes it and colors one's reception of it" (502). Fair enough.

But there are enough instances in the Lipstadt trial that make it plain that structures of belief are not at issue. One piece of evidence Richard Rampton brings to the court's attention late in the Irving trial is on the latter's association with racist groups in the United States. In a written interrogatory, Irving has denied up and down—as he has done in the past—that he'd had any association with a white-supremacist group called the National Alliance, and denied in particular that he'd attended any meetings of the group. After Rampton produces a letter of invitation to Irving from the Alliance and an entry from Irving's diary describing the meeting, Irving becomes testy, saying "There is not the slightest reference either in that diary entry or in any other diary entry to the NA or the National Alliance which confirms what I said about having had no knowledge of them" (Guttenplan 250). Rampton then reads a further entry in the diary:

> "Drove all day to Tampa, phoned Key West, etc. Etc. Etc. Arrived at the Hotel Best Western at 4:00 pm. Sinister gent with pony tail was the organizer. Turned out the meeting here is also organized by the National Alliance and the National Vanguard Bookshop. Well attended." Now, Mr. Irving, do you want to revise the answers you have just been giving me? (Guttenplan 250)

While it is certainly the case that this evidence—Irving's diary and the letter of invitation on National Alliance letterhead—doesn't "just sit there," Irving's lie does.

There are indeed multiple narratives that might account for the evidence left from the Final Solution, the countless memos, lists, speeches, and other documents produced by the SS, the Wehrmacht and the Order Police; and there are multiple narratives, too, that might account for the evidence left of Irving's work in archives, his meetings with racist groups and his travels and phone conversations. But that evidence has a materiality to it. As Fish says in an earlier essay, "If you set out to determine what happened in 1649, you will look to the materials that recommend themselves to you as the likely repositories of historical knowledge and go from there. [. . . Y]ou and those who dispute your findings (a word precisely intended) will be engaged in empirical work" (*There's No Such Thing* 253); the work of establishing the textual nature of the history that the evidence seems to suggest is a different sort of work entirely. But it's this latter sort of work, I think, that Fish associates with Holocaust deniers and those who would stand against them; what the *Irving v. Lipstadt* trial has shown over and over again, however, is that what's at issue isn't the historical accounts produced of the evidence—the matter of the "truth" of the Holocaust's occurrence or nonoccurrence—but of the evidence itself and of its durability.

DENIAL, FORGETFULNESS, AND THE WITNESS

It's the evidence's durability—its materiality, the fact that it simply cannot speak for itself—that leads us to try to draw lessons from that evidence, to construct narratives that make sense at some level. That the Final Solution and the destruction of Jewish culture in Europe seems to make no sense from the very beginning makes the job of historians of the Holocaust that much harder; the evidence leads to a narrative of utter unreality and that seems so contrary to human reason that the denial of those events on the grounds that they are too unreasonable to contemplate—how, paraphrasing Yehuda Bauer's question, could the most civilized nation in Europe contrive to eliminate an entire people in a systemic and scientific way?—might in the end seem easier than accepting them (see Bauer 14). But it's the evidence's durability which seems to exert a pressure on the narratives that would seek to explain them. Fish takes Alex Grobman and Michael Shermer to task for seeing the work of the historian as "the combined product of past events and the discovery and description of past events" (Shermer and Grobman 21). Fish worries that "[a]ccording to this language, events exert a pressure on their own discovery and cooperate, in a way that remains unspecified, with the task of describing themselves" (Fish, "Holocaust Denial" 509). Well, not exactly. What Grobman and Shermer, along with Fox-Genovese, imply is that history, and historical work, is constrained by reality which, according to Amos Funkenstein, is "beyond the modes of narrative, the mythopoetic intensity of the narrator, the intervening subconsciousness and superego," which is "never isolatable yet all pervasive" (34). The real—both the material dimension of the world that affects individual memories and the affective and counterrational element of the individual memories themselves—"escapes our control, [and] forces itself upon us whether or not we welcome it," but it is also "that which we make relevant, construct, manipulate" (Funkenstein 35). History and historical work shows the impingements of the real and tries hard to gain some control over them. Historians write to produce in the reader a sense of what was recollected by the original witness and collected in the material evidence. But what the witness saw, and the materiality of the evidence, are beyond the modes of narrative ("the event," reality as it impinges upon us and our conventions of thought and language), and though the event impinges upon us, it may or may not be narratable, though it is most certainly visible as it works against the grain of the narrative of collective memory. Fish is right: evidence doesn't just sit there unencumbered; but neither does it easily fit any one of the narrative accounts built to subsume it into history, whether it is the account of a Deborah Lipstadt, or a Christopher Browning, or the amateur historian named David Irving.

This is why, in spite of National Socialism's "arguing away" of the facts of Jewish citizenship, or the fraudulence of the *Protocols of the Elders of Zion*, Holocaust deniers in France, the United States, and elsewhere, the impingements of the real—the reality of the gas chambers, of antisemitism, and the destruction of the Shoah—will ultimately disturb the narrative of denial and show the revisionists for the liars they are. Their "arguments" make sense of the crimes of the Final Solution that are otherwise not sensible or rational: "Many of us say that the Nazi crimes were 'incomprehensible,' that the sheer limitless inventiveness in degradation and killing of that regime defy all our historical explanatory schemes. . . . Precisely this incomprehensibility of the crimes makes their denial into a much more rational account of a possible world (better than ours) in which people act out of rational, or at least pre-dictable motivations" (Funkenstein 47). But individual memory—that which is out of reach of the rational—"'shines through'" and affects that rational, collective narrative. The effect of the event stands in the way of this sort of "diabolical worldmaking," preventing it from becoming an arbi-trary concoction altogether removed from what happened. Though this real-ity is something outside the narrative that is brought to bear upon history in order to adjudicate accountings, it is nonetheless also embedded into the accountings themselves.

And yet it is individual memory which seemed to be entirely missing from the proceedings. In summing up the trial, D. D. Guttenplan writes:

> And so we take refuge in history, in documents, in facts—cool, detached, silent, precise. [. . .]
> But witnesses, memories, testimony—all that was left outside the courtroom. And that seems to me cause for regret.
> Witnesses area always partial. Memory is by definition selective. And testimony—not the sworn responses of expert witnesses, but the still-vivid responses of people whose history is lived, not studied—can be treacherous. (307–8)

While Fish—and I—would disagree with Guttenplan's sense of facts as "cool" or "detached," it is the witnesses who do, in fact, seem oddly absent both in the *Irving v. Lipstadt* trial and also in Fish's account of the problem of Holocaust denial. Fish tells us over and over again that historians do their work "by telling a story that fits with the stories we already know to be true and telling it in ways that corresponds to our by now intuitive and internal-ized sense of how one connects the dots between observations on the way to a conclusion" ("Holocaust Denial" 510). This "fit" is achieved by hewing closely to the practices and protocols established by historians whose work is more or less conventional, and which has effects inside the academy whose "freedom" Fish sees as specific not universal. The argument that Irv-ing was unjustly prevented from purveying his version of events in the Nazi Reich because, as an academic, he was simply doing what academics do is corrupt; he was justly prevented from purveying that version because he was not hewing to those conventional methods of inquiry that makes a historian a historian.

But what about witnesses, real people, like those survivors in Skokie who would be harmed by a neo-Nazi march through the city, or like those who saw what they saw in hiding and in the camps but whose reality is impugned by those like Irving whose academic credentials are in shreds but who nonetheless tell a certain tale and have a ready audience? Individual witnesses—as well as individuals whose encounters with the events of the Shoah either as second-hand witnesses, or as "people of good will and good sense," or as those so troubled by its tropes and images they, like Binjamin Wilkomirski, come to identify with its horror—have a real stake in *Irving v. Lipstadt* and the phenomenon of denial. And the deniers themselves, particularly those unlike Irving who have no claim upon history and who have no other stake in denying the Shoah except their racism and anti-semitism, must also be accounted for, and their work must be explained in terms broader than the purely disciplinary and academic. It's true that Holocaust denial, as a phenomenon, can't be allowed on the grounds of academic freedom because what the deniers are doing is not academic work, and that their ideas cannot be promulgated on the grounds of free speech because what they're selling is not the contextless expression of an idea. It's also true that if we want to do away with the deniers, one way to do this is simply to tell them "that they have not met our criteria for being considered seriously and that we are sending them away" ("Holocaust Denial" 524). Lipstadt "made the bastards pay" by dissolving Irving's reputation as an historian.

But denial isn't only about history and about how one responds—through law, or through discourse, or through other rational, political means—to false claims. "Denial hurts people," Raul Hilberg told Guttenplan before the trial (302), and therein lies an aspect of Irving's pronouncements about Hitler or the CODOH's insinuations about what really went on at Auschwitz that is a byproduct of the blurred line between words and deeds. It isn't so much that "every idea is an incitement to somebody" (Fish, *There's No Such Thing* 106) but that in the case of Holocaust denial there are real harms—harms to memory and to being—that "are finally not taken seriously" (*The Trouble with Principle* 82) either by those clinging fast to the First Amendment or those who want to see the consequences of work done by historians and faux-historians alike as bearing only on Lipstadt, Irving, and their circle.

Guttenplan is right: "Irving does represent a real danger" (298), whether or not he's been rendered toothless (and certainly now penniless) by the British courts. Deniers really do assault memory as is implied in Lipstadt's title. Recall the *Donahue* show taped in 1994, in which the deniers David Cole and Bradley Smith share a stage with Michael Shermer and Judith Berg, a camp survivor. While Berg's facts are wrong, her memory isn't; or rather, the facts of the event have disappeared for Berg behind a narrative that attempts to make plain, to serve as an index, for very real suffering. Her conflation of her memories and others' results from the need to create a language that has an effect that may make others "see" or remember what has become lost for the witness. But the effect that it has upon Smith is to make him revert to the language of historical and memorial consistency: he discounts her testimony altogether, regardless of the event which that testimony clearly indicates (though perhaps fails to represent clearly), and the historian's explanation is seen as hair-splitting.

It is finally memory on which denial has its most profound and damaging effect: not history, not academic freedom, not "the truth," but the events of the Shoah which reside in the memories of those who were there and, more and more through the projections of history, and of fiction, and of images, those who weren't. The battle has already been won, Fish tells us, "because the vast majority of mainstream researchers support Holocaust affirmers and reject Holocaust deniers" ("Holocaust Denial" 511), and I'm taken by the way Fish ends his essay: if all else fails in fighting off the deniers' lies, "make the bastards pay." But if the battle's been won by the historians, it's precariously unresolved in the much larger field of memory, because denial hurts people by filling the silence that inevitably comes from the "damage" of denial with the deniers' false but apparently plausible explanation of the destruction of central European Jewish culture. The Holocaust really is a limit case in which the testimonies which bore the "traces of the *here*'s and *now*'s, the documents which indicated the sense or senses of facts" (Lyotard 57) have been destroyed. The witness, as much as the historian, is charged with "breaking the monopoly over history granted to the cognitive regimen of phrases" and must lend an ear "to what is not presentable under the rules of knowledge" (57).

In the end, when Lipstadt and some of those who are working against Holocaust denial make claims for historical "truth" they're going too far. And "academic freedom" may indeed be squishy ground on which to silence the deniers. But I'm not sure that this is, in the end, just an argument about history or about the force of language and reason. Though these arguments may function as a strong rebuttal to the deniers' arguments, they don't go to the heart of why the deniers should be able to make their case in the first place, and they fail to consider arguments from witnesses—problematic as they might be—that might provide a stronger rebuttal still. It's true that the historian must follow lines of inquiry, and based on documentary and testimonial evidence find a convergence of that evidence that seems to explain a preponderance of it under a controlling if sometimes complicated narrative. But accounts of it are stronger or weaker in part because of the story they *don't* tell as much as for the story that they do; the survivor on *Donahue* may have provided a weak account of her experiences in the camps because of her error regarding the soap supposedly produced in Dachau, but her insistence on the fact that she saw what she saw, despite its inability to tell us precisely *what* she saw, provides another kind of evidence, in another kind of language, that has nothing to do with reasonability, or the conventions of history, or the archival work that sustains it. Bradley Smith's denial of the witness's memory, and his willingness to provide an alternative narrative in the face of her inability to respond to charges of falsification, has a real historical effect upon those for whom the work of the historian matters little and barely registers on the radar. Even in the face of reconstructions of the past in all sorts of narratives, that past nonetheless makes itself apparent, though perhaps not rationally so. This, finally, is the historians' predicament: as Vidal-Naquet constantly reminds us, the historian *writes*, and that writing is neither neutral nor transparent. The difficulty is finding a way for that "historical discourse [to be] connected—by as many intermediate links as one likes—to what may be called, for lack of a better term, reality" (110–11).

SEVEN

Conflations of Memory; or, What They Saw at the Holocaust Museum after 9/11

AS VISITORS IN THE United States Holocaust Memorial Museum leave the permanent exhibit, they find an open, loose-leafed binder, in which they are invited to write comments about what they saw. Many visitors do so, sometimes leaving a single word or sentence, and sometimes covering an entire page with writing, attempting in one way or another to make clear what they've just experienced. Yet what they write isn't quite a record of memory, and it isn't quite a testimony either. The visitors act as witnesses to the chronology of the Holocaust, and see visual representations of some of the atrocities committed immediately before and during the Final Solution to the Jewish Question in Europe. But what they testify to—and what they remember—is often a curious conflation of memories, one that involves impossible connections between the events of the Holocaust and other events, sometimes only tangentially related to it. In their complexity, these comments reveal that far from using the narrative of the Holocaust as a screen memory, using Freud's terms, for other (absent) events (see Sturken), these visitors frequently see the "events of the world"—and in the aftermath of the attacks in New York and Washington in September 2001 those events and those taking place in Afghanistan were very much on the minds of visitors to the USHMM—as screen memories for the Holocaust.

In the next several pages I'll describe this conflation of memory as it makes itself visible in the comments left by visitors to the Holocaust Museum in the wake of the events of the fall and winter of 2001–2002. I'll argue that this conflation of memories is due in part to the design of the museum itself, a design that began as a site of memory but that evolved, in the meetings of the US Holocaust Memorial Council, into a didactic exhibit meant to create memories in a very particular context of Holocaust "seeing." But more inter-estingly, the visitors' use of contemporary events as screens for their under-standing of the Holocaust is due to what I've been calling "forgetful mem-ory," in which aspects of events seen but not remembered as such insinuate themselves into individual and cultural memories so well-wrought as to be (presumably) hermetic. The strands of collective and individual memory as they are shot through with forgetfulness produce something altogether dif-ferent from memory as such, a memory-effect which—like Walter Ben-jamin's flash of memory at the moment of danger—causes the viewer to see something that eludes memory and which is nonetheless related to the real. It's this memory effect that may provide the viewer a kind of memorial agency which—contrary to Stjepan Mestrovic's sense of post-emotional inertia in the face of the culture (or memory) industry—prevents the con-flation of memory from becoming an endless cycle of memorial repetition, in which the Holocaust becomes 9/11, and atrocities simply stand in for one another. The upshot of this analysis may be that we've paid too much atten-tion in recent years to the ways memories make present—or represent—a past, and we haven't paid enough attention to how aspects of memory inter-vene in and make possible a future. I think it's possible to say that the USHMM's permanent exhibit produces witnesses. It doesn't produce mem-ories; the question is, just what did these witnesses see? Ultimately, even the witnesses themselves can't say, and it's this spontaneity of seeing—a kind of uncontrollable witnessing that isn't easily integrated into the narrative of either the Holocaust of the "events of 9/11"—that shows forgetfulness as a positive aspect of memory-making.[1]

MEMORY AND FORGETFULNESS AT THE USHMM

It is the discontinuity of forgetful memory that confounds the work of the his-torian and the storyteller alike. David Krell has suggested that memory includes a void, a kernel at its center that is irrecuparable, like the event itself (19). Forgetful memory is like a flash of seeing, in which the witness isn't quite sure what he's seen, but understands its connection to his present (tem-poral and spatial) location. Forgetful memory inheres in memory itself though, as soon as that which inheres in the memory makes itself present— as soon as one calls to mind those whom Levinas referred to as the closest among the six million by name—that kernel is subsumed by representation, and the risk of conflation begins again: those named become the name; the destruction of the Shoah becomes "the Shoah."

It is just this risk that the United States Holocaust Memorial Council and its various design teams wished to avoid as it planned the site that would eventually become the USHMM. Three memos make this quite clear. The first is a 1979 document entitled "Summary of Views Received to Date, Museums and Monuments" ("Museum Planning and Design"). It makes explicit the idea that "the Holocaust Memorial should consist of a *living memorial* and a *memorial monument*" (1, emphasis in original), and that it should include, ideally, three parts, "a monument, a museum, and an education center" (3). These three functions of the museum were each designed to produce a different effect upon the visitor, according to the Council: a monument, along with individual museum artifacts, would evoke a memory radically particular to each visitor; an education center would evoke a collective memory, scripted primarily through a timeline and by the "pathway" through which visitors experience the permanent exhibit; and a set of exhibits would move the visitor between a radically individual and a collective or cultural memory to produce not so much a knowledge of events or objects as what might be called a "memory effect."

But the "Summary of Views" memo is interesting as much for its confusion and contradictions as its attempt to script memory. While the third point of the memo makes clear that a "living memorial rather than a statue or other form of art presentation" is called for in a Holocaust Center, it also notes that while the commission favors the former, "a monument is in order" as well. "People respond to living reminders," tangible expressions "of the empathy which this country has for the martyrs." In addition, the Center's educational mission should

> provide multi-media type of educational displays, that would be informative for all age groups of our society. These displays would focus on both the "unique" Jewish as well as "universal" meaning of the Holocaust. The committee urged that the display expose . . . the danger [fascism] poses for society, American "constitutional rights" and Western civilization. (Berenbaum, "Correspondence" 2)

Unique, universal, American, Jewish, suitable for all ages: at this stage the committee's views on the nature of its "Holocaust Center" runs the gamut. The memo makes concrete the tension between a collective or cultural memory, whose narrative will be made clear in the informative or educational mission of the Holocaust Center, and an individual recollection invoked by a monument, a memory which may be informed by the material constraints of contemporary concerns. In fact one could argue that, in Stjepan Mestrovic's terms, this document reveals the design team's post-emotional investment in the Holocaust. It intends visitors to understand the Holocaust (a difficult event to experience even for second-hand witnesses) in terms of other events more clearly understood in distinctly American tones. Its design is not simply meant to help visitors script only what he knows about the Holocaust, but also what he feels ("the dangers [fascism] poses") about it.

During a two-day planning session on the 2nd and 7th of May 1984, the question of just what sort of memory the memorial/museum should evoke was raised again, this time by the Development Committee. Anna Cohn, the museum's first Director of Museum Development, described the proposed Hall of Witness as a place to evoke in visitors "a particular sadness" (Berenbaum 1). To do this, she suggests using close-up photographs of individuals, like "this one, who committed suicide by grasping electrified wire" in order to make the viewer witness, at second hand, a single victim and—conflating the terms again—to remember that death as a connection between the witness's present and her past. Chris White, the designer hired to draw conceptual plans for the museum, makes the problem with such an approach clear:

> I'm afraid that the visitor will look at these photographs and immmedi-
> ately seek to remove them from their own time and space. "Oh . . . some-
> thing that happened long ago in a far-off place . . . something that could
> not happen here." [. . . U]nless the visitor can relate a message to his own
> or her own time and space, the story will never penetrate or provoke.
> (Berenbaum 2–3)

The radically particular "memory" invoked in the witness by the photo will be so strong as to refuse integration into the historical narrative that leads from the Shoah to the historical present. The danger of giving the visitor what White called an "easy out" (Berenbaum 6–7) is that she will lock what she sees in a prison-house of memory, and the effect of what she has seen will remain unconnected to her present. The risk of reinserting what has been witnessed into the present, as Eli Pfefferkorn unwittingly suggests in the 7 May meeting, is that it turns the event into "categories of experience," which fills the void of memory with a historical narrative. In a point raised by Cohn on how to make the memories and experiences of children central to the per- manent exhibit, Pfefferkorn tells committee members, "You can't ask a [child] survivor, 40 years later, to distill his experiences through the mind's eye of a child. Everything he does and thinks is colored by his later life as an adult. So the use of primary materials—materials created by children during the Holo- caust—is critical here" (Berenbaum 7). The witness's "retrospective opin- ions," in Pfefferkorn's terms, are impossible to eliminate unless one allows the testimonies and authentic, primary materials, speak for themselves. But there's no guarantee that the second-hand witness will hear what they have to say, since that witness, too, will retrospectively provide a historical con- text—in his or her present reading of history—for what they may have to say. By the late 1980s the Museum's mission became largely an educational one, and it came to subsume the memorial and monumental goals enjoined in the enacting legislation of 1979. Nonetheless, these other aims would continue to exert a pressure on what visitors saw in the permanent exhibit, and allowed them to construct memories associated not only with the Holocaust or their contemporary history but also circumstances over which they themselves could not control as memories.

It could be argued, I think, that the documents cited above—and others like them—speak to the Memorial Council's attempt to manipulate the visitors' emotion, and not just their knowledge, of the Holocaust, to use Mestrovic's vocabulary of the post-emotional. The fact that there is a museum to the Holocaust at all—and that it exists in the American capital, several thousand miles away from the sites in which the Final Solution took place—speaks to the American desire to avoid genuine emotional connection with contemporary events by referring instead to (in Reisman's terms "nice") representations of past events. Those representations become more authentic that the events they mean to represent. In the case of the Holocaust museum, the designers tried hard to seal off the Holocaust from other representations of atrocity, rather than to allow visitors to link it with other atrocities, for fear that the Holocaust would become lost in the memorial shuffle. If Mestrovic is right about the "post-emotional" tendency to rationalize victimization by representing perpetrators as victims and one instance of atrocity as being not unlike other instances of atrocity—suppressing any sense that something should or can be done to prevent acts of violence (since everyone's to blame, and therefore no one's to blame)—then the USHMM's decision to avoid connecting the events of the Holocaust to other genocides and atrocities could be seen as an attempt to ensure that its narrative would not be coopted by visitors to name other events as "holocausts." In other words, though the museum seems intent on manipulating the visitors' knowledge and emotional response to the events of the Holocaust, its purpose seems to have been avoid giving the visitor the "easy out" by allowing him to dissipate that emotion by reinserting it into other narratives of atrocity thereby naming the Holocaust as simply one more instance of "evil" or "inhumanity."

But what would an authentic (or "forgetful") memory of the Holocaust look like, and how would the museum create a space in which the visitor could experience or see it? If my hypothesis is right, the museum's design would need to make room for something like "forgetful memory" to intrude upon the narrative of the Holocaust in both personal and collective terms. Just this possibility becomes visible in a debate over the USHMM's need to recognize the Balkan war around the time the Museum opened to the public in 1994. It's possible to see the response of Elaine Heumann Gurian to a memo written by Ralph Grunewald on the events in Bosnia as a set of criteria with wich the USHMM could create in the visitor an act that involves not just individual and scripted memory but something like a spontaneous act of seeing. Grunewald had made some suggestions for how the USHMM might respond to world events and in particular to the war in Bosnia. At the time, Americans had been confronted with images and newspaper and newsmagazine stories "that might have been extracted from the liberation of the camps at the end of World War II" for nearly two years (Linenthal 264), and one of Grunewald's suggestions was for the USHMM to sponsor a fact-finding mission to the Balkans; this after he brought officials from the Department of State and other national leaders to the USHMM to discuss other international issues. As Linenthal writes, surely the ethnic cleansing taking place in Bosnia represented an opportunity for the institution to exert some moral authority on a subject—genocide—for which it has some historical responsibility. Gurian writes that as much as the educational work of the museum can be seen in and of itself as contributing to the work of diminishing racism and intolerance, it may also represent the limit of the museum's work with regard to specific world events. "[W]henever we act in a direct and public way about current events, we risk reducing rather than enhancing our effectiveness as a moral force" (Weinberg 1). What we need, the memo goes on, are "criteria for action. It is not enough to suggest that we should act when 'innocent women and children' are affected, or in ethnic or tribally based civil war, for, unfortunately, we have plenty of examples of each of these on the world scene today" (2). But museum officials can take on "the responsibility of speaking out when clear aspects of the Holocaust exist and are reminiscent or (worse still) prognosticative of that tragic event. 'Ethnic cleansing,' 'cultural genocide,' 'starvation as a political tool' while only aspects of the Holocaust could serve, in part, as criteria" (2). In short, Gurian insists that before acting, the USHMM "define [its] activity" and "understand [its] position" (3).

I quote this memo at length because on its face it seems perfectly consistent with the USHMM's educative, rather than its memorial, aim: the construction of a public memory of the Holocaust—one that is clear on the event's chronology, the facts of the event's history, and its "uniqueness" as a Jewish tragedy that nonetheless was a strand in a larger historical tapestry—instead of a memorial function which allows visitors to bring the void of particular, and particularly traumatic, individual memories into contact with the names and the faces of those lost in the Shoah. Its writer essentially warns Grunewald that while action is needed in the case of Bosnia, it should be taken by the USHMM only insofar as the disaster in Bosnia bears historical and methodological similarities to that in central Europe in the 1930s and 1940s. To the extent that the facts of the war on the ground in the Balkans are connected to the historical facts of the Holocaust—to the extent that ethnic cleansing is motivated by the same circumstances or ideologies as the Nuremburg race laws; or to the extent that forced or voluntary removal of Bosnians by train is not simply visually reminiscent but also materially and factually similar to the transports of the Reichsbahn—then there are some avenues of action for the museum. The striking visual and memorial similarities—in the photos of the trains, or the emaciated Muslim men held prisoner behind barbed wire—may well call up a certain horror for witnesses to the then-current tragedy of Bosnia as it does for the historical horror of the Holocaust.

But the memo also reveals just how difficult it is to keep forgetful memory at bay. There are at least three strands of memory at work in Grunenwald's memo and Gurian's response. The first, historical memory, is what the USHMM is charged with producing as knowledge in the permanent exhibit, and through its educational mission to bring its visitors to know. The second is individual memory, through which the individual witness—to the Bosnian conflict and, as second-hand witnesses, to the images of the Holocaust presented at the Museum—sees what Cathy Caruth calls the "terrible accident" and literally forgets what she saw but produces an image—perhaps in the "moral imagination"—that is correlative to neither Bosnia nor the Holocaust but something else, some kernel of disaster. This individual memory is fleeting, the result of an image too terrible to bring to knowledge but terrifying enough to leave an imprint—to interrupt—knowledge. But it is forgetful memory—neither collective memory nor individual memory but the effect of the latter intserting itself into the fabric of the former—that compels it. Ralph Grunewald seemed to think it possible that the Bosnian crisis and the Holocaust bear enough similarities to insist that the USHMM make a statement or sponsor a delegation, and that compels Gurian to worry that reading one in light of the other will lead to inertia rather than ethical action or political intervention. The criteria Gurian mentions in her memo would allow her to remain faithful to the collective memory sponsored by the museum while providing evidence as to whether the images presented by CNN or in the *New York Times* elicit authentic memories of atrocity, atrocities whose context (historical, narrative, legal, political) might be shared with the USHMM's definition of "Holocaust." And the phrases she cites—"ethnic cleansing," "cultural genocide," "starvation as a political tool"—while evocative of the TV and newspaper images, also take on other valences when connected to some of the images that confront the viewer in the USHMM (and resonate with the deformations of language—*endlösung, nacht und nebel, transport, lebensraum*—from fifty years earlier). Both Grunewald's memo and Gurian's response suggest that there must be something that resides between correspondence between event and event through memory, and a disjunction of events in memory (leading to an ethical impotence and, in Mestrovic's terms, a voiding of agency) that will create an act of seeing that disorients the viewer and unmoors him from the present. If the object of witnessing is to be "authentic," it is created figurally— metonymically, mnemonically—and not because it has its temporal origins in the events of the Holocaust or of Bosnia. As Mestrovic puts it, "it is not the 'reality' question that determines authenticity, but the spontaneous emotion that works . . . in apparent defiance of social conventions . . ." (75), a defiance that is both entirely real and entirely resistant to memory. The only way the Holocaust may be connected memorially to other instances of atrocity is by means of representations that create an effect upon a reader or viewer. That effect is neither a merely personal memory evoked by the representations in the Holocaust Museum nor a recollection of the narrative spun out by the permanent exhibit, but an indication of an event as it is seen by the viewer but not recognized as either a memory or as knowledge.

CONFLATIONS OF MEMORY

The memories of 11 September 2001 and its aftermath—in both Afghanistan and in Israel and the occupied Palestinian territories—as they were inscribed in the Museum's book of comments clearly troubled museum visitors in the winter of 2001–02 and the following spring, in defiance of the "memorial conventions" the museum attempted to inscribe in the narrative of the permanent exhibit. In the remainder of this chapter, I want to show not only how forgetful memory impresses itself upon what the viewer saw in the permanent exhibit, but also suggest how forgetful memory may in fact provide a kind of post-memorial agency, one that Mestrovic, Sturken, and others worry isn't available in a post-emotional, post-traumatic era. Those comments— written in over a dozen languages (mainly English, but also Hebrew, Spanish, Portugese, French, German, Dutch, Swedish, Russian, Italian, Malaysian, Thai, Korean, and Japanese), by children as young as five years old and by visitors from school and tour groups; by families and single visitors; by many who were alive during the events of the Shoah, including survivors and rescuers— ranged from the banal ("it was great") to the shocked ("words fail me") to the rude ("boring!"). Visitors left poems, prayers, diatribes, political statements, memories, and imaginings; a few left drawings.[2]

What visitors to the museum "saw" in its permanent exhibit was an interanimation of both the collective memory that the museum itself tried to shape through the contours of the displays and its choices of artifacts and texts, and of a much more particular memory, one that visitors brought with them to the exhibit. Often visitors' comments record a clash of memories, in which the disjunction between what they saw in the museum, and the images and experiences they saw first-hand, created an interstice, what Krell calls a "crux" of memory. In this crux something other than the object of memory— the Holocaust, 9/11, the *intefadeh*—is visible. Of course, in reading the comments left by visitors, maybe the best we can do is identify instances of forgetful memory. But I want to note too how these spontaneous acts of seeing—remembering forgetfully—give these witnesses an agency outside the memory screens identified by Sturken, Mestrovic, and others. In reading these comments we can see visitors attempt to find a language that makes some sense of memory's void, a void triggered by a juxtaposition of images from the Holocaust and other, related images that they may well not have been able to shake: airplanes flying into buildings, New Yorkers covered in ash, the collapse of the Pentagon and the World Trade Center, and the individual instances of loss and trauma that affected them unbeknownst to us. Some of these utterances are uncanny in their power, in the images juxtaposed in them; some appear as shockingly inappropriate expressions of hate, or pain, or anger. But each works against the grain of the narrative of the Holocaust, and each makes clear that the memorial, if not the educative, function of the USHMM is at work in ways unanticipated by its designers.

A number of remarks record a visceral connection to the events of 11 September, and make explicit a memorial link between it and the Holocaust, as if the images in the museum were mnemonics for images of the destruction in New York and Washington. The link is perhaps most explicit in an anonymous comment written on 30 December 2001.

> May the memory of the righteous be a blessing. In this day all people can now know what it feels like to be a jew—when we can be hated just for being an American who does no harm to anyone—but can be killed while we are at work—or on a plane—at the whim of a maniac and his followers.

For this writer, the museum makes plain the injustices done to the outsider, the lower-case "jew" persecuted for no other reason but her identity. Particularly on the fourth floor of the permanent exhibit, a good deal of space is devoted to National Socialist racial policies and the Nuremburg Laws that made legal what racial ideology had already forged as a groundswell of opinion if not as scientific fact. But there is a certain irony that the outsider—the "jew"—is, in this writer's memory, "American," here conflated with those individual "innocents" who were at work in their offices in Washington and New York. The litany of photographs and biographies printed in the *New York Times* and, less formally, on posters and flyers in and around lower Manhattan, may well match, in this writer's imagination, the photos and biographies of those individuals that appear in the museum, particularly on the fourth floor, where mug-shot-like images of those whose "racial" traits appear typical to Nazi science are juxtaposed with photos of attacks upon old men and experiments done on children. The metonymic association of name with name, and face with face, creates here the sense that all Americans, like the Jews of Germany and German-speaking Europe, are innocents—the righteous—who do no harm to anyone. What one sees here is that the events of 9/11 become a screen memory for the Holocaust. But because the relation is reversed—the Holocaust doesn't function as a screen for 9/11—it's not clear that the closer traumatic memory of the destruction in New York is being "domesticated" by the Holocaust narrative, which has been fully interiorized by this writer. Instead, there seems to be a confusion of race and nation, of religion and culture, all bound up in the metonym "jew," that escalates into a kind of panic at the vulnerability expressed in the writer's concern that s/he could be singled out and killed because she functions as the object of some-one's hate. This conflation of memories produces an anxiety that belies any easy equation, and it suggests instead that this visitor sees something—as a "jew"—he hadn't seen either on TV or in the museum.

Several visitors to the museum make clear equations among individuals, most often between Hitler and some despot (if not a national government official), and so it is unsurprising that a number of comments reflect a moral equation between the German führer and Osama Bin Laden. Janey R., in late February, writes that "my dad couldn't stop crying. I definitely have a new look and perspective on everyone. I hate Osama Bin Laden. He is just like Hitler—where he went and put some crazy idea in people's heads and then went and killed innocent people." But remarks like these are most often not based upon what the visitor saw in the museum. Two comments make star-tlingly clear how the images of 9/11 and those found in the permanent exhibit function together. Gabriel M., in mid-January 2002, writes:

> I read and see here about Holocausts, genocides, gassings, exportations, tor-tures, all of it, nearly every horror we can imagine, and yet in my own life, I have personally witnessed so little violence, besides the smoke and ashes rising from the Twin Towers in my home of New York. I respond to this with bewilderment, numbness, sadness that our world seems to have forgotten the lessons of the Nazi regime, and gratitude.

On the face of it, Gabriel's response attempts to place the destruction of the WTC towers into perspective, by noting the enormity of the Holocaust, and the writer seems a bit overwhelmed by the litany of "Holocausts, genocides, gassings, exportations, tortures" in the face of the very little violence he him-self has seen "besides the smoke and ashes rising" from ground zero. Things get a bit more complicated, though, in the last sentence: it's unclear what the referent of the pronoun "this" is—New York or the Holocaust—and it's unclear, too, which lessons of the Nazi regime he has in mind. The attempt to distinguish the two events, the Holocaust and the terrorist attacks, falls apart in the second half of the comment, and history—the lessons of the Nazi regime—is both forgotten and remembered at a stroke: remembered in that history is no longer to be held at bay but is instead something that may be "personally witnessed" in the writer's home, and forgotten in that the repeti-tion of the violence ("all of it") and the images associated with it seem to erase the carefully crafted narrative that concludes with "never again," since—as one of the museum's visitors puts it ("If only it hadn't happened again . . ." [X. E. 2/1/2002])—it has.

Robby S.'s grandmother, a German, was on this visitor's mind as he vis-ited the museum. He begins his comment by suggesting that the destruction of the innocents during the Holocaust was further complicated by the vast number of innocent Germans ("they know not of what their country did") who were nevertheless implicated in the horror of the event. "My German grandmother is embarrassed to tell the story; she still never has." Then Robby writes:

> Sometime my grandmother on 9/11 says, "You don't know how living in a war is." Quite often she says, "How could they kill that many people without knowing." I didn't know what she was talking about until now.

There are three strands of memory here: the writer's recollection of the permanent exhibit, his grandmother's recollections of both the war (which she never spoke of and which formed, apparently, a silence between them) and of September 11th, and the writer's "historical consciousness" of the link between the two, particularly the killing of vast numbers of individuals. The writer speaks here of a knowledge, a knowledge that he didn't have until his visit to the USHMM. It is knowledge that has to do with the destruction of thousands and the experience of war, though it was something his grandmother had attempted to keep from him but which nonetheless had a pedagogical effect upon him. But like the individual memory that binds these three acts of witness together, such knowledge can't be distilled into a narrative history or a chronology. The three images—of his grandmother, of the museum, and of what he saw in September—fall into one another in the writer's memory and create not a collective memory whose understanding promises lessons, but a void or absence ("you don't know how living in a war is"; they know not what they did) defined as knowledge's opposite.

These last two comments—Robby's and Gabriel's—make clear something Marita Sturken writes in connection with the Vietnam memorial and the AIDS quilt. "The survivors of recent political events often disrupt the closure of a particular history; indeed, history often operates more efficiently when its agents are dead" (5). So too when its witnesses are dead. But Robby and Gabriel are themselves historical agents and witnesses and like Robby's grandmother have seen the events—of 9/11 and of war either on TV or in person—whose memories flash before their eyes as they pass through the museum. Though the Holocaust may function as a screen on which to project the memory of 9/11 for these witnesses, I think it's also accurate to say that both 9/11 and the Holocaust—as memories—function as a screen for witnessing, though just what the object of witness might be is not clear; neither is it clear how their historical agency will play itself out.

The second largest group of comments has to do with the second intifadeh in Israel, which escalated—since its beginnings in September 2000—to suicide bombings and periodic reoccupations of the West Bank. Like some of the writers who link Hitler with bin Laden, those who take as their focus the war in Israel most often link Hitler with Palestinian Authority chairman Yasir Arafat. Among such comments there are these: "Arafat = Hitler," "The new Nazi is now in the PLO—> Arafat. We have to face them with guns in our hands," "Arafat must be stripped of his Nobel Prize, and brought to justice! [Signed] grandson of survivors/veterans," and, in full block letters covering most of the page, "Arifat [sic] the Jew killer," a comment that has been scribbled out by (apparently) another visitor. Others see things differently. One writes, "Knowing what I learned now I'm surprised to see Sharon acting like a Nazi"; another has drawn a large star of David and a large Nazi swastika with an "=" sign between them. As Jeffrey Carter suggested only half-kiddingly, it is sometimes typical of visitors to write down the first thing that comes to their minds, and these comments seem to reflect a desire to find villains to blame for the destruction of which visitors have just seen evidence in the USHMM, and which they see on CNN and in the newspapers outside the museum's walls.

Other comments seem to make direct reference to the museum's explicit (metaphorical) aim, which is to create a particular narrative of the atrocity of the Holocaust that then allows individual visitors to make memorial connections between aspects of that event and similar aspects of world events. An anonymous writer asks, "Look at the Middle East today! Have we learned nothing?" while another warns, with reference to the destruction of Jews during the Holocaust, "Arafat's going for double. Let's learn from our mistakes. Do we have to expand this place in the future to make room for all of his stuff?" (both comments are dated 1 April 2002). The narrative of the destruction of Judaism in Europe, and the threat of anti-semitism in Europe, the United States, and particularly in the middle east—references to all three are sprinkled throughout the comments—seem to have come around full circle, and in spite of the similarities or dissimilarities in those histories, visitors understand the point of connection as the survival of Jewish culture, this time in Israel. But if the historical narrative of the Holocaust is seen to have a parallel in the narrative of the struggle for Israel's survival fifty years later, that narrative seems to have its negative image in other visitors' memories, in which Israel now plays the role of the oppressor and disenfranchiser, and the Palestinians play the part of "the jew." Rich H. notes on 26 January that we rightly

> condemn what happened to the Jews during the Holocaust. It is a dark part of human history. However, it is also sad to see today that the jews are passing their experiences to Palestinians by bombing homes and killing innocent people. When are they going to learn to be a human being? Now, Jews use the Holocaust to justify their act to Palestinians.

And four months later, a teacher from Pittsburgh writes:

> [Our] high school appreciates this. And takes all of the images to the heart. This day will be with us forever. Remember the Palestinians.

Taking these two remarks together, we see an interesting dynamic of memory and forgetting, in which the memory of the Holocaust—forged, presumably, by the narrative contours and the historical objects woven together in the permanent exhibit—is overtaken by a more recent memory, one having to do with images of the violence of suicide bombings in Netanya and Jerusalem and Haifa, and of Israeli Defense Force snipers and tanks in Ramallah and Bethlehem. More problematically, because the narrative force of the Holocaust is so strong, and because that narrative has been used to justify, at least in these visitors' memories, the Israeli defense of its "historical homeland" and the survival of the Jewish people, the historical complexities of the Final Solution are elided with the equally complex historical present since the Camp David accords. Both the Final Solution and the prospect of a peaceful middle east are forgotten in favor of a memory—though it is, of course, not a memory at all but a narrative account designed to fill in a void that is otherwise unspeakable involving violence and terror—of the intefadeh, of Israeli and Jewish violence, and of the Palestinian victim, who is, according to the teacher from Pittsburgh, something like the new "jew" of the middle east.

Of those who connect the present situation in Israel directly with the destruction of the Final Solution, many do so by following out the narrative trajectory of the museum's exhibit: the second floor of the museum, devoted to the aftermath of the Holocaust in Europe (including liberation, the DP camps, repatriation, and the emigrations to Palestine, the United States and other countries), which concludes with the transformation of the Jewish resistance movements (particularly those in Poland and in Palestine) from local terrorists to nationalist freedom fighters and Zionist pioneers. Sandy P. writes in April of the "real struggle for the continued existence of Israel"; an unnamed writer does the same, only with reference to the "Arab nations, that would see [the Jews is Israel] eradicated, from the face of the earth."

But there is an equal, if not larger, group of writers who see the destruction of the Holocaust and the redemption of Israel in purely apocalyptic—and purely Christian—terms. One writer who bemoans the Arab nations surrounding Israel concludes, "Their only hope is GOD. Sincerely, a human being." Two other comments are characteristic: Steph G. and Roslyn S., from Montreal, write on 10 April 2002 that "We shall always remember what had happened, and never ever forget. Hopefully there will be peace in the world, especially in Israel." Dave D., on the same day, exhorts, "Please 'pray for the peace of Jerusalem.'" It would be heartening to conclude that these museum visitors have also taken the lesson from the USHMM's narrative and collective memory of the Holocaust that the solution to the destruction of the Shoah is the work of peace-making in a troubled world (including a very troubled Israel). But it is far more likely (and this was a sentiment confirmed by Carter) that they have been written by charismatic or evangelical Christians, by whose reading of the book of Revelations the rapture—the bodily ascension of the righteous into heaven at the end of days—can only occur

when the Jews have rebuilt the temple in a peaceful Jerusalem. Far from reading Israel's survival as the political conclusion of the Shoah, these writers
more likely read the creation of a peaceful Israel as the penultimate step
toward their own Christian salvation, a salvation in which Jews play only an
instrumental part. Here the memory of the Holocaust is merely ancillary to a
much larger cultural narrative of redemption whose prime mover is Christ.

It isn't just the violence in Israel, the attacks on the United States, and
the war on terror that occupy visitor's minds as they leave the permanent
exhibit. It's inevitable that the world's events, particularly its atrocities, will
impinge upon the memories of those who witness to the Holocaust at the
USHMM. Weighing on visitors' minds were events that included the civil war
in Sudan, the drug-funded violence in Colombia, Timothy McVeigh's bombing of the Federal Building in Oklahoma City in 1995, the genocide of nearly
a million Tutsis in Rwanda, Pol Pot's reign of terror in Cambodia, violence in
the United States perpetrated by the KKK and homophobes, repression in
post-revolutionary Cuba, the use of the atomic bomb on Japan during the second World War, the disintegration of Yugoslavia, the racism and violence during the Raj in India, and the "killing of unborn babies" since Roe v. Wade. In
some ways, the concerns of these visitors would seem to confirm the success of
the museum's mission—teaching the lessons of the Holocaust so that events
like it can't recur—though one wonders if, given the prevalence of such
events, the lessons were really learned at all. One could argue that the way
individual visitors' memories were triggered suggests a metonymic, rather than
a metaphoric recollection, speaking to the overwhelming strength of anamnesis in the midsts of a collective or historical memory.

Though it would be easy to dismiss the comments of a visitor like
Rebecca L.'s as those of a religious fundamentalist who would see her disdain
of abortion in just about any depiction of atrocity ("Today I minutely experienced the sadness of what people experienced in the holocaust. May we learn
from this and stop killing millions of unborn babies"), it's less simple in the
case of J.S. This visitor's memory is not only a visual memory but one that
seems founded in a sense of a terrible injustice. S/he writes

> The silent cries of the unborn as they are aborted remind me that like the
> Jews who needed a strong voice of support for their lives, I too need to raise
> my voice to the slaughter of the unborn in my generation. (8 January 2002)

Her comment is reminiscent of Pastor Niemoller's often-quoted aphorism,
which begins, "When they came for the Communists I did not speak up,
because I was not a Communist," and ends with the speaker being taken away
himself, with no one left to speak up for him. The museum's fourth floor is a
record of injustices perpetrated not only by legal fiat in National Socialist
Germany, but by other countries—the United States, Great Britain—that
abdicated a role in opening their borders to German and other Jewish

refugees at the conference at Evian and under other circumstances. For J.S., the unborn children, like the Jews sixty years ago, seem to cry out for justice so far delayed.

For J.S., Roe v. Wade disenfranchised the unborn in the same way that the Nuremburg Laws disenfranchised German Jews, and it was this legal foundation that led to the destruction of both. And in spite of the "legality" of the disenfranchisements in both cases, righteous people remained silent in their home countries and abroad, and it is this "lesson"—the dangers of silence and complicity—that she has taken from the USHMM. So in this sense, the web of narrative created by the museum seems to have provided the criteria by which legal abortion in the US and the destruction of the Jews in the Final Solution are parallel, if not coequal. But J.S.'s logic is undermined by the less logical but no less figural connection provided by the visual image. The term "slaughter" in J.S.'s comment is a commonplace in the anti-abortion vocabulary ("the slaughter of the unborn"), and its visual images on placards and posters are (to choose a polite term) arresting: they included images of dismembered and discarded fetuses, of children, and the bloody aftereffects of abortion procedures. These images are strikingly like a series of images found on the museum's third floor, where the depictions of medical experiments performed by Nazi doctors on Soviet POWs, Jewish camp inmates, and the medically and mentally disabled in the T-4 campaign are located behind viewer screens to prevent the museum's younger visitors from being disturbed by them. As Dominick La Capra and others have suggested, however, the weird attraction to (and borderline voyeurism associated with) these images has little to do with their historical specificity, but only with their violation of the norms of decorum and the commonplace. The film loops depicting pressurized Soviet airmen, drowning Auschwitz inmates, and the amputated limbs of Jewish prisoners aren't attractive to visitors because of their historical context, just as the posters of anti-abortion protesters aren't arresting because of their cause. These images are disturbing regardless of their historical context, and it is this contextlessness that allows the images to be metonymically conflated by J.S. and by other museum visitors, and which circumvents the historically specific criteria by which collective memory could be constructed.

Some of the most heartfelt comments found at the museum are from those who have themselves been witnesses to atrocities and their motivating ideologies and these comments, like those of J.S. and Rebecca L., display various "criteria" of connection between the memory of the Shoah and their own memories. One visitor writes:

> I am from Rwanda, the country in central Africa, where took place a geno-
> cide of Tutsis in April–June 1994, and were killed 1.5 million of my people.
> I think all peoples of the world could do all possible so that this genocide

never more could be done anywhere. That is the reason peoples of Israel, people of Rwanda, have right to fight those killers who want to exterminate them anywhere they are. It is not understandable to hear some persons, responsibles at so great level as UN, or some government, defend Palistinian terrorists or Rwandan [illegible] (genocidaires). When those killers were killing the innocents, the nation, the governments, did nothing for us. They condemned us to death; and where we want to live, they defend the killers. (14 April 2002)

Clearly parallels between Israel and Rwanda (sovereign entities) and Palestinian "terrorists" and the Hutu genocidaires (whose aim is the extermination of those entities) override the historical complexities of both contexts, and in fact reduce the Holocaust in this comment to silence. An unnamed visitor from the US, apparently impressed that the museum's content committee included material from National Socialism's attempt to eliminate male homosexuals along with Jews and Communists from its national body, writes

> Thank you for honoring the gay victims of the Holocaust alongside the 1000s [sic] of Jewish persons murdered. Please continue to tell this story to the "Christian Right," who would condemn me to the incinerator, given a choice. Gay American, Gay father, Gay teacher, Gay Christian, Gay Brother of Humankind. (22 March 2002)

Like a visitor from earlier in March, who links the devastation of Jews to the actions of the Klan across the US and the murder of Matthew Shepard in Wyoming, the historical narrative of the Holocaust is inextricably tied to the individual visitor's memories of his own feelings of deprivation and disenfranchisement as a gay man living in a largely straight and largely Christian country. And while the historical precedent is available in the Holocaust narrative—the metaphorical, textual link between disparate moments in time— the suggestion that the Christian right would condemn him to the incinerator seems to be an historically unsubstantiable, but nonetheless very real, intimation borne of a memory to which we (and perhaps the visitor himself) do not have immediate access, and certainly no knowledge as such.

The memory of Takashi, or more accurately his second-generation remembrance of what his mother saw, is perhaps the most striking of the comments I found in my research. After visiting the museum with his mother, who survived another "holocaust"—the bombing of Hiroshima at the end of the second World War—he wrote the following:

> I came here from Tokyo. My mother was born in Hiroshima and of course her house was burn[ed] down in 1945.8.6. She has been suffering from some unhealthy physical problems because of irradiation for over 50 years. She was lying on her bed, when I was a kid, and told me about "Holocaust" so long long time. And said "You never, never forget about it." So many time.

First time I was scared but I strongly recognzied that I should do so. Today.
I came here from Japan, at last, I could watch and see around this museum
with my mom. It was [such a] good time. I am a pediatric neurosurgeon. I
strongly feel my destiny that I have to continue to save the children's life,
including all the children's lives that were lost in this story. Thank you very
much. (16 March 2002)

The link between the devastation witnessed by his mother and the evidence
of destruction Takashi himself witnessed, at second hand, in the USHMM, is
a single word, "holocaust," uttered by his mother over fifty years ago. It is this
word, and its historical referent—the moment when the bomb destroyed his
mother's house and caused her to become ill forever afterward—that presumably functions as the object of the pronoun "it," as in "you never forget about
it." Again one can imagine that it is the visual connection—the photographs
of the dead and the dying in the camps, or the inhabitants of the ghettos starving to death—that forged the connection, in Takashi's mother's recollection,
to what she saw in the aftermath of the atom bomb. But for Takashi, the word
"holocaust" and the parallel destructions, in Japan and in central Europe, are
here connected to another memory, one that is peculiar to Takashi: the memories of the children with whom he has worked in his capacity as a neurosurgeon. Here, in perhaps one of the most complex webs of recollection inscribed
in the book of comments, are nearly half a dozen strands of memory: the
mother's recollection of the bomb, her son's recollection of her stories of the
destruction, his much more immediate memory of the historical narrative told
in the USHMM's permanent exhibit, and the recollection of his pediatric
patients. These memories are woven together with Funkenstein's "historical
consciousness," his ability to see a connection between the "children's lives
that were lost in this story," the story of the Holocaust, and the children's lives
that he has saved, and may continue to save, in his work as a neurosurgeon.
Takashi's narrative is also a narrative of loss and redemption, but it is founded
upon a loss not only of the children of Hiroshima (and, presumably, its grand-
children) and of nearly three generations of Jews in the Shoah, but also the
loss of memory. What one sees in Takashi's own narrative is a suppression of
historical criteria—the metaphorical links that could in fact reasonably connect the "holocaust" of August 1945 in Japan and the Holocaust of the Final
Solution to the Jewish problem in Europe—in favor of a metonymic link of
child to child: the child Takashi recalling his mother's stories; the mother, herself as a child, witnessing the firestorm of Hiroshima; the children lost in the
Shoah; and the children saved (and perhaps those lost) in the medical prac-
tice of a single pediatric neurosurgeon from Tokyo. Takashi's memory is a conflation of the collective memory of the Holocaust and the particular, uncanny
memories of other "world events," some of which register in the consciousness
of other museum visitors, and others of which are his alone.

One of the difficulties we contend with during a time when images seem to take precedence over text—during a time when, as W.J.T. Mitchell has put it, we have taken a pictorial turn—is how to avoid taking their incessant repetition as a substitute for the real or for history. My students told me, with little irony at all, that as they watched the planes crash into the World Trade Center they thought it looked just like a movie, evidence enough that the effectiveness of a visual representation has come dangerously close to supplanting evidence of the event as the benchmark of authenticity. Barbie Zelizer reminds us that the repetition of the image, if it works to produce a collective memory of atrocity unconnected to a place and a name—to the materiality of the historical event itself—empties the image of the particularity of the disaster and we are left only with a shell: this, we think, is the Holocaust; Rwanda and 9/11 and Iraq are simply reinstantiations of "the Holocaust." Treating the image of the atrocity as one more vehicle through which we and our students can produce knowledge of the events that form their object simply repeats the two dangers of narrative representation, the dangers of "writing" the Holocaust—we are either lulled into believing that images and narratives are interchangeable, both of them substitutions for the event in the past, or we see the image as somehow giving us a better or more "real" representation of the event because it seems to fix that event in ways of which the written text, with the endless possibilities for interpretation and revision, seem incapable. Photographic representations, like textual representations, of atrocity may indeed be instruments of knowledge. But at least in the case of the representations I've cited here, and in the case of other—and more recent—examples, their repetition doesn't just repeat instances of the same; each instance is distinct from the one just before or just after it, and it is this nonidentity that eventually makes itself apparent and shatters the collective memory that has no point of origin in the atrocity itself. To put it in my students' terms, the still photographs taken of the aftermath of the destruction of the WTC call up aspects of the event that cannot be easily integrated into the narratives of the death of innocents, or the war on terror, or American imperialism, aspects that prevent them from easily making connections between atrocities, between the name of "the Holocaust" and the name of "9/11." Those images produce, in Hirsch's terms, a memory effect that invokes a forgetfulness rather than a memory, since the memories produced or invoked—collective or personal—aren't memories of the event at all, since none of us was there on the spot.

Because forgetting is not memory's opposite but its double, forgetful memory requires not a looking back—the desperate attempt to make out the details of the image so that we may see some passing resemblance to it in future atrocities—but a looking forward. The disaster of the Holocaust that has been, we presume, captured on film and in other visual images, cannot be remembered. But it exists as a crux that is embedded in the images and makes itself present only as a rupture of historical and individual memories, and it requires a writing that works against what Lyotard called "the monopoly of the cognitive regimen of phrases," that narrative of history that is so well-worn and well-understood that it runs the risk of letting us think we can "know what it was like." It should be a writing that lends an ear "to what is not presentable under the rules of knowledge" (57), that which is forgotten. Like those working on the top floors of the WTC or like those rushing there to save them, the images we saw at the time passed before our eyes and passed away. They are degraded, disincarnated, and forever lost to memory. What is left is the contemporary image, which opens a space beyond representation and the object, a space that is "homologous with the nondiscursiveness" of the event itself.

EIGHT

"Difficult Freedom"

Levinas, Memory, and Politics

IN THE DECADES immediately following the establishment of the state of Israel, Emmanuel Levinas wrote a group of essays, many of which were collected in the volumes entitled *Difficult Freedom* and *In the Time of Nations*, which took the practicalities of politics as their subject. These essays explored what it would mean for a collection of individuals to exist as a nation, how a nation should engage with others, and how it should establish a set of laws governing the interaction of its citizens. For a philosopher whose primary attention—in works like *Totality and Infinity* and *Otherwise than Being*—had focused on the individual's relation to others, and whose writing made clear that any attempt to establish a collectivity (a "we") worked against ethics, what Levinas called first philosophy, these essays seemed like odd forays, even a contradiction of that larger body of work. In the years just before and immediately following Levinas's death in 1995, ethicists, philosophers, and political scientists tried to make sense of the political essays in the context of Levinas's philosophical thought. So David Campbell, in 1993, noted the affinities between Levinas's thought and that of Jacques Derrida and Simon Critchley, and spoke of the former's political thought as an attempt to "reterritorialize the space . . . of responsibility, subjectivity, and ethics" (quoted in Campbell and Shapiro 32) in Israel/Palestine. Michael Shapiro, writing in 1997, sees Levinas as reading time "otherwise," arguing that the Israeli's understanding of national time is radically different from the displaced Palestinian's, thereby working against what he calls one of "Levinas's more egregious blind spots" (65), namely his failure to understand the rights of Israel's dispossessed. Working from a theological perspective, Adam Newton and Marie Baird tie together the philosophical, political, and Talmudic writing by focusing on Levinas's notion of the "other" and the "neighbor," noting that what binds the three genres together for Levinas is the sense that the neighbor and the other are not the same, but quite distinct national/familial engagements, and that Israeli— and world—politics are vexed by the distinction.

But analyses like those cited above tend to excuse Levinas's "blind spots," acting as if disjunctions between the philosophical/religious and the political writing were unfortunate lapses, or (as in the case of someone like Alain Badiou or, more recently, Martin Hagglund and Slavoj Zizek) fundamental errors, in Levinas's formulation of the realities of politics as such. In this chapter, I want to make the case that Levinas's political thinking, particularly those instances that appear contradictory to his other writing, can be seen as consonant with his work on language and ethics. In doing so I want to avoid two lines of argument that have been pursued in the last dozen years concerning Levinas's politics and political thought. The first—this is Badiou's—is that Levinas's philosophy of the "other" is fundamentally flawed and inevitably leads to a politics that apotheosizes a bland "tolerance of difference" that celebrates multiculturalism. I think this fundamentally mischaracterizes Levinas's notion of the other, causing Badiou to miss how close his notion of ethics is to Levinas's. The second line of argument—this is the political scientists' and the theologians'—is to see in Levinas's Jewish exceptionalism a kind of pro-Israeli chauvinism. In fact, the biblical notion of "chosenness," coupled with the Talmudic injunction (both ethical and "religious") to orient oneself toward both the other (the one close by) and the neighbor (the one far off) forces the individual to consider those with whom he considers himself kin and those who are bound to him by other means—territorially and nationally, extraterritorially and exilic. Religion and politics are two sides to the same coin, and exert a tension on one another; the former does not subsume the latter.

Because Levinas's position depends so much on individual relations, and works so antisystemically (or so the argument goes), it can't be developed into a useful articulation of a politics. Gayatri Spivak—in her seminar at the School of Criticism and Theory at Cornell during the summer of 2004— makes much the same point: Levinas' rejection of rhetoric, ethics, and politics, at least as we've understood them for two thousand years, and his development of a notion of "otherness," seems to render his thought useless for political underlaboring in the world as we know it. But what I'll do here is lay out the relation among Levinas's understanding of language, memory, ethics, and politics, and describe how Israel can be seen as a testing ground for a contemporary politics based in forgetful memory—in political parlance, perhaps the better term is "exiled memory"—though it may be that we are failing that test.

LANGUAGE AND ETHICS

It could be said that if ethics is first philosophy for Levinas, then a theory of language or utterance (rhetoric) might be fundamental to ethics. For Levinas, an utterance is by definition an "approach" to another individual. In any such encounter, I am compelled to approach that other; more specifically, any encounter with another compels speech. Levinas puts this in terms of what he calls "proximity": in *Otherwise than Being*, he writes that "in the non-indifference to a neighbor, . . . proximity is never close enough, the difference between me and the other, and the undeclinability of the subject are not effaced" (138). Not only can the neighbor—the person we approach—not be met with indifference; we have to act as if we are responsible both for and to that other person. What makes this more complicated is that, though "proximity is never close enough"—though we have to put ourselves in the other's place—such a substitution isn't possible ("the difference between me and the other . . . [is] not effaced") and so we're met with the first difficulty in Levinas's ethics. Though I am responsible for the other and am enjoined to engage with the other as if our lives depended upon it, I can't ever fully understand him. The subject—and here Levinas means not just the other but myself as well—is "undeclinable."

This incommensurability is reflected in what we can say in our encounter with the other. In the same way that I can't ever *be* or understand that other individual, I also can't produce an utterance that reflects my position with regard to that other individual. Just as I can't substitute myself for others, neither does the language I use rest on the principle of substitution. Levinas asks what the difference between language (what he calls the "said") and what compels language (the "saying") tells us about our position as subjects relative to others. Utterance always indicates incommensurability, and this can best be described by noting the distinction between the pronominal "I" and the subject the pronoun describes. I can never be contained by that pronoun; more to the point, if I could, that "I" shifts from the present to the past very, very swiftly. So not only is an individual never able to substitute himself for the other; neither is the individual able to utter his or her position as a subject. The best one is able to do is to note the problematic relation between what we've said and that which compelled us to speak in the first place.

In a way that's reminiscent of Geoffrey Harpham's notion of ethics, as laid out in his essays in *Getting it Right* and *Shadows of Ethics*, Levinas's moment of approach is the ethical moment *par excellence*: it's the moment at which all possible options for action are as yet unforeclosed, the moment just prior to choosing what for better or worse might be called the proper course for acting. The moment of proximity for Levinas, as the ethical moment for Harpham, is radically open, in which no name has been supplied for either one's self or the other, and in which the question of how one ought to act has not been definitively decided. Ideally, any utterance at such a moment attempts to hold that moment open: it resists the temptation to name the other, to foreclose courses of action, or to describe the situation in which the speaker finds herself. Of course, this isn't possible: choosing is inevitable, as is producing an utterance will necessarily be at odds with the open moment that compels it.

What such radical openness also makes clear, though, is that the individual—not to mention her interlocutor—is exceptionally vulnerable in such an encounter. Exposure "identifies me as the unique one, not by reducing me to myself, but by stripping me of every [identity], and thus all form, all investiture" (OTB 49). Elsewhere Levinas writes that exposure—the moment of ethical openness—is a "giving," where the individual gives up his or her name ("I am I") in favor of being responsible to and for the other with whom she has contact. The moment isn't reciprocal—there are no guarantees that the other individual will respond with the same openness or willingness to engage—and with that nonreciprocity comes vulnerability: the other could respond by foreclosing the encounter in any number of ways: by falling back into what he already knows, the familiarity of names and of precedents, which for Levinas is a kind of violence. His has sometimes been called a trauma theory of ethics, in which the speaker has to essentially empty herself of names, regularities, and knowledge at the moment of her encounter with the other, a literal turning inside out (a *denucleation* or coring out). But this coring out of the self is the heart of Levinas's ethical system: it is the only way in which individuals as subjects can catch a glimpse of what resides beyond the regularities of reason which restrict human action and which foreclose the possibility of real contact between and among individuals one person (one "face") at a time.

One of the reasons Alain Badiou, in *Ethics*, rejects Levinas's notion of otherness is that it works against the possibility of establishing what he calls "truths," the enactment of or engagement with the consequences of an event. For Badiou as for Levinas, knowledge is static, objective, encumbered by institutions, names, and what Lyotard has called—in a different context—"the monopoly of the cognitive regimen of phrases" (57). The ethical imperative is to break with this monopoly by "identify[ing] in thought of singular situations. There is no ethics in general. There are only—eventually—ethics of processes by which we treat the possibilities of a situation" (Badiou 16). To engage in the production of truths is to "treat [the situation—the moment of engagement—] *right to the limit* of the possible," to "draw from the situation, to the greatest possible extent, the affirmative humanity that it contains" (15). For Badiou, the problem with an ethics of otherness is that it devalorizes the term "humanity" as something essential, as part of the problem: it names individuals as a "we." The *denucleation* of the self—the notion that individuals are defined by their suffering—is precisely what ethics should seek to avoid. Badiou provides the example of the doctor in a national medical plan: because he is forced to work for the national Good, that doctor must refuse to treat those who are aliens, who are "without legal residency papers, or not a contributor to Social Security." In such a situation, the doctor ignores that he must work to alleviate the suffering of the individual, regardless of the national Good, "using everything he knows and with all the means at his disposal, without taking anything else into consideration" (15). It is the doctor's ethical obligation to affiliate himself with the sick person, regardless of national or institutional affiliation, and to engage with him "right to the limit of the possible."

But Badiou misunderstands, I think, the degree to which Levinas's notion of approach, and the radically open nature of the encounter with the other (in this case, the patient), is ethical under criteria—Badiou calls them axioms—not unlike as his own. "[E]very situation, inasmuch as it is, is a multiple composed of an infinity of elements, each one of which is itself a multiple. Considered in their simple belonging to a situation (to an infinite multiple), the animals of the species *Homo sapiens* are ordinary multiplicities." To put it another way, "infinite alterity is quite simply *what there is*" (25). When Levinas writes that responsibility should be unhitched from "logical deliberation summoned by reasoned decision" (*OTB* 111) and instead should be reconfigured as a response anterior to knowledge of being, to the "nakedness [of] a face" (*TI* 213), he's getting at much the same thing. This is the command that we engage with individuals, from one moment to the next, without regard to the singularity of names, "to the limit of the possible." As Marie Baird puts it in an essay that accounts for the theological dimension of Levinas's work as much as the political promise, "the ethical subject is held hostage by the human face"—the face of the nonresident alien, who has fallen ill and is without papers or insurance—"and takes up responsibility for the life of the other—before being for itself" (156). Without thinking; without naming; without knowing; simply doing. Such an encounter, for both Badiou and for Levinas, is resistant to knowledge precisely because "concepts suppose an anticipation, a horizon within which alterity is amortized as soon as it is announced precisely because it has let itself be foreseen" (Derrida, "Violence and Metaphysics" 95). Both Levinas and Badiou are working to ensure that "there is no circumstance under which we could declare that" human situations like that faced by the doctor, or crises like those in Israel or in other parts of the world, "[are] not our concern" (Campbell 35).

ETHICS AND POLITICS

The difficulty is that Levinas's ethics, like the doctor's encounter with the sick patient, takes place one individual and one situation at a time. But "[i]n the real world there are many others" ("Ideology and Idealism" 247). If we think of politics in its classical formulation as the art of statecraft, then the radically individual nature of ethics on Levinas's terms seems to require an intermediate step between it and an the formulation of consensus or the development of policy. If we think of politics in a more contemporary sense—the development of a communitarian or national identity that can be deployed so that benefits may be accrued to its members—then Levinas's principle of nonidentity (the idea that the pronominal "I" cannot name or substitute for the subject) seems to rule that sense of politics out of court as well. But as with his approach toward language and ethics, Levinas's politics works against the orthodoxies of the classical (and even modern) tradition. As Derrida puts it in *Adieu*, it "require[s] us to think law and politics otherwise" (20–21). Derrida goes so far as to suggest that there is a "hiatus" between ethics and politics in Levinas's work, which may well be true. But it's precisely that hiatus—the idea of a rupture or aporia between that which can be known and that which compels us to know it—that lies at the heart of Levinas's political thought.

One of Levinas' principal notions in *Totality and Infinity* is that of hospitality or of welcoming, a notion that is connected very closely to the idea of proximity and approach in *Otherwise than Being*. Playing on the double meaning of the French *hôte* as both "host" and "guest," Levinas' implication is that when an individual engages another in discourse—at the ethical moment—he acts at once as host and as guest. Derrida glosses the term's double meaning this way: *apropos* Rosenzweig, there is a divine law "that would make of the inhabitant a guest [hôte] received in his own home, that would make of the owner a tenant, of the welcoming host [hôte] a welcomed guest [hôte]" (42). The displacement involved here is not just a conceptual or epistemological one; it's also, potentially, a physical one. When the individual engages the other, she resides in a kind of no-man's land, in which she is both at home and in exile, neither completely apart from, nor completely a part of, the community or the location from which she speaks.

Derrida goes even further—the host is a not only a host or a guest; the host [hôte] is also a hostage [ostage]. He writes in *Adieu*, paraphrasing *Otherwise than Being* (111–12) that

> the host is a hostage insofar as he is a subject put into question, obsessed (and thus besieged), persecuted, in the very place where he takes place, where, as emigrant, exile, stranger, a guest from the very beginning, he finds himself elected to or taken up by a residence before himself electing or taking one up. (56)

In ethical terms, the individual is vulnerable because she is troubled by the presence of that other. She is, in this sense, the other's hostage, forced to put herself in the other's place with no way to know whether her (charitable) act will be returned in kind. In political terms, the subject is both non-coincident with herself, but also noncoincident with the location of her utterance: there is no place that she can comfortably call home, or domi-cile, or community, or nation. Though she may speak from a location that is home, or domicile, or nation, her relation to that place is, like her rela-tion with the other, "thrown out of phase with itself": it isn't "natural," a point of origin from which everything else may be easily understood. The state, not unlike biblical cities of refuge, should be seen as places for the exile—the individual "put into question"—to find respite; in that respite, the individual becomes committed (or, in the case of the refugee, recom-mitted) to the possibility that what sent him into exile—what is beyond being, beyond what the utterance—might be redeemed (see *Beyond the Verse* 38–47).

What allows for the possibility of an *other* politics is what Levinas calls "the third." While the subject's relation to the other is always fraught and always tenuous, what raises the stakes is the presence of a third party to whom both the speaker and the other are also responsible. The third—"the neighbor and the one far off" (Isaiah 57:19)—introduces the notion of jus-tice. "The third introduces a contradiction in the saying. . . . A question of conscience, consciousness. Justice is necessary, that is, comparison, coexis-tence, contemporaneousness, assembling . . ." (*OTB* 157). Not only must individuals be responsible for one another; they must also be responsible for those they cannot see. This is different from the Kantian categorical imper-ative whereby one must assume that his actions would be determinative of the law for everyone else. Instead, Levinas's third acts as a witness: anything I might do or say will be seen, even only potentially, by the third, and forces me to compare my individual, unique act with other acts, other utterances, that might be carried out by someone I do not know. It forces, in Levinas's terms, "a weighing, a thinking, a calculation, the comparison of incompara-bles, and consequently, the neutrality—presence or representation—of being" ("Peace and Proximity" 168). And yet it is justice, ironically, that potentially corrupts ethics—the ethics in which the other's response might be violent, and in which the speaker's utterance itself may require a certain traumatic undoing (*denucleation*) of the self—but makes politics possible. It is this comparison of incomparables that allows the ethical actor to think the radical individuality of his act as something other than solitary or unique, despite (oddly) its uniqueness.

While saying and acting make evident an aspect of being that is beyond language and beyond action, the act and the utterance are made in the con-text of "the calculations, knowledge, science, and consciousness that nonetheless condition it" (*Adieu* 116). Acting in the context of justice gives a "content" to what we do—meanings can be assigned to it by our neighbors in spite of whatever meaning or meaninglessness we ourselves assign—

thought that content must always be acted upon in its turn ethically. For Levinas, ethics and politics occur in the same act; one acts ethically, politics comes after ("whether in logical consequence or chronological sequence" [*Adieu* 83]): one acts toward one individual at a time, knowing—given the presence of the third, the neighbor—that that act takes place in a community of other individuals who we can't see at the moment but on whom our action may have a palpable effect.

Levinas at times talks about the possibility that the political process invented in Israel might bring peace, and of these instances Derrida asks whether "this political invention in Israel ever [will] come to pass." He then goes on to say that "this is perhaps not the place to pose this question, certainly not to answer it" (81). But Levinas has in fact answered the question himself, for he sees in Israel—struggling with its Jewish identity and its identity as a city of refuge of sorts—something like a testing ground for the ethics/politics he lays out in the philosophical works. Perhaps the first and most important influence on Levinas's political and philosophical texts is a pair of events that neither he nor political philosophy in general can ignore: the destruction of the Jewish communities of Europe in the Final Solution, and the war of 1947–9 that led to the creation of the state of Israel. As he says in the afterword or "signature" to *Difficult Freedom*, his biography "is dominated by the presentiment and the memory of the Nazi horror" (291). Levinas actively works against a notion of politics in which the name of the individual is subsumed—and in the case of the Final Solution, eliminated—by the name of the universal. The name—the "we" of nation, or community, or race—produces the sense of an origin, and what doesn't originate from it is a surplus that must be consumed. Levinas works from the opposite assumption: *all* action produces a surplus; the danger to it is a politics that reduces it to a repetition of the same. In the philosophical texts, Levinas is alert for a politics "for itself": justice is necessary because (to paraphrase Simon Critchley) its relation to the one-to-one, face-to-face continually interrupts the tendency toward totalitarianism (see *The Ethics of Deconstruction* 223); the

> *metaphysical* relation of the I to the Other moves into the form of the We, aspires to a State, institutions, laws, which are the source of universality. [P]olitics left to itself bears a tyranny within itself; it deforms the I and the other who have given rise to it, for it judges them according to universal rules, and thus as in absentia. (*Totality and Infinity* 300; emphasis added)

The difference between the ethical which *aspires to* the law and the ethical which *becomes* the law—the metaphysical relation—is the difference between a kind of politics which acknowledges a place for the guest and the host, and one which sees the exile, the Other, as a corrupt instance of the same and thus in need of elimination.

POLITICS IN THE TIME OF THE NATIONS

Levinas sees in Israel the possibility of a state that makes room for both the individual—the host (hôte)—and the universal, and that aspires toward providing a refuge for all comers. Israel was founded essentially by strangers—by those who had arrived from Europe in the generations before the UN Partition Plan and by those who had arrived immediately after the war—and by fellow-Jews, so it is Judaism, rather than national community, that establishes the "universality" of the nation. And yet that Judaism is itself not exactly universal: the Jew, because he is "exiled on this earth," discovers his fellows "before discovering landscapes and towns" (DF 22). Individuals matter more than geography: "The world becomes intelligible before a human face and not, as for the great contemporary philosopher who sums up an important aspect of the West, through houses, temples, and bridges" (23). If Israel is to become a country among countries, a political entity, it must see itself as "non-original, stripped of all local colour." To the extent that such a country might lose its "'curiosity' value, [it will become] increasingly difficult to define [itself]." It stands to lose hypocrisy and gain in its place a generosity, an openness that comes from the attempt to understand itself beyond origins (52).

Levinas is careful to suggest that while the "concern for the other remains utopian in the sense that it is always 'out of place' (u-topos)" (Entre Nous 114), Israel itself is no utopia: though its residents may conceive of what he calls a "supernatural order," they see themselves as both hosts and guests, at home and exiled at one and the same time. What Levinas says of the self-other relation in Otherwise than Being might also be said of the residents of Israel: that they live in time "out of phase with itself" (OTB 9). Each of Israel's citizens is both a resident and a usurper, and Israel is a home to aliens and an instigator of exile: "what is signified by the advent of conscience, and even the first spark of spirit, if not the discovery of corpses beside me and my horror of existing by assassination" (DF 100)? To act ethically and politically at once is to understand one's actions as both radically individual and, through justice, universal: Israel and the Bible both understand the founding of an ethical community must take place "inside [the situations of wars and slavery and sacrifices and priests] which it must assume in order to overcome them" (DF 101). The citizen of such a state "uproot[s himself] from his recent past . . . and seeks his authenticity" (DF 164). This doesn't mean ignoring wars and slavery, sacrifices and priests; it means that the citizen has to act ethically in the face of all this—uprooting himself from the context in which he finds himself mired—in order to affect his neighbor, to act justly in his encounters with his fellow citizens, one by one. It is only in such a particularism—in such a notion of authenticity found in justice—that the citizen of any state, let alone the state of Israel, might also become a member of a broader community.

This radically particular politics is made manifest in the notion of "chosenness" which has vexed both Israel and Judaism, a notion that is closely related to Levinas's notion of engagement. Levinas writes that the idea of being chosen doesn't involve exceptional rights, but instead involves exceptional duties: "the rabbinic principle by which the just of every nation participate in the future world expresses not only an eschatological view. It affirms the possibility of that ultimate intimacy, beyond the dogma affirmed by the one or the other, an intimacy without reserve" (DF 176). The intimacy referred to here is the intimacy of approach, of utterance, of the individual encounter or engagement with the other. If Israel is indeed "chosen," it is because its citizen is "alone in being able to answer the call, [she is] irreplaceable in [her] assumption of responsibility. Being chosen involves a surplus of obligations for which the 'I' of moral consciousness utters" (DF 177). Chosenness is related to the notion of sanctity or sanctification—in Hebrew, kadosh—which also means apartness. To be chosen is to be radically separate and individual in one's relations to the other: you have to engage with individual others as if your life depended upon it; and you have to do so in the midst of your neighbors and "the ones far off" as if your life depended upon their witnessing of that act. Here ethics doesn't substitute for the political, but creates an excess of—and for—politics.

The political situation on the ground in Israel, of course, is exceptionally difficult, and has been since the creation of the state. Its most pressing problem has been, to paraphrase Paul Claudel—the "Bedouin caper," the Arab neighbors in Israel's midst, the Palestinians who formerly resided in what is now the state of Israel. It's worth considering this issue at some length, since it represents perhaps the single most significant limitation on Levinas's political thinking. Perhaps the most controversial of his statements about the Palestinian issue came in the wake of the massacres at the Sabra and Shatila refugee camps in Lebanon in 1982, for which the Israeli armed forces were said to be at least tacitly responsible. In a radio exchange with Alain Finkielkraut and Shlomo Malkin, we get the following. Levinas says that for him the essence of Zionism is that

> It signifies a State in the fullest sense of the term, a state with an army and arms, an army which can have a deterrent, and if necessary, defensive significance. Its necessity is ethical—indeed it is an old ethical idea which commands us precisely to defend our neighbors. My people and my kin are still my neighbors. When you defend the Jewish people, you defend your neighbor; and every Jew in particular defends his neighbor, when he defends.

> SHLOMO MALKIN: Emmanuel Levinas, you are the philosopher of the "other." Isn't history, isn't politics the very site of the encounter with the "other," and for the Israeli isn't the "other" above all Palestinian?

LEVINAS: My definition of the other is completely different. The other is the neighbor, who is not necessarily my kin but who may be. But if your neighbor attacks another neighbor, or treats him unjustly, what can you do? Then alterity takes on another character, in alterity we can find an enemy, or at least we are faced with the problem of knowing who is right and who is wrong, who is just and who is unjust. There are people who are wrong. (cited in *The Levinas Reader* 293–4)

Of this passage Michael Shapiro writes that "Levinas's attachment to the venerable story of state sovereignty . . . makes him veer away from his commitment to an ethical bond that precedes all such ontological/spatial attachments"; he does "not heed the Other's stories of self and space" (69).

I think Shapiro's comment is illustrative both of Levinas's shortsightedness on the matter of Israel as a political entity—the "Zionist" question—and the problems that it causes for those who'd want to see Levinas as a political thinker. Levinas is clearly a Zionist, if we take that term to mean an affiliation with the idea that there should be a national homeland for Jews. Given that Levinas's work is so indebted to that of Franz Rosensweig, who rejected the march of history and its political correlatives in favor of history's *beyond*, this affiliation would seem problematic at best, and contradictory at worst. Shapiro is right to suggest that Levinas is attached to the "venerable story of state sovereignty" when it comes to the question of Israel. One reason for Levinas's shortsightedness on this matter is the very historical and palpable fact of the Holocaust, in which Levinas's family, along with his wife's family, in Lithuania were killed either by Nazi *Einsatzgruppen* who followed the Wehrmacht during the invasion of the Baltic countries and the Soviet Union or by pro-Nazi Lithuanian antisemites. Levinas, like many other Jewish thinkers at the time, saw the nation of Israel as a haven for Jews in the wake of the Holocaust, with protected borders and a standing army. Israel functions, for Levinas, as a place for Jews to "teach the new generation the strength necessary to be strong in isolation" (*Proper Names* 121). Because it is impossible to live, physically and historically, in a utopia, or in no place at all, a location must be established, and Israel is that place (see, in *Difficult Freedom*, the essay "Place and Utopia," especially 101).

But it's also true that Zionism for Levinas functioned as an idea that went beyond the notion of borders and national entities—the "venerable story of state sovereignty"—and was as much a placeholder for strength in isolation as anything else. For Levinas, more important than Israel was the idea of Judaism. In an essay on contemporary Judaism and politics, "Judaism and the Present," Levinas writes that "Judaism, disdaining false eternity, has always wished to be a simultaneous engagement and disengagement" (*DF* 213). He has in mind here Sartre's notion of engagement, and notes that those who think of the philosopher as stressing commitment miss the point that he wanted to guarantee the thinker's and the politician's *disengagement* in the midst of engagement. The one who is politically engaged is separate from—disengaged—from the consensually-built community in which he otherwise resides. The tension that results creates what Levinas calls a "negation" of human essence, and it's just this negation that Levinas sees in Judaism and, potentially, in an Israeli state. It must be "a noncoincidence with its time, within coincidence: in the radical sense of the term it is an anachronism" (212). So while Zionism insists on an eternal relation with the land, Judaism resists that idea of eternity, disengages from it. Israel is an existing entity; but the idea of Israel as eternal is mythic, and to "return to the land" is impossible, because that land to which one might return never existed. What exists in its place is Judaism, "attached to the here below" (DF 100) but never of it. And what is here below are Palestinians, nonreligious Israelis, a land fought over with guns and bombs, and large swaths of the community that for any number of reasons are quite materially dispossessed. What makes the idea of politics—and of Israel—so difficult for Levinas is that the Jew must negotiate between Judaism and Israel, the eternal and the anachronism in the here below. It's fair to say that—whatever else we might adduce from Levinas about politics—he was never able to become comfortable in that tension, nor should he (or we) have been.

To return to the question of the Palestinians in the Israelis' midsts, and of Sabra and Shatlia in particular, Shapiro asks, "what makes Palestinians wrong?" But the question should be, what makes the one who attacks another wrong? The answer to *this* question is, this time according to Levinas, the third: not the one "close by" in Isaiah's formulation but "the one far off." In a point I'll elaborate in the conclusion of this chapter, Levinas's other and neighbor aren't precisely the same, and which is which depends very much on the relation of proximity and on a relation of *kin*. In the case of the one who attacks one's neighbor, neither the attacker nor the neighbor is necessarily in proximity to the speaker. Neither is the speaker's (in this case, Levinas's) interlocutor-other. Yet each functions as the other's neighbor: each approaches the other—ideally through utterance in an open relation of giving, but in the case of the attack upon the refugee camps, through violence, something Levinas understood full well is always a possibility. The determination of who is right and who is wrong in this case falls not (only) to those engaged in the immediate relation, but (also) to their neighbors, namely, someone like Levinas (in the court of public opinion) or the civil and national courts (of Israel or Lebanon in this case).

Moreover, the question of who is kin and who isn't in this case isn't a question of nationality: Levinas isn't asking which is the national host and which the national guest (who is Jewish kin to Levinas, and who is the outsider). "The other is the neighbor, who is not necessarily my kin but who may be." The one who is unjust may be a kinsman—a fellow Jew—and if this is the case, then the matter of justice becomes complicated, but only because of the relation of proximity, and not because of any essential identity bonding one to the other. It is complicated because in such a case, the other's identity as host, guest and hostage become conflated (perhaps the better way to put it is that they collapse upon one another). It thus becomes exceedingly difficult for those neighbors "far off" (now perhaps also kinsmen) to mete out justice. So the matter of whether the Palestinians or the Israelis are in the wrong in this case is ancillary to the matter of justice. Levinas is simply making clear that in the Sabra and Shatila massacres, as in the territorial claims made by settlers, Palestinians, and the Israeli government, the question of who is right and who is wrong is a matter of deciding relations among individuals, not necessarily among nations. Any drawing of boundaries or meting out of justice constitutes not just the formation of identity relations but also constitutes exclusions. Israeli and Palestinian identities, questions of who owns which land (the matter of "local color"), matter less than the immediate question of justice for those who committed violent acts, regardless of whether the acts have been committed by Druze militia, stone-throwing Palestinians, armed Fatah members, or the Israeli Defense Forces. If Levinas is right, no answer to that question can be pinned down to questions of "I" and "we," let alone national identities.

CONCLUSION: THE FENCE AND THE NEIGHBOR

Is a politics founded in an ethics of radical otherness possible given the often violent realities on the ground? There are a number of obstacles to answering in the affirmative, whether in Israel or any national community. If we think about Israel as a state that is inescapably religious, we might also see in it a model for other national entities that have a religious character: the Islamic states in the middle east, particularly Iran, Sudan, and Saudi Arabia; the Catholic countries of Europe, particularly Ireland, Poland, and Italy; and, increasingly, the United States with its conservative politics heavily inflected with a religious fundamentalism of its own. It is extremely difficult to separate the "universalism" implied by religious belief—regardless of the exclusionary character of their belief systems—and the particularity of an ethical social law. In Israel, this tension is borne out in religious parties in which the conflict between the constitution, statute law, and representative democracy on the one hand, and the adherence to religion doctrine on the other, creates political paralysis. Levinas writes that "religion and religious parties do not necessarily coincide" because the engagement of ritual belief and the engagement of ethics are at odds. It's only when justice and religion are seen as operating on the principle of an open law—a Torah loved more than God—that the parties of religion and the parties of the state function in concert. Levinas insists that "the relationship of the Jewish State and the Jewish religion . . . [must be] one of study" rather than seeing the latter as a guide to policy for the former. For the Talmudist, the Torah might be understood as the word of God, but only as vehicle for negotiating its significance—its "eternity"—in the here below. Clearly, looking at the state of parliamentary politics in Israel today, this hasn't happened yet.

One reason why it hasn't is that the state hasn't reconciled itself to being both host and guest, host and hostage. But Israel is not the only nation having trouble dealing with this issue: recent work in diaspora studies and on the influence of emigration on world culture and politics has suggested that this century more than any other might be seen as one of both cosmopolitanism and of exile. And it is fundamentally difficult to understand oneself as both a stranger and a host, which is precisely what the state of Israel has become: torn between establishing a city of refuge for Jews around the world and erecting barriers to the stranger, Israel's policy for the Palestinians has become abhorrent in the eyes of many of its own citizens. Repulsed by Paul Claudel's question—"What does all this Bedouin caper matter to us?"—Levinas warns that we are prisoners of "outmoded sociological categories" (131). And yet to approach the other is to become vulnerable, and to do so exposes the individual to the possibility that she will be rebuffed, in some cases violently. For Levinas the most horrifying example of the consequences of exposure was the Shoah, which haunted Levinas—the individual was crushed by the "we" of National Socialism—as much as it haunts Israel. While he recognizes that "the Arab peoples would not have to answer for German atrocities, or cede their lands to the victims of Hitler" (131), Levinas also recognizes that Arabs *have* ceded their land, often involuntarily, and also suffer. Though the right to a birthplace is important, the "local colour" of the landscape is less important than engagement. "*Every survivor of the Hitlerian massacres—whether or not a Jew—is Other in relation to martyrs.* [Each one] is consequently responsible and unable to remain silent" (132; emphasis in original). Suffering, noncoincidence, and survival require engagement, regardless of any individual's location of origin or her personal or national affiliation with the dead; but that engagement does *not* guarantee a successful political outcome.

Engagement's demand can be nonetheless obeyed in political terms in two ways. The first is, in Derrida's terms, to "invent new gestures, discourses, politico-institutional practices that inscribe the alliance of [political movements and political margins], of these two promises or contracts" (*The Other Heading* 44). To do this—to work against "the identity stories that construct actors as one or another type of person . . . [and] provide the foundations for historical and contemporary forms of antagonism, violence, and interpretive contention over the meaning of actions" both political and ethical (Shapiro 59)—is to engage in discourse that doesn't anticipate concepts in which alterity is denied, in which one cannot imagine oneself as anything but host or guest, resident or alien (in which the Jew is *defined as* a member of an Israeli "we," or in which the Palestinian is *defined as* a member of an exiled community). In a passage reminiscent of Walter Benjamin's notion of "messianic time" in his "Task of the Translator" essay, Levinas writes that though Israel's Jews have a sense of themselves as an "eternal people,"

> there is an incessant reference to the time of the nations, an unfailing presence to their presence and their present, to the acme of their actuality, to their eventual modernity, their trials and hopes, despite the indistinguishable consciousness of the "time lag" between the clock of Universal History according to which Israel cannot be late, and the time of Holy History. (*In the Time of the Nations* 2)

This is the ethical orientation that challenges the predicates—both spatial and temporal—of traditional moral thinking, and that takes cognizance of the variety of times, or memories, of collective consciousnesses that move in parallel with, and sometimes cut across (with sometimes violent effects), the space-times of what we call, for lack of a better term, modernity.

But we will have to find some other language, some other terms, in which to do so. Lyotard and Blanchot have suggested that after Auschwitz, the disaster which has ruined everything, the language of history and of politics may not do justice to the future. To find a model for this other language, we might look to poetry. Lyotard puts it this way: to do the work required by both history and politics, we must "break with the monopoly over history granted to the cognitive regimen of phrases, and he or she must venture forth by lending his or her ear to what is not presentable under the rules of knowledge" (*The Differend* 57). Such a break, suggest Blanchot, doesn't foreclose speech, but marks the very advent of speech, what Levinas called "saying." "He is consequently not able to remain silent" (*DF* 132). That which transcends Being, politics' guide to action, is "the poetic vision," not one that is "doomed to remain 'belles lettres' and perpetuate phantasms" but one that "makes language possible" (132).

Where might we find such language? Its model can be found—as I suggested earlier—in the poetry of a Yehuda Amichai, or in the prose of a Mahmoud Darwish, writers who have been displaced (Amichai from Germany immediately prior to the Shoah, Darwish from northern Palestine which, in his absence, became Israel) and who attempt to make a space for the exile without displacing the homeborn, in politics' imagination if not in its reality. Both Amichai and Darwish have had to contend with memories—which aren't their own memories so much as they are collective invocations—of places forcibly abandoned (Germany, Palestine) and the ways in which the narrative of memory confounds the language with which each poet attempts to come to terms with their displacement, both geographical and memorial, in his present. Levinas's politics acknowledges that between the other and the neighbor there is a space—like the imaginative space between an Amichai and a Darwish—that as often as not can't be traversed. In terms as much theological as political, Adam Newton calls this a recognition of both the fence and the neighbor. To go back to Levinas's response to Shlomo Malkin in the context of Israel's invasion of Lebanon, his formulation of "the neighbor" is taken from the biblical phrase "strangers, the orphan, and widow"—according to Adam Newton, "the Bible's own phraseology for alterity" (64)—making clear that one's status as neighbor means that s/he is also, simultaneously, a stranger. At the same time, one's status as a kinsman—a fellow Jew, a fellow resident of a community or a nation, even a sibling or parent—does not preclude that person's otherness. In Levinas's writing on the Talmud, he cites instance after instance in which Hebrews and Israelites are defined by their differentiation from one another and themselves as much as they are by filial continuity. For Newton, the fact that Levinas takes Genesis as his key text for defining the other as stranger is important. It is that text "where insiders divide, partition, and fence off one another, where [a blessing] is intimately tied to [intrafamilial choice]. . . . Levinas does not say that others and strangers are akin to family, but rather '[kin] are my others, like strangers, and demand justice and protection" (Newton 73). If the Jew is to be made a political model for "peoplehood," it's because the Jew is a person outside peoplehood; Jews are "a people capable of diaspora, of remaining outside," an outside involving "a different sort of universality, . . . [one that] is noncatholic . . . [and that] consists in serving the universe" (*Difficult Freedom* 95). But it's a diaspora that also involves the reality of others, not just their ethical status as interlocutors but as individuals who may do harm as well as good, and between whom both imagined, ethical fences must be erected as well as real, palpable ones. It also means that politics always involves work that may not necessarily also build a knowledge of the consequences that result.

Levinas writes that "to be with the nations is to be for the nations" (*In the Time of the Nations* 144), which amounts to an insistence that politics involves constant engagement—what he calls "vocation, not nationality"— with one's neighbors regardless of the possibility that they will not respond in kind, reciprocally; and it insists also that fences are not only to keep out those neighbors but also to ensure that even our kinsmen are recognized as necessarily distinct from ourselves, lest we form a name for ourselves, a "we," that becomes insurmountable, and leads to politics for itself, and raises the specter of totalitarianism. What politics ultimately requires is a language in which the real may be written. While such a language doesn't establish a foundation for political thought, it nonetheless establishes the ethical ground on which such a politics might he enacted. It remains to be seen whether, in the language of displacement and of patient and painful encounters with individual others, a politics will ultimately emerge (in Israel or anywhere else) that finally abandons claims to the land, or to language—in Hebrew terms to *yad vashem*—in favor of claims on individuals as hosts, hostages, and guests.

NINE

Conclusion

Forgetful Memory and the Disaster

The disaster is related to forgetfulness—forgetfulness without
memory, the motionless retreat of what has not been treated—the
immemorial, perhaps. . . . If forgetfulnesss precedes memory or
perhaps founds it, [then it is] the passive demand that designat[es
in the past] what has never taken place.

—Blanchot

YOSEF YERUSHALMI SAYS of the contemporary moment that "perhaps the
time has come to look more closely at ruptures, breaches, breaks, to identify them more precisely, to see how Jews endured them, to undertstand that
not everything of value that existed before a break was either salvaged or
metamorphosed, but was lost, and that often some of what fell by the wayside became, through our retrieval, meaningful to us" (*Zakhor* 101). It has.
been my claim that we should see memory as just such a break or a rupture—not as the material kernel of historical knowledge, but as a void or
hollow. Rather than see the relation between history and memory as that
between what happened and what can be retrieved of those events, we
should it as a relation between what has been retrieved and what is lost to
that retrieval and yet which haunts it incessantly. Rather than understand
testimonial accounts and descriptions of the most profound historical break
in the fabric of Jewish culture as a record of the events that, taken one by
one, can be understood as "the Final Solution" or "the Holocaust," it may
be more useful to understand those accounts as indications of a loss, not of
life or of family but of knowledge and experience. If memory is both a

retrieval and a construction—both the instantaneous and often involuntary glimpse of things that happened, things that the witness would often
rather not see; and the creation of a language or set of images with which
to make sense of those events that have imprinted themselves on the waxen
surface of the mind—then it is in the movement between the seeing and
the saying (between, as I've suggested elsewhere, witness and testimony)
that the void of memory lies.

In *Zakhor* Yerushalmi made use of a distinction that is productive for
understanding memory as void or a forgetting. There he notes the difference
between memory (mneme) and recollection (anamnesis), where "memory,
for our purposes, will be that which is essentially unbroken, continuous," and
where "anamnesis will serve to describe the recollection of that which has
been forgotten" (107). To put this into other terms, mneme can be seen as
cultural memory, that which is seen to be important for the transmission of
cultural knowledge or the survival of a people and its traditions, what is continuous and unbroken. Anamnesis can be seen as the intrusion of those elements of a culture of events that have occurred either to individual members
of a culture of to groups or the entire culture itself that have lurked at at the
edges of the continuum, and that break into that continuum in often unex-
pected (and often destructive) ways. "When we say a people 'remembers' we
are really saying that a past has been actively transmitted to the present generation and that this past has been accepted as meaningful. Conversely, a
people 'forgets' when the generation that now possesses the past does not
convey it to the next. . . . The break in transmission can occur abruptly or by
a process of erosion" (109). To see the two terms this way is to seen anamnesis not so much as a recollection that comes unbidden but as a void or break
in recollection. Anamnesis functions as a flash of seeing, a moment that is
both glimpsed and lost at the moment of seeing, and the pain that comes with
the recognition that it can't be recuperated as cultural memory (as mneme),
and that it has in fact—at least for the moment—shattered it altogether. By
way of conclusion, I want to investigate, on Yerushalmi's own terms (and on
the terms of those who have written and thought a great deal about his work),
how memory—that which is collective and which, taken critically and
sorted, becomes history—is destroyed by anamnesis, that which is forgotten
and lies at the core of memory. In particular, I want to begin where
Yerushalmi leaves off—at speculation about the Holocaust as the most recent
and perhaps most violent break in Jewish memory—and describe the effects
of forgetful memory (in Blanchot's terms, the disaster of memory) upon what
we take to be memories of the event itself.

But that break—both historical catastrophes that destroy collective
memory and the break that defines memory itself—has been with us for a
long time, not just since 1945 (though since 1945 it has appeared more pronounced). Part of the aim of *Zakhor* is to understand how "the secularization

of Jewish history is a break with the past, [and] the historicizing of Judaism itself has been an equally significant departure" (91), one that began with emancipation but only became fully fledged in the middle of the twentieth century when the tragedy of the Shoah showed once and for all that the analogies to the past (the expulsions, the destructions of the temple) didn't work anymore. But such a break has been a structural element in memory, and particularly Jewish memory, from the beginning. In fact, contrary to what Yerushalmi claims, there are "uses of forgetting" to be found in the Torah and in other canonical theological and legal writing (108) that trouble and haunt injunctions to remember.

MEMORY: HISTORICAL, COLLECTIVE, INDIVIDUAL

In "Collective Memory and Historical Consciousness," Amos Funkenstein provides a useful distinction—though for him it is only a "reservation" that is dropped as soon as it's mentioned—as he inaugurates the dialogue (in Saul Friedlander's journal *History and Memory*) that Yerushalmi began seven years earlier.

The reservation? That we need to distinguish between individual, personal memories, and memories of a more collective kind. He goes on: "even the most personal memory cannot be removed from its social context" (4); the relationship between individual memory and the broad material realities that constrain it is a dialectical one. "No memory, not even the most intimate and personal, can be isolated from the social context, from the language and symbolic system molded by the society [in which it is embedded] over centuries" (5). Memory as retrieval—as the sometimes unbidden glimpse of events that had for all other purposes been taken as lost—becomes insinuated in the fabric of knowledge, in the language and symbolic systems of a culture that any individual takes for granted. Taken together with the distinction made in *Zakhor* between mneme and anamnesis, it's possible to understand both terms as referring to memories recalled by individuals, rather than seeing the first referring only to collective memory and the second referring only to memories occurring in individuals. Those lost events—memories of "even the most personal" kind—that indicate something that has fallen outside the sanction of the collective, cannot be removed from the language of knowledge with which it is incommensurable. Funkenstein provides this example: "When I remember (and none too happily) my first day at school, I recall the city, the institution, the teacher—through and through social entities or constructs" (4). But the memory of the "first day at school" is not the memory of the city, or the teacher, or the institution, but of what falls between those interstices, interstices marked precisely by system, language, social fabric. The memory of the first day at school may have only tangentially to do with teacher, institution, and city, and perhaps everything to do with what falls outside those indices but which are palpably present to Amos Funkenstein decades later. The point here is that anamnesis and mneme function in relation to one another, though the latter does not resolve the former and regularize it; instead, the language and symbolic systems the witness has at her disposal are incommensurable with what has been lost, and indicated by, recollection.

Funkenstein makes another useful distinction in this essay, the one indicated by his title, between "historical consciousness" and "collective memory." Historical consciousness is "the degree of creative freedom in the use of interpretation of the contents" of the latter (10), the writer's or historian's understanding that the constraints of knowledge and language can also be seen as tools with which to construct the collective memory. The one is the articulation of the other. The result is a triadic division of memory, history, and recollection, whereby history (or historical consciousness) is the critical manipulation of collective memory—presumably to recuperate the events of the past the reside behind it—that is itself comprised by individual memories. One way to theorize the distinction is to suggest that historical consciousness (and the language or tools of historiography) mediates collective memory (mneme) and individual memory (anamnesis). On such a view, the work of the historian is a work not of retrieval but of construction, in which she has a great deal of freedom to create a written record comprised by the testimonies and available recollections of individuals who were there at the occurrence of the event. "The more a culture permits conscious changes and variations of the narrator in the contents, symbols, and structures of collective memory, the more complex and less predictable the narrative of history becomes" (9). And for Funkenstein—and certainty for Hayden White—this is an advantage: on such a view, the work of the historian is the work of the writer. Inasmuch as historical consciousness is an act of mediation, what it mediates are constructions. To the extent that individual memories, inscribed or insinuated in the fabric of the language and rhythms of a people, are available to the historian to be woven into the different fabric of collective memory and taken as history, they are available only as interruption or discontinuity rather than as an object already given. Like Funkenstein's memory of his first day of school, it is located somewhere among descriptions of a city, or of a teacher, or of an institution, but it isn't the same as any one of these descriptions, and may in fact be indicated most clearly by his parenthetical throwaway, "and none too happily." The historian's critical consciousness, in other words, is to find a language with which to indicate anamnesis as imprints intself upon, and undoes, meneme.

In the middle ages, Funkenstein suggests that "the writing of history . . . was guided by the implicit assumption that the historical fact is immediately given: it does not need to be *interpreted* in order to be meaningful except at a deeper theological level (*spiritualis intelligentia*). The eyewitness thus seemed to them the most reliable historian . . ." (14, original italics). At least in this period, historical writing is more closely connected to individual eyewitness testimony than it is to collective memory; what happened happened, and we have the authority of the eyewitness to rely upon. Individual memory (anamnesis) and the historical consciousness were closely aligned. What this suggests of the medieval historian is that historical writing was meant to produce in the reader a moment of seeing, in which the eyewitness, through the mouth of the historian or chronicler, describes what she saw so that the reader herself can see it as well. At the very least, in the medieval historians' view, the writing of history was not meant to provide a collective or mnemonic (that is, contextual) understanding of events. Instead, historical writing that had as its aim a kind of witnessing seems to work against a collective understanding. Here seeing is more important than knowing, and glimpsing the event (insofar as it is possible) is more important than forging the collective consciousnes that would allow its transmissibility; the "none too happily" is privileged over the language of institution, and the historian's job is to create a language through which seeing—individual memory—was possible for the reader as much as for the witness. What is important in both distinctions is the elaboration of a "third term," individual memory, that seems to be closer to an understanding of Yerushalmi's term anamnesis that recognizes its ability to cut against the grain of collective memory, and that is associated with certain kinds of writing, though not necessarily with the kind that we usually think of as the transparently historical.

It is through the *writing* of history that memory has an effect upon the individual writer as well as the reader of the account. Like the freedom associated with historical consciousness—a freedom whose result is often "complex" and "unpredictable"—it is understood here that writing intervenes in and mediates memory. Funkenstein is primarily interested in how the choices historians make—of voice, selection, plot, genre—consciously and sometimes unconsciously alter the historical work and as a result the collective memory of those who read it. He says that "it had to occur to some ancient and medieval authors—as indeed it did—that the historian, rather than being a mere spectator, possesses an *ius vitae nocendi* of sorts over that which he should record. He or she can make and unmake history, can obliterate names, events, identities by not recording them" (30). By writing history, those writers "found themselves admitting that by writing, they act upon history" (31). But what about memory? If it's true that historical consciousness mediates collective memory (the received understanding of what happened) and individual memories (the absent events that lie at the margins of history and return not in narrative but in narrative's interruption), does the historian also act upon memory? If we take historical consciousness also be a kind of "freedom" to inscribe what has been seen but not necessarily integrated into the languages of history, then one way to see the writing of history is as the creation of something quite apart from the events that are apparently its focus. But if we go farther, and take anamnesis to be that nagging suspicion that the events that make themselves apparent to us are entirely incommensurable with whatever narratives we may have at our disposal with which to render them, then the writer of history doesn't render memory; he renders something else entirely. The goal of the historical writer is to make present what lies at the foundation of memory—namely, what has been forgotten or, better still, what is unavailable to memory at all—and to replicate the effect it has on the individual who recalls it in the reader.

All individual memories are constrained by reality, that which is "beyond the modes of narrative, the mythopoetic intensity of the narrator, the intervening subconsciousness and superego," which is "never isolatable yet all pervasive" ("History, Counterhistory, Narrative" 68). The real—both the material dimension of the world that affects individual memories and the affective and counterrational element of those individual memories themselves—"escapes our control, [and] forces itself upon us whether or not we welcome it," but it is also "that which we make relevant, construct, manipulate" (68–9). We write both to indicate the impingements of the real—the reality of memory as it forces itself upon us—and to gain some control over it and (at least insofar as the historian is able) to make it into something that resembles collective memory and, eventually, history. We write both as a result of the real's violence in the midst of the order of knowledge—"the language and symbolic system molded by society over centuries" (Funkenstein, "Collective Memory" 5)—and as a way to produce in the reader a sense of what was recollected by the original witness. Memory, as anamnesis, is an instance whereby that which is beyond the modes of narrative ("the event," reality as it impinges upon us and our conventions of thought and language) is an instance of just this facet of the real. And though it impinges upon us, it may or may not be narratable, though it is most certainly visible as it works its way against the grain of the narrative of collective memory.

This is why Funkenstein can argue that, in spite of National Socialism's "arguing away" of the facts of Jewish citizenship or the fraudulence of the *Protocols of the Elders of Zion*, Holocaust deniers in France, the United States, and elsewhere, the impingements of the real will ultimately disturb the narrative of denial. As I tried to make clear earlier, their "arguments" make sense of the crimes of the Final Solution that are otherwise not sensible or rational: "Many of us say that the Nazi crimes were 'incomprehensible,' that the sheer limitless inventiveness in degradation and killing of that regime defy all our historical explanatory schemes. . . . Precisely this incomprehensibility of the crimes makes their denial into a much more rational account of a possible world (better than ours) in which people act out of rational, or at least predictable motivations" (79). But individual memory "'shines through'" and affects that rational, collective narrative.[1] It is to the degree to which the real makes itself apparent in the narratives that try to bring the events of history into the collective consciousness that an event like the Holocaust is (in Funkenstein's terms) comprehensible (see "The Dialectical Theology of Meaninglessness" 334–7). It is an event that imprints itself on the memories of those who were there and—through writing—on those who weren't, and these memories shape the lives and actions of all involved. That those memories are precisely voids of memory—that they are inaccessible to the very language and context that is at their disposal and that would, for lack of a better term, transmit them—doesn't make the Holocaust incomprehensible, or absent from memory. However it makes whatever we can say or do with those forgetful memories is susceptible to misreading if we are not exceptionally on guard for the reality that shines through but is not represented, and it means that those accounts—testimonial, historical, literary—that appear seamless or transparent may be the most suspicious of them all. What we say cannot be made equivalent to knowledge. Memories of events like the Shoah, then, need to be seen instead as knowledge's other. "Closeness to reality [in a testimony derived from memory of the catastrophe] can be neither measured nor proven by a waterproof algorithm. It must be decided from case to case without universal criteria" ("History, Counterhistory, Narrative" 79). The predicament of individual memory is indeed a complicated one.

And yet measure we do. David Roskies, among others, has been taking the measure of memories of catastrophe for almost thirty years. In the introduction to the book that established him as perhaps the best historian of Jewish memory and disaster, he writes:

> When Jews now mourn in public, . . . they preserve the collective memory
> of the collective disaster, but in doing so fall back on symbolic constructs
> and ritual acts that necessarily blur the specificity and the implacable contradiction of the event. (*Against the Apocalypse* 4)

During the yizkor and Yom Ha'Shoah services in synagogues around the world, and when Jews say kaddish, the liturgical recollections and the prayers themselves are attempts to weave together the strands of individual memory—of deceased parents and children, and those six million dead of no relation but certainly kin—to form a collective. And yet those memories called to mind during the recitation of kaddish or the yizkor prayers do not take as their object the destruction or deaths but are specific beyond the representation of a name or a location or the language of the prayerbook. The event is in fact implacably contradictory, incommensurable with the collective or the liturgical language wrought to present it, and indicated as such by the effects those individual memories have upon the congregants as they stand to recite the public prayers. Like the Moroccan Jews with whom Roskies opens his book—who have "kept the keys to their ancestral homes in fifteenth-century Spain and Portugal," and who, when they were dispersed again to France, Quebec, and Israel, carried with them "their most tangible link to their great Sephardic past" (1)—the prayers are indices of specificity that is nonetheless irreducible to the representations of memory that are uttered collectively and in unison.

Roskies, in other words, is working actively against Yerushalmi's (and Funkenstein's) collective memory of "the Event" as such by focusing upon the work of remembrance, but work that doesn't involve retrieval so much as it involves (in Hegel's terms) presentation (*darstellung*). "[T]o approach the event as closely as possible and to reach back over it in search of meaning, language, and song is a much more promising endeavor than to profess blind faith or apocalyptic despair." The focus on "the Event" itself, as far as Roskies is concerned, "rob[s] the dead of the fullness of their lives and invit[es] the abstraction of . . . the Holocaust into Everything" (9). Rather than forge a collective memory and a name for the event, thereby allowing it to be substituted—in the never-ending chain of substitutions that we think of as writing—for other events (Inquisition, Exodus, or, perhaps more banally, the legal termination of pregnancy), the more apt response is to see the event as unnameable as a memory, unavailable to our use in the present, and to—in Funkenstein's terms—engage in acts of historical consciousness that write the immemorial event. Acts of commemoration do not produce or retrieve memory; rather, collective acts of commemoration, historical understanding of events, and individual memories comprised by language both our own and not our own function to indicate the event at their interstices, and as such work against the (mere) collective tradition that stands in for history.

And yet such an error is doomed, ultimately, to failure from the beginning. Like Funkenstein, who believes that the intransigent and immemorial reality at the center of memory exerts a pressure upon narratives that would endeavor to regularize it, the event taken as a whole is not something that is available to recollection, any more than its details are available to knowledge. As Pierre Vidal-Naquet has said in the context of Holocaust denial, "events are not things" (*Assassins of Memory* 97) and while the narratives that attempt to bring the memory of events into the material reality of the now exert a pressure on the present moment only by indirection, it has an effect that is often more disruptive and more counterrational than the presentation of irrefutable evidence and is more troubling to narrative than any transparent historical representation would be. Nor is it desirable to integrate the event, through ritual recollection, into a tapestry of destruction that flattens out the Holocaust so that its name may be recited in a litany of destruction.

One productive way to understand the act of "reach[ing] back over [the abyss] in search of meaning, language" is as a precocious one. As used by Shoshana Felman in connection with the trauma associated with events like the Holocaust, it refers to a "relentless talking" that comes as an immediate and uncontrollable response to the break, the limit event.[2] If we see the events of the Shoah as a break, and the relation between mneme and anamnesis also as a discontinuity rather than a continuum, then we might also see the production of discourse—a relentless talking that is often beyond the control of the speaker—as the counterpart to memory seen as the indication of a void or an elemental forgetfulness. If the event itself swallows memory, and what memory we have is a sense that though the event is irretrievably lost it nonetheless compels a telling—a testimony—then memory's counterpart is writing. The forgetfulness of memory, the event's relentless retreat from the present, compels writing, it compels the need to remember forgetfully but not necessarily the need to remember the event itself and that might best be understood as the creation or presentation of memory that troubles the collective.

In his analysis of the members of the Oneg Shabbas organization and other diarists and chroniclers of ghetto life, Roskies suggests that the initial impulse of these writers was to record the events as clearly as possible, but to embed them into the larger chronicle of other disasters: in a way that is consistent with Yerushalmi's thesis that Jewish history succumbed to the desire to see the trials of its people as simply a restaging of the abrogation of the covenant followed by an eventual but earthly redemption, the ghetto writers saw their travails as of a piece with earlier ones. "After 1940 everyone became a historian, from forty-year-old Ringelblum to fourteen-year-old Yitskhok Rudashevski of Vilna, both of whom recognized the ghetto as a 'return to the middle ages'" (202). Part of this sense of was due to Nazi calculation, to be sure: their coordination of violence with the Jewish calendar had its precedents in imperial Rome, and its internal government of the ghettos through the *judenrat* was taken out of historical accounts of Jewish ghettoes from hundreds of years earlier (202–4). But it was also due to the long tradition of Jewish historical writing that took individual trials and worked to integrate them into a larger collective memory.

But Roskies argued that this sense of déjà vu only came to be truly realized—with its indication of the difference that is the same or of the uncanny—once the diarists and pamphleteers tried to write in the older traditional forms. The older forms of writing began to break down precisely where the intrusions of the real, the incomparable sufferings that were only impoverished and made incredible by comparing them to sufferings understood by many only through stories and the recollections of the seder table, put so much pressure on those forms as to make them untenable. Before this recognition, many Jews in the ghettos fell into a sense of resignation or precedent, in which the collective memory—Judaism's traditional way of dealing with disaster—was the default position. These primitive conditions in the ghetto, they may well have reasoned, are like the primitive conditions experienced during the first World War, in older ghettos, and in earlier pogroms. But once the conditions worsened, and there appeared to be no eventual redemption at the end of the road (and no conceivable transgression that would warrant what many clearly saw by 1942 as complete extermination of the Jews of Poland if not of Europe), writers had no recourse but to record suffering as individual rather than as collective. As Roskies puts it, what became the focus of writing in 1942 was "the use or abuse of those archetypes [of memory] by individual writers as they stood facing the void" (220–1), and the result was testimonies of seeing but not knowing, of facing the void of memory at the loss of the collective context inside of which any knowledge or reason might be found. "The people . . . had to be recreated before a memorial could be built in its memory. 'I have imagined you!' [the poet] exclaimed from his last and temporary refuge" (224). The suggestion seems to be that there is no possible way to integrate into collective memory the individual instances—memories—of suffering. They are memories that are not the reader's (she was not there) or even the writer's (the event is past and unavailable at the time of the writing); the writer's only recourse is to create—not remember, but create out of the void of memory—an imagined people to memorialize.

Oddly enough, we have come full circle. Yerushalmi ends his book with the following rumination: "Though modern historiography may give the illusion of both *mneme* and *anamnesis*, it is really neither collective memory nor recollection in any of their prior senses, but a radically new venture" (114). What lies between the two—or, rather, what we might better understand as the interanimation of them—is neither a retrieval or a construction but an indication, whose vehicle isn't the transparent language of history or the flat and repetitive rhythms of narrative, but the language of literature. But how could it be the language of literature (which, after all, includes fiction) should be the language of memory? Such an argument would seem to roll back Funkenstein's insistence that reality, after all, must shine through the language of history and of memory.

JEWISH MEMORY AND DISASTER

Let's return now to Yosef Yerushalmi's theses on the convergence of memory and history, particularly as he enjoins writers to examine the break of the Holocaust, to see in such a retheorization of memory—as itself a break or a crux, as forgetful—it compels us to move forward. One thing that becomes clear is that, in spite of the critical foundation Yerushalmi sets up that puts memory and history into a sometimes vexed relation with one another, there is a third term lurking in the background of Yerushalmi's study: forgetting. In fact, the more interesting relation, in the history of Jewish historiography traced out in *Zakhor*, is between memory and forgetting, and what that relationship's impact has been upon history, particularly as we attempt to deal with the rupture of the Shoah. Memory and forgetting are always (though sometimes silently) paired in historical understanding, and become even more so, as we've seen, when faced with the limit event.

The principal claim that memory and history are established together in the injunction to Israel to "remember" appears early in *Zakhor* as it does in the canonical texts. Yerushalmi cites Deuteronomy ("Remember the days of old"), Isaiah("Remember these things, O Jacob, for you O Israel, are my servant . . . O never forget me"), Exodus ("Inscribe this as a memory, blot out the name of Amalek"), Micah ("O my people remember now that Balak plotted against you") and the ever-present "remember that you were slaves in Egypt" to establish the almost anxious demand that neither God, nor God's covenant—the connection between the human and the divine—be forgotten. But because the historical is only as good as the memories and the testimonies of those who bear it, there comes a problem: there will come a time when the children of several generations removed will wonder about the memorials, divorced as they are by distance and time, and ask how they might possibly be connected to the events they were designed to call to mind. It is almost too obvious to say that this is precisely the problem now faced by the second and third generation after the Shoah, who have only the most tenuous connection to the historical circumstances to the Shoah, let alone the individuals in their families who survived (or who didn't), and whose living memories are now failing or exist not at all. Yerushalmi's response, following Joshua, is that it is "not the stone, but the memory transmitted by the fathers, [that] is decisive if the memory embedded in the stone is to be conjured out of it to live again for subsequent generations" (10). Hence the testimony— the narrative of history—is a sign of the lost event, not a representation or simulacrum of it. And yet the memory itself is also not "in" the sign but independent of it. In this defense of memory and history there are two senses of memory: the one transmitted by the fathers and the one to be conjured from the stone. There is the cultural, collective sense (mneme) which is borne by the narrative but which, oddly, becomes corroded and repetitious with time and the magical incandescence (anamnesis) that is conjured from the stone, unconnected (or only tangentially so) to the events represented in the story. What becomes clear from this example is not necessarily the conjunction and potential conflict between the sensible didacticism of the narrative history and the barely synechdochic stone from which memory might be conjured, although this is a startlingly vivid depiction of the clash of collective memory and historical consciousness that Funkenstein draws from Yerushalmi's work. More interesting is that neither the stone nor the story, neither the indication or mark of events that takes the form of a pile of stones or a vast museum nor the story of the exile to Egypt and return to Canaan or the tale of destruction in Europe and redemption in Palestine, contains the memory. Both mark, instead, an absent memory—a forgetful memory—and between the two lies the void that is only filled by incantation. Whether this memory belongs to the person narrating the story or to the person who hears the story or who sees the sign is not clear. What is clear, though, is that Yerushalmi means for the memory to belong to the person who is at the receiving end of the incantation.

The "incantative" transmission of memory—the question of how this nearly impossible thing, this void makes its way from the one who was there to those who were not and could not have been there—here seems unrelated to the kinds of historical writing we're used to, or at least the kind that we normally think of as "historical." Like Amos Funkenstein or Pierre Vidal-Naquet, one wants to be sure that the narrative freedom borne by historical consciousness is constrained by the connection to reality, that it pushes against the precociousness of discourse enough so that we don't open to the door to preposterous versions of what happened. And yet, if we follow Funkenstein and Vidal-Naquet, it is precisely this incantative, this figural, dimension of testimony that seems to mark a memory as having that connection to the event itself. Like the ghetto-fighter's eventual realization that what they were trying to mark as a memory for future generations couldn't be done by setting those memories into the "language and symbolic systems molded by society over centuries" (Funkenstein 5), Yerushalmi too notes the need for incantation for the transmission of memory.

> Oral poetry preceded and sometimes accompanied the prose of the chroniclers. For the Hebrew reader even now such survivals as the Song of the Sea or the Song of Deborah seem possessed of a curious power to evoke, through the sheer force of their archaic rhythms and images, distant but strangely moving intimations of an experience of primal events whose factual details are perhaps irrevocably lost. (11)

"Perhaps" understates matters: the details *are* irrevocably lost to history. But so, too, do the words "archaic" and "primal" overstate the mystery of the language of the songs and the nature of the event that their language is meant to indicate. But the event—its details—is not what matters here, but the memory of the event, and the rhythms of the Song of the Sea are not meant to be archaic or call to mind a primal or mythical time before time but instead are meant to open, in the present, a sort of disturbance. The story of the escape from the Pharaoh's soldiers is as exciting as it is bland, wrought from the language of narrative, of event following event: the Israelites come to the brink of the sea, the chariots follow, Moses raises his hand at the command of the Lord, at which the sea parts, and so on. The Song of the Sea, with

God's flaring nostrils and his desire to bring destruction to any people that dares to do them harm, punctuated as it is with description and retribution, God as glorious and God as wrathful in nearly equal measures, seems as out of place as it could be, particularly given that it is followed by Miriam's two-line song that is more in keeping with the narrative itself. But as an interruption—as a block to the narrative, to a collective memory meant to explain the train of events that led to Israel's delivery—the poetry is neither archaic nor primal but certainly, in Yerushalmi's words, "evocative." Perhaps indicative is the better term, since it notes the disconnection between the narrative force of history and the affective force of the song. Placed together, they call to mind something other than what is represented in the parsha: call it an anxiety over the force of a divinity that seems to exceed easy explanation, or an odd but guilty pleasure over the fate of the Egyptians who should have known better than to follow the pillar of fire; whatever it is called, it is not a memory of the events but a memory of that which is not and perhaps was never present at all. But it does mark a moment in the present—a nexus—in which the coordinates of narrative understanding and aesthetic pleasure (or sublime pain) meet to rupture knowledge. The stone, as a sign, is an impetus for writing, as is the crashing of the sea over a pursuing army, a writing that "intimates," a void of the event. The stone and the song are each a "recollection" (anamnesis) of a seeing—a kind of witnessing—that works against the conceptual understanding of events as historical.

The witnessing, though, is not the same thing as bringing to mind the object of seeing. Seeing, as forgetful memory, is—like the place of the Socratic dialogue in *Phaedrus*, outside the polis and the rhythms of the day—both out of place and out of time. This, too, is supported by Yerushalmi's understanding of rabbinic historiography (if one could call it that), particularly their willingness to eschew the narrative or chronological order normally associated with historical writing in favor of a condensation of time that associated events from different ages in a single narrative, phrase, or liturgy. (That the ninth of the month of Av is the calendrical marker of the destruction of the first and the second Temples is not odd; what is odd is the rabbinical insistence that their destruction did in fact fall, over six hundred years apart, on the very same day.) He notes that "the rabbis seem to play with Time as though with an accordion, expanding and collapsing it at will. Where historical specificity is the hallmark of the biblical narratives, here that acute biblical sense of time and place often gives way to rampant and seemingly unselfconscious anachronism" (17). Yet where Yerushalmi sees this as supporting his claim that at this point through the middle ages Jewish historical consciousness is being sloughed off in favor of a kind of collective (or even divine) memory, it seems instead to suggest something else: a sense of the anachronic as an indication of a void or crux of memory. Moshe Idel, speaking of the same phenomenon in sixteenth century mystical commentaries, suggests that this kind of anachronism was meant as a way to understand the integration of the divine and the material world: in the writings of Moshe Cordovero, he sees this kind of overlapping as "cairological moments" that had less to do with history than with a kind of divine memory. Linear time, *chronos*, is collapsed into no-time, *anachronos*, in which the events of the past—those "factual details [which] are perhaps irrevocably lost"—give way to the intrusions of what Walter Benjamin called "now times," in which one calls to mind not historical moments but the crux that is formed among or perhaps between them.

For the rabbis, this came to be concrete in their belief that the (messianic) future was assured and the (biblical) past was known. The real task at hand was to forge a collective memory in the present that could be situated bewteen the two. Historical time marches apace while the everyday—the real—is what should concern the community of Israel and occupy its time. This "meant the study and fulfillment of the written and oral law, the establishment of a Jewish society based fully on its precepts and ideals and, where the future was concerned, trust, patience, and prayer" (24). But it is the "inbetweenness" of the now where the command to remember is situated. And it is a command to remember that is at once a command to pay attention to what lies between the historical and the momentary, the the narrative of history (mneme) and the sign of its events (anamnesis). That is to say that it is a command to remember forgetfully, to recognize that what we are enjoined to remember is lost, tumbling forever into the past that is simply accepted as past, and yet always having an effect—though one that exceeds our capacity to explain it—in the present. If—in this post-Temple understanding—history records the past while memory connects the present to past, it is a connection to a void, in part a recollection of lost events that intervenes in and tears the connective fabric of collective memory. The task of forging a collective memory, then, is a task that will always be incomplete not because time marches ever onward but because the events which comprise it resist representation and can be called to mind only individually, and only fleetingly, and only indicatively.

Another place to see this phenomenon is in Yerushalmi's picture of the medieval rabbis, whose tendency was to submerge contemporary horrors into the theodicy of the biblical narrative. For the rabbis, "even the most terrible events are somehow less terrifying when viewed within old patterns rather than in their bewildering specificity" (36). As we saw in Roskies' analysis of the writers in the ghettos during the Shoah, viewing horrors through a well-tried lens can only take you so far.[3] But more fundamental to the event's resistance to this kind of "biblical regularization" is that the very same reistance can be seen in the biblical narratives themselves. As the events are recalled—as they are remembered—they are remembered forgetfully in part through the sheer force of the event's absence and in part because of language's (in)ability to simply "record" or "represent" events mimetically. One example Yerushalmi cites is that of the Crusade chroniclers, who witnessed the destruction of entire Jewish communities as the crusaders made their way to the Holy Land.

> Confronted with the intolerable—the gruesome scenes of Jewish mass suicide in the Rhineland, in which, by mutual consent, compassionate fathers took the slaughterer's knife to their children and wives and then to themselves rather than to accept baptism—the chronicles of the crusades turn repeatedly to the image of Abraham ready to slaughter Isaac on Mount Moriah. (38)

The world shook for the one on Mount Moriah as it must certainly have for the events in Mainz, and "the appeal to the binding of Isaac . . . provided desperately needed understanding of what had occurred" (38). But even this bridge of collective memory (what Yerushalmi calls the bridge to Abraham) is built on shifting soil. To see the Akedah as blithely redemptive is to profoundly misunderstand the degree to which even that story is founded upon a forgetting: Isaac, not a young boy at the time, has only one line, which he utters in a sort of biblical monotone. "I see the wood for the fire, but where is the sacrifice?" The Akedah ends with God's words to Abraham, but as for Isaac, we have no ending at all. And this is precisely the point. The biblical narrative meant to regularize suffering, and that serves to connect one act of destruction with another in a collective memory built to explain suffering, in fact rests upon a void of memory, the memory of Isaac's suffering on a sacrificial altar under his father's knife, a moment to which we have no access except as a kind of emptiness or crux. But it is a crux that does quite the opposite from Yerushalmi suggests it might, namely, anchor the narrative of sacrifice in the Rhineland. Instead, it seems to untether both stories from the collective memory and in an instant cause the reader to wonder just what it is that he's missed. Rather than act as a bridge for the tragedies, the Akedah itself acts as a rupture in the connective tissue of Jewish memory.

Again and again, we are faced with the disconnection between the object of memory and remembrance itself in *Zakhor*; rather than the past being made clear in a moment of remembrance—either collective or individual—we get instead a kind of apodeictic "thereness," a collapse of time and space, in which a testimony doesn't provide a description of what is remembered but, quite oddly, an indication of what was not. It is an apodicity that is produced discursively—artistically—and it doesn't provide the scene of the event but its absence or trace. The ritual liturgies, like the Song of the Sea or the Song of Deborah, function in the same way: the antiphony of the lament from the Tish'ba Av prayer cited by Yerushalmi is a case in point:

> A fire kindles within me as I recall—when I left Egypt, But I raise laments as I remember—when I left Jerusalem. Moses sang a song that would never be forgotten—when I left Egypt, Jeremiah mourned and cried out in grief— when I left Jerusalem.

The memory of exile here is not a memory at all—the departure from Egypt and from Jerusalem are, now, part of a narrative of prayer and of history that is recognized as much by American Jews as it is by members of the Knesset negotiating the case of Palestinian sovereignty—but between that narrative and the rhythmic repetition of the "stones" (Egypt, Jerusalem, Egypt, Jerusalem, over and over) is a "there," a crux—not temporal or spatial but certainly palpable—that is produced by the language of the prayer itself. It is a fairly radical claim: that memory is produced through poetry or literature. But this is what Yerushalmi claims about liturgical utterance. Of this prayer he says that what is remembered is "the realization of a structural contrast in Jewish historical experience, built around the dramatic polarity of two great historical 'departures'" (44), departures—Cathy Caruth would call them traumas—that simply cannot be experienced collectively but *only* individually, and that are not experienced in the language of the narrative but in the breaks of the narrative, the breaks located precisely in the repetition of the first-person "I": "I left Jerusalem," "I left Egypt." As suggested by Funkenstein, and as suggested by Blanchot, the disaster of memory here is experienced through the language that follows it—that follows the void of memory—and it is experienced individually as it interrupts the collective and the contextual. The "messianic vibrations" Yerushalmi sees in the juxtapositions of present and past in early modern Jewish responses to the Inquisition and expulsion from Spain were designed to "find within [those juxtapositions] hints, configurations, and meanings that lay beyond them" (64). It is not the language of history but the language of literature that produces memory, but it produces a forgetful memory that is most productively seen as a crux or a kernel—not anamnesis, exactly, but anamnesis's rupture of the fabric of what we're sure we remember.

Let me return to the two theses integral to a view of "forgetful memory," issues that are implicit in writers like Josef Yerushalmi, Amos Funkenstein, and even Pierre Vidal-Naquet, but that are made more clear through the lens of theorists of memory whose interest is in the epistemological break inherent memory in as much as it is in the historical circumstances in which memories are played out. The first is that Yerushalmi's claim—that "only in the modern era do we really find, for the first time, a Jewish historiography divorced from [and at times thoroughly at odds with] Jewish collective memory" (93)—is not quite right. As I've tried to suggest here, historical consciousness and collective memory have played against one another at least since rabbinic times, and likely find their precedent in the Torah. What is more accurate is to say that between history and collective memory fall moments of individual memory related to witnessing or seeing, moments that are themselves a structural part of memory, but that evidence precisely the loss of the event rather than its recuperation. The neat distinction between mneme and anamnesis is not so neat after all, and in fact if there is a distinction at all it is supplied by a third term—or perhaps a null term—that represents what lies between them: the crux or void of memory, the presence of events that are irrecuperable because they did not, for our purposes, occur as "experience" at all. They precede our ability to know them, though we see them, and they register on us and result in Felman's "relentless talking," that precocious testimony that is so maddeningly difficult to map onto history.

The second thesis is that historical writing, while it "cannot replace [the] eroded group memory" (Yerushalmi 94) of the Jewish people after the annihilation of the Shoah, doesn't have to. In fact, historical writing of a sort—like the intransitive writing favored by someone like Hayden White—produces the disjunction between meneme and anamnesis that produces the uncanny reaction. Such writing is neither collective nor historical but indicative, producing what Idel calls "cairological" or apodictic effects that let the memory—the loss of the event—"shine through." Like the Akedah and the Song of the Sea, and like the ghetto poetry and the work of a Yehuda Amichai or a Claude Lanzmann, it presents moments of seeing that are more memorial—though immemorial, in that they indicate loss as much as they indicate presence—than collective memory. When Yerushalmi suggests that the Holocaust is the most recent and violent historical break in Jewish culture, and that it will have its image "shaped not at the historian's anvil but in the novelist's crucible" (98), he is exactly right.

Zakhor ends with a lament: "The divorce of history from literature has been calamitous for Jewish as for general historical writing, not only because it widens the breach between history and the layman, but because it affects the very image of the past that results" (100). In fact, the recuperation of literature as an instrument of history is worthwhile because it is literature—read as "writing" in Blanchot's formulation—that produces an effect of memory that is a break. It presents the trace of "the real" that is unrepresentable otherwise. As a break, we need to see the writing produced by the Shoah as being at once memorial and immemorial, as disastrous and forgetful writing that makes clear what cannot be, and perhaps should not be, called to mind.

Notes

CHAPTER FOUR. MEMORY AND THE IMAGE IN VISUAL REPRESENTATIONS OF THE HOLOCAUST

1. The editors for the collection in the Bildarchiv Preussicher Kulturbesitz are Sybil Milton and Roland Klemig (see Friedlander, Henry and Sybil Milton, eds. *Arvhives of the Holocaust: An International Collection of Selected Documents*, vol. I, part 2, Bildarchiv Preussicher Kulturbesitz, Berlin (1939–1945); the captioning on the photos is limited to a line of description, a date, and where the photo was taken. Klarsfeld's collection, published as *French Children of the Holocaust: A Memorial*, contains a fair amount of text, though that which accompanies the photos themselves is mainly limited to names, ages, domicile, place of arrest, and the convoy on which those depicted were transported.

2. See Christine Busi-Glucksmann's essay, particularly the section on the connection between the image and "screen," in Ettinger, *Halala-Autiswork* (60–68).

CHAPTER FIVE. "THOU SHALT NOT BEAR FALSE WITNESS": WITNESS AND TESTIMONY IN THE *FRAGMENTS* CONTROVERSY

1. *Representing* 205–23; *History and Memory* 180–210.

2. *Fragments* is one of a number of Holocaust representations written by those born during or immediately after the war. To mention only two, Art Spiegelman's *Maus* and Bernhard Schlink's *The Reader* do not attempt to render (only) the events of the Shoah but (also) to critically examine the relation of history, memory, and text (which, in the case of Spiegelman is partly pictoral and in the case of Schlink is largely discursive). *Fragments*, it seems to me, occupies a curious place in the literature of the post-Holocaust generation because of the book's broad claims for historical authenticity, and because (unlike Spiegelman or Schlink) the author's purpose seems to be primarily to testify to a witnessing. For these reasons I'm not willing to extend the claims I make here to other second-generation Holocaust texts.

3. See Caruth, "Unclaimed Experience"; Felman, "Education and Crisis;" Bernard-Donals and Glejzer, "Between Witness and Testimony."

4. See Ganzfried's "Die geliehene Holocaust-Biographie" in *Weltwoche* 35.98 (27 August 1998). Two essays on the Wilkomirski affair appeared in English during the summer of 1999: Philip Gourevitch's "The Memory Thief," in *The New Yorker*, and Elena Lappin's "The Man with Two Heads," in *Granta*. The historian Stefan Mächler published *Der Fall Wilkomirski*, which exhaustively reviews the research and establishes definitively that *Fragments* is not historically verifiable. Though I rely primarily on the two English-language sources because they are the most widely available in the US, Mächler's book will quickly become the definitive text on the affair.

5. See Rudolf Braun for details on child welfare in Switzerland during its transition to industrialism from the 1660s through the twentieth century, particularly 154–60. Mächler's book doesn't take up the question of Bruno Doesseker's welfare status.

6. See Lawrence Rosenfeld's "The Practical Celebration of Epideictic"and "Central Park and the Celebration of Civic Virtue; " and Dale Sullivan's "Kairos and the Rhetoric of Belief."

CHAPTER SIX. DENIALS OF MEMORY

1. Though their discussion focuses on the German context, Jeffrey Olick and Daniel Levy's description of the complexities of the "Holocaust myth" as a taboo subject in cultural memory, one which creates prohibitions and obligations for individual memory, is instructive. The essay, "Collective Memory and Cultural Constraint: Holocaust Myth and Rationality in German Politics," was published in the *American Sociological Review* in 1997.

2. Many of the responses to Gross, including Strembosz's and the others published in *Wiez*, have since been collected together in a book, *The Neighbors Respond*.

3. This, incidentally, is also the danger of dealing with trauma in a strategy of "working-through:" by connecting one's traumatic memories, which are by definition contentless, to those emotions and images that seem best able to mediate the traumatic break, the break and the images become inseparable. In Maechler's words, "Wilkomirski has said that in his therapy . . . the point was to tie 'an existent memory . . . to its appropriate emotions.' Everyone who was involved thus turns out to be an adherent of a well-established therapeutic philosophy that promises healing through the integration, abreaction, or working through of disssociated experiences. . . . For Wilkomirski, though, it was a catastrophe. It only made the sufferings from which he was to be freed that much worse—and gave birth to countless new ones" (271). See Michael Kenny's "The Proof is in the Passion: Emotion as an Index of Veridical Memory."

4. Fish's side of the debates, staged in 1991 and 1992, are published in *There's No Such Thing as Free Speech (and it's a Good Thing, Too)*.

5. The memo reads in full:

Besuch bei Schwarz.
Koksagys.

Verwaltungsfuhrer der SS
haben zu bleiben.
Lappenschuhe u. Finnenstiefel

In the fourth line, Irving has changed the "h" to a "j," the "a" to a "u," and a "b" to a "d," thus rendering it "Juden zu bleiben," the Jews are to stay where they are. Irving tried hard during his testimony to suggest this was an honest mistake having to do with the sloppiness of Himmler's handwriting (though Himmler's handwriting is fairly clear according to Evans, an historian who has seen the relevant documents), and he tries to ignore the fact that "Juden zu bleiben" is ungrammatical (whereas "haben zu bleiben" is perfectly grammatical).

CHAPTER SEVEN. CONFLATIONS OF MEMORY; OR, WHAT THEY SAW AT THE HOLOCAUST MUSEUM AFTER 9/11

1. A note on method: In May and July 2002 I examined 4400 pages of comments collected and saved by the Museum's office of communication. The communications office periodically removed the pages from the binder, and culled the pages for what Jeffrey Carter—the USHMM's chief records management officer—called the most "poignant" comments and excerpts; once the selected comments had been recorded, the pages themselves were destroyed. (At my urging, Carter convinced the communications office to keep these and other pages for three years before they are destroyed.) Most of them were written between 29 December 2001 through late April 2002, though I also found some 500 pages of comments from the months of April, May, June, and September 1996 and January 1997 (the pages from 1996 and 1997 were misfiled with the more recent pages, which explains why they were not destroyed along with the other pages form those years), and I was given a several-page selection of comments culled from the months between September and November 2001. The communications office sometimes uses the culled comments in its publicity for the museum; it may be the case that those comments providing recommendations or criticisms are forwarded to members of the museum staff as appropriate. (Several comments, though very few in the context of the thousands which I read, made specific suggestions about crowd control, the use of cameras, the helpfulness of the staff, and about the age appropriateness of parts of the permanent exhibit.)

I also examined correspondence, memoranda, meeting minutes, and other documents dating from the inception of the museum during the Carter administration through the present. Most of the material from these records was catalogued by year of acquisition and document type; each will be cited parenthetically in the text by title (when available), document type, and accession number. Since the publication of Linenthal's *Preserving Memory* (New York, 1994) the new material cited here and that cited by Linenthal earlier was moved to a suite of offices in L'Enfant Plaza in Washington, DC.

Obviously, then, what follows isn't based on a statistical analysis of the comments left at the museum. But the comments are quite clearly conceptually significant, since even a small number of comments show how the memories of the visitors work.

2. The vast majority of comments left in the binder at the conclusion of the permanent exhibit are comprised of one or two lines, and generally record the impres-

sions of the visitor. Of the over four thousand pages of comments, nearly three-fourths consisted of one or two lines, and often listed only the visitor's name and city. Because so many of the these visitors are from tour groups, and so many of these from middle and high schools, the comments come in waves, and in most cases are unremarkable. Thematically, comments which comprised more than a few lines (about a thousand pages) fell into several categories: the nature of evil, the danger of totalitarianism, the disastrous effects of war, the racism associated with National Socialist and other national policies, and comparisons of the Holocaust to other atrocities. A large number had to do with America's role in the Holocaust, both for good and for ill, and many simply were expressions of nationalism or patriotism (including phrases like "God Bless America," "Thank God for the United States"). The numbers of comments referring to 9/11 or the wars in the middle east were small in comparison to the vast bulk of the total array of more significant comments (about seven hundred), though a surprising number (nearly a third of those that were unusual in their length or scope—over two hundred) referred directly to these events. The other large number of comments from the months after 9/11 noted the connection between the Holocaust and other atrocities, and comments that reflected upon the role the United States plays in the wars in Afghanistan, Israel, and against terrorism (another two hundred comments).

CHAPTER NINE. CONCLUSION:
FORGETFUL MEMORY AND DISASTER

1. Resilience—the shining through of the real—is sometimes aggravating to those in charge of collective memory, as is the case in Israel, where collective memory, the histories that are written in response to it, has not yet taken account of the reality of the Palestinian experience (or individual Palestinians' lived lives), a "silence" that wreaks havoc with Zionist narratives. "By destroying the identity of the other we will destroy our own." (See "History, Counterhistory, Narrative 79–91).

2. See "Education and Crisis, or The Vicissitudes of Teaching." *Trauma*, ed. Cathy Caruth. Baltimore: Johns Hopkins University Press, 1995. For now it is enough to note that Felman sees writing, particularly literary writing, as perhaps the best way through which to transmit memory, but a memory that can at best be called "traumatic" and—in its most extreme formulation—forgetful, a memory from which any access to the event has been irretrievably lost.

3. For an instance of a ghetto diarist whose encoding of the event of the Shoah as biblical seems to have tapered off quite quickly, see Bernard-Donals' essay on Avraham Lewin's diary of the Warsaw ghetto in *Clio*.

Bibliography

Ajami, Fouaz. *The Dream Place of the Arabs*. New York: Pantheon, 1998.

Amichai, Yehuda. *Open, Closed, Open: Poems*. Translated by Chana Bloch and Chana Kronfeld. New York: Harcourt, 2000.

——. *A Life in Poetry, 1948–1994*. Translated by Benjamin Harshav and Barbara Harshav. New York: Harper Collins, 1994.

Aristotle. "On the Soul." *Parva Naturalia*, translated by W. S. Hett (vol. VIII). Loeb Classical Library. Cambridge: Harvard University Press, 1975.

Augustine. *Confessions*. Loeb Classical Library. Cambridge: Harvard University Press, 1979.

Badiou, Alain. *Ethics: An Essay on the Understanding of Evil*. Translated by Peter Hallward. London: Verso, 2001.

Baird, Marie L. "The Movement toward Personalism in Israel and Revelation and Emmanuel Levinas's Ethics of Responsibility: Toward a Post-Holocaust Spirituality." *Voegelin's* Israel and Revelation: *An Interdisciplinary Debate and Anthology*. Edited by William Thompson and David Morse. Milwaukee: Marquette University Press, 2000.

Baudrillard, Jean. *The Transparency of Evil*. Translated by James Benedict. London: Verso, 1993.

Bauer, Yehuda. *Rethinking the Holocaust*. New Haven: Yale University Press, 2001.

Benjamin, Walter. "Theses on the Philosophy of History." *Illuminations*. Translated by Harry Zohn. New York: Schocken, 1968.

——. *Reflections*. Translated by Peter Demetz. New York: Schocken, 1986.

Benvenisti, Meron. *Sacred Landscape: The Buried History of The Holy Land Since 1948*. Translated by Maxine Kaufman-Lacusta. Berkeley: University of California Press, 2000.

Berenbaum, Michael. "Correspondence, Memos, other Documents," 1998–011. Archives of the US Holocaust Memorial Museum.

Bernard-Donals, Michael. "Beyond the Question of Authenticity: Witness and Testimony in the Fragments Controversy." *PMLA* 116.5 (October 2001): 1302–15.

———. "History and Disaster." *Clio* 30.2 (Winter 2001): 143–68.

———, and Richard Glejzer. "Between Witness and Testimony: Survivor Narratives of the Shoah." *College Literature* 27.2 (Spring 2000): 1–20.

———, and Richard Glejzer. *Between Witness and Testimony: The Holocaust and the Limits of Representation.* Albany: State University of New York Press, 2001.

Blanchot, Maurice. *The Writing of the Disaster.* Translated by Ann Smock. Lincoln: University of Nebraska Press, 1996.

———. "Our Clandestine Companion." *Face to Face with Levinas.* Edited by Richard Cohen. Albany: State University of New York Press, 1986.

Blom, Philip. "In a Country . . ." *The Independent* (London). 30 September 1998. Features 1 +.

Braun, Rudolf. *Industrialization and Everyday Life.* Translated by Sarah Hanbury Tenison. Cambridge: Cambridge University Press, 1990.

Campbell, David. "Deterritorialization of Responsibility: Levinas, Derrida, and Ethics after the End of Philosophy." *Alternatives: Social Transformation and Humane Governance.* 19.4 (Fall 1994): 78–111.

———. *Moral Spaces: Rethinking Ethics and World Politics.* Minneapolis: University of Minnesota Press, 1999.

Carlebach, Elisheva, John Efron and David Myers, eds. *Jewish History and Jewish Memory: Essays in Honor of Yosef Hayim Yerushalmi.* Hanover, NH and London: Brandeis University Press, 1998.

Carruthers, Mary. *The Book of Memory: A Study of Memory in Medieval Culture.* Cambridge: Cambridge University Press, 1990.

Caruth, Cathy. *Unclaimed Experience: Trauma, Narrative, and History.* Baltimore: Johns Hopkins University Press, 1996.

———. "Unclaimed Experience: Trauma and the Possibility of History." *YFS* 79 (1991): 181–192.

Chalier, Catherine. *Figures du feminin: Lecture d'Emmanuel Levinas.* Paris: La Nuit Surveillee, 1982.

Coles, Timothy. *Selling the Holocaust.* New York: Routledge, 2000.

Critchley, Simon. *The Ethics of Deconstruction: Derrida and Levinas.* Oxford: Basil Blackwell, 1992.

Darwish, Mahmoud. *Memory for Forgetfulness: August, Beirut, 1982.* Translated by Ibrahim Murwani. Berkeley: University of California Press, 1995.

———. *Unfortunately, It was Paradise: Selected Poems.* Translated by Munir Akash and Carolyn Forche. Berkeley: University of California Press, 2003.

———. *The Adam of Two Edens: Poems.* Translated by Husain Hadawi, et al. Edited by Munir Akash. Syracuse: Syracuse University Press, 2000.

———. "Interview." *Hadarim* 12 (March 1996): 167–98.

De Beauvoir,Simone. *The Second Sex.* Translated by H. M. Parshley. New York: Vintage, 1974.

Department of Exhibitions and Educational Publications, 1997–005.7. Archives of the US Holocaust Memorial Museum.

Derrida, Jacques. *Of Grammatology.* Translated by Gayatri Spivak. Baltimore: Johns Hopkins University Press, 1974.

———. "Passages—From Traumatism to Promise." *Points: Interviews 1974–1994.* Translated by Peggy Kamuf. Stanford: Stanford University Press, 1995.

———. *Adieu: to Emmanuel Levinas.* Translated by Pascale-Anne Brault and Michael Naas. Stanford: Stanford University Press, 1999.

———. "Violence and Metaphysics." *Writing and Difference.* Translated by Alan Bass. Chicago: University of Chicago Press, 1978.

———. *The Other Heading: Reflections on Today's Europe.* Translated by Pascale-Anne Brault and Michael Naas. Bloomington: Indiana University Press, 1992.

Ettinger, Bracha Lichtenberg. *Halala-Autiswork.* Aix en Provence, France: Louis-Jean Depot, 1995.

Evans, Richard J. *Lying about Hitler: History, Holocaust, and the David Irving Trial.* New York: Basic Books, 2001.

Feinstein, Stephen C. "Mediums of Memory: Artistic Responses of the Second Generation. *Breaking Crystal,* Edited by Efraim Sicher. Urbana: University of Illinois Press, 1998. 201–51.

Felman, Shoshana. "Education and Crisis, or The Vicissitudes of Teaching." *Trauma,* Edited by Cathy Caruth. Baltimore: Johns Hopkins University Press, 1995.

Fine, Ellen. "Transmission of Memory: The Post-Holocaust Generation in the Diaspora." *Breaking Crystal.* Edited by Efraim Sicher. Urbana: University of Illinois Press, 1998. 185–200.

Fish, Stanley. *There's No Such Thing as Free Speech, and it's a Good Thing, Too.* Oxford and New York: Oxford University Press, 1994.

———. *The Trouble with Principle.* Cambridge: Harvard University Press, 1999.

———. "Holocaust Denial and Academic Freedom." *Valparaiso Law Review* 35.3 (Summer 2001): 499–524.

Friedlander, Henry and Sybil Milton, eds. *Archives of the Holocaust: An International Collection of Selected Documents. Volume I, Part 2: Bildarchiv Preussicher Kulturbesitz, Berlin (1939–1945).* New York: Garland, 1990.

Friedlander, Saul. "The 'Final Solution': On the Unease in Historical Interpretation." *Lessons and Legacies: The Meaning of the Holocaust in a Changing World.* Edited by Peter Hayes. Evanston: Northwestern University Press, 1991.

Funkenstein, Amos. *Perceptions of Jewish History.* Berkeley: University of California Press, 1993.

———. "Collective Memory and Historical Consciousnesss." *Perceptions of Jewish History*. Berkeley: University of California Press, 1993.

———. "History, Counterhistory, and Narrative." *Perceptions of Jewish History*. Berkeley: University of California Press, 1993. 11–18.

———. "Perceptions of Historical Fact." *Perceptions of Jewish History*. Berkeley: University of California Press, 1993. 19–34.

Ganzfried, Daniel. "Die geliehene Holocaust-Biographie." *Weltwoche* 35.98 (27 August 1998). <http://www.weltwoche.ch/3598/35.98.wahrodernicht.html>

Ginzburg, Carlo. "Just one Witness." *Probing the Limits of Representation: Nazism and the "Final Solution."* Edited by Saul Friedlander. Cambridge: Harvard University Press, 1992. 82–96.

Gourevitch, Philip. "The Memory Thief." *The New Yorker* (14 June 1999): 48–68.

Gross, Jan T. *Neighbors: The Destruction of the Jewish Community in Jedwabne, Poland*. Princeton: Princeton University Press, 2001.

Gruneberg, Michael and Peter Morris, eds. *Aspects of Memory*. Vol. I, *The Practical Aspects*. London and New York: Routledge, 1992.

Gutman, Israel. "Introduction." *Thou Shalt Not Kill: Poles on Jedwabne*. Special issue of *Wiez*. http://free.ngo.pl/wiez/jedwabne/main.html.

Guttenplan, D. D. *The Holocaust on Trial*. New York: Norton, 2001.

Hagglund, Martin. "The Necessity of Discrimination: Disjoining Derrida and Levinas. *Diacritics* 34.1 (2004): 40–71.

Handelman, Susan. *Fragments of Redemption: Jewish Thought and Literary Theory in Benjamin, Scholem, and Levinas*. Bloomington: Indiana University Press, 1991.

Harpham, Geoffrey Galt. *Getting it Right: Language, Literature, and Ethics*. Chicago: University of Chicago Press, 1992.

———. *Shadows of Ethics: Criticism and the Just Society*. Durham, NC: Duke University Press, 1999.

Hart, Peter D. "Results of Visitor Surveys Conducted 1989–." 2002.022. Archives of the US Holocaust Memorial Museum.

Hirsch, Marianne. "Surviving Images: Holocaust Photographs and the Work of Postmemory." *Visual Culture and the Holocaust*. Edited by Barbie Zelizer. New Brunswick: Rutgers University Press, 2001. 214–46.

Jay, Martin. "Of Plots, Witnesses and Judgments." *Probing the Limits of Representation: Nazism and the 'Final Solution.'* Edited by Saul Friedlander. Cambridge: Harvard University Press, 1992: 97–107.

Kenney, Michael, "The Proof is in the Passion: Emotion as an Index of Veridical Memory." *Believed-in Imaginings: The New Construction of Reality*. Edited by Joseph de Rivera and Theodore Sarbin. Washington, DC: American Psychological Association, 1998.

Klarsfeld, Serge. *French Children of the Holocaust: A Memorial*. New York: New York University Press, 1996.

Krell, David. *Of Memory, Reminiscing, and Writing: On the Verge*. Bloomington: Indiana University Press, 1990.

La Capra, Dominick. *History and Memory after Auschwitz*. Ithaca: Cornell University Press, 1998.

———. *Representing the Holocaust: History, Theory, Trauma*. Ithaca: Cornell University Press, 1994.

Langer, Lawrence. *Holocaust Testimonies: The Ruins of Memory*. New Haven: Yale University Press, 1998.

Lappin, Elena. "The Man with Two Heads." *Granta* 66 (Summer 1999): 7–65.

Levinas, Emmanuel. *Otherwise than Being; or Beyond Essence*. Translated by Alphonso Lingis. Pittsburgh: Duquesne University Press,1981/1998.

———. *Totality and Infinity*. Translated by Alphonso Lingis. Pittsburgh: Duquesne University Press, 1969.

———. *Difficult Freedom: Essays on Judaism*. Translated by Sean Hand. Baltimore: Johns Hopkins University Press, 1990.

———. *Beyond the Verse: Talmudic Readings and Lectures*. Translated by Gary D. Mole. London: Athlone Press, 1994.

———. "Peace and Proximity." Translated by Peter Atterton and Simon Critchley. *Emmanuel Levinas: Basic Philosophical Writings*. Edited by Adrian Peperzak, Simon Critchley, and Robert Bernasconi. Bloomington: University of Indiana Press, 1996.

———. *Proper Names*. Translated by Michael B. Smith. Stanford: Stanford University Press, 1996.

———. *Entre Nous: On Thinking-of-the-Other*. Translated by Michael Smith and Barbara Harshav. New York: Columbia University Press, 1998.

———. *The Levinas Reader*. Edited by Sean Hand. Oxford: Blackwell, 1990.

———. "To Love the Torah More than God." Translated by Richard Sugarman and Helen Stephenson. *Judaism* 28 (1979): 217–22. (Reprinted in *Difficult Freedom*.)

———. *In the Time of Nations*. Translated by Michael Smith. New York: Continuum, 2007.

———. "God and Philosophy." *Of God who Comes to Mind*. Translated by Bettina Bergo. Stanford: Stanford University Press, 1998.

———. "The Ark and the Mummy." In *Difficult Freedom*. Baltimore: Johns Hopkins University Press, 1992. 54–55.

———. "Poetry and the Impossible." In *Difficult Freedom*. Baltimore: Johns Hopkins University Press, 1990. 127–32.

———. "On the Trail of the Other." Translated by Daniel Hoy. *Philosophy Today* 10 (1966): 34–36.

———. "'Between Two Worlds.'" In *Difficult Freedom*. Baltimore: Johns Hopkins University Press. 181–201.

Linenthal, Edward T. *Preserving Memory: the Struggle to Create America's Holocaust Museum*. New York: Penguin, 1995.

Lipstadt, Deborah. *Denying the Holocaust: The Growing Assault on Truth and Memory*. London: Penguin, 1993.

Lisus, Nicola A., and Richard V. Ericson. "Misplacing Memory: The Effect of Television Format on Holocaust Remembrance." *The British Journal of Sociology* 46.1 (March 1995): 1–19.

Lyotard, Jean-Francois. *The Differend: Phrases in Dispute*. Translated by Georges Van Den Abbeele. Minneapolis: University of Minnesota Press, 1988.

Mächler, Stefan. *Der Fall Wilkomirski: Über die Wahreit einer Biographie*. Zurich: Pendo 2000.

Mary, R. Interview with Lucy Stanovick. St. Louis, MO, March–April 1997.

McLaughlin, Thomas. "Figurative Language." *Critical Terms for Literary Study*. Edited by Frank Lentricchia and Thomas McLaughlin. Chicago: University of Chicago Press, 1990, 1995. 80–90.

Meltzer, Françoise. "Unconscious." *Critical terms for Literary Study*. Edited by Frank Lentricchia and Thomas McLaughlin. Chicago: University of Chicago Press, 1995. 147–62.

Merleau-Ponty. *Phenenomenologie de la Perception*. Paris: Gallimard, 1945.

———. *Visible and Invisible*. Translated by Alphonso Lingis. Evanston: Northwestern University Press, 1968.

Mestrovic, Stjepan. *Postemotional Society*. London: Verso, 1997.

Mink, Louis O. *Historical Understanding*. Ithaca: Cornell 1987.

Molloy, Patricia. "Face-to-Face with the Dead Man: Ethical Responsibility, State-Sanctioned Killing, and Empathetic Impossibility." *Moral Spaces: Rethinking Ethics and World Politics*. Edited by David Campbell and Michael Shapiro. Minneapolis: University of Minnesota Press, 1999.

Museum Planning and Design. 1999–115 and 2000–051. Archives of the US Holocaust Memorial Museum.

Myers, David. "Of Marranos and Memory." *Jewish History and Jewish Memory*. Edited by Elisheva Carlebach, John M. Efron and David Myers. Hanover: Brandeis University Press, 1998.

Nemo, Philippe. *Job and the Excess of Evil*. Translated by Michael Kiegl. Pittsburgh: Duquesne University Press, 1998.

Newton, Adam Z. *The Fence and the Neighbor: Emmanuel Levinas, Yeshayahu Leibowitz, and Israel Among the Nations*. Albany: State University of New York Press, 2001.

Olick, Jeffrey K., and Daniel Levy. "Collective memory and Cultural Constraint: Holocaust Myth and Rationality in German Politics." *American Sociological Review* 62.6 (December 1997): 921–36.

Ozick, Cynthia. "Towards a New Yiddish." *Art and Ardor*. New York: Knopf, 1983. 151–77.

Plato. *Phaedrus*. Edited and translated by James H. Nicholls. Ithaca: Cornell University Press, 1998.

Polonsky, Antony, and Joanna Michlik, editors. *The Neighbors Respond*. Princeton: Princeton University Press, 2002.

Radstone, Susannah, ed. *Memory and Methodology*. Oxford: Berg, 2000.

Rosenfeld, Lawrence W. "Central Park and the Celebration of Civic Virtue." *American Rhetoric: Context and Criticism*. Edited by Thomas W. Benson. Carbondale: Southern Illinois University Press, 1989. 221–66.

———. "The Practical Celebration of Epideictic." *Rhetoric in Transition: Studies in the Nature and Uses of Rhetoric*. Edited by Eugene E. White. University Park: Penn State University Press, 1980. 131–56.

Roskies, David. *Against the Apocalypse: Responses to Catastrophe in Modern Jewish Culture*. Cambridge: Harvard University Press, 1984.

Sarna, Nahum. *Exploring Exodus*. New York: Schocken, 1986.

———, ed. *JPS Torah and Commentary: Exodus*. Philadelphia: Jewish Publication Society, 1991.

Shapiro, Michael. "The Ethics of Encounter: Unreading, Unmapping the Imperium." *Moral Spaces: Rethinking Ethics and World Politics*. Edited by David Campbell and Michael Shapiro. Minneapolis: University of Minnesota Press, 1999.

Shermer, Michael, and Alex Grobman. *Denying History: Who Says the Holocaust Never Happened and Why do They Say It?* Berkeley: University of California Press, 2000.

Sicher, Efraim, ed. *Breaking Crystal: Writing and Memory After Auschwitz*. Urbana: University of Illinois Press, 1998.

Stoekl, Allan. "Lanzmann and Deleuze: On the Question of Memory." *Symploke* 6.1 (1998): 72–82.

Strzembosz, Tomasz. "Covered-Up Collaboration." *Thou Shalt Not Kill*. Special issue of *Wiez*. http://free.ngo.pl/wiez/jedwabne/main.html.

Sturken, Marita. *Tangled Memories*. Berkeley: University of California Press, 1997.

Sullivan, Dale L. "*Kairos* and the Rhetoric of Belief." *Quarterly Journal of Speech* 78 (August 1992): 317–32.

Vidal-Naquet, Pierre. *Assassins of Memory: Essays on the Denial of the Holocaust*. Translated by Jeffrey Mehlman. New York: Columbia University Press, 1992.

———. "Apropos of *Zakhor*." *The Jews: History, Memory, and the Present*. Translated and edited by David Ames Curtis. New York: Columbia University Press, 1996.

———. "The Holocaust's Challenge to History." *Auschwitz and After*. Edited by Lawrence Kritzman. New York: Routledge, 1995.

Weinberg, Jesjahu. "Correspondence, memos, and other documents," 1997–014. Archives of the US Holocaust Memorial Museum.

White, Hayden. *Metahistory: The Historical Imagination in Nineteenth Century Europe*. Baltimore: Johns Hopkins University Press, 1978.

Wiesel, Elie. "Correspondence, memos, and other documents," 1997–013. Archives of the US Holocaust Memorial Museum.

Wieseltier, Leon and Adam Michnik. "An Exchange." *The New Republic*, 4 June 2001: 22.

Wilkomirski, Binjamin. *Fragments: Memories of a Wartime Childhood*. Translated by Carol Brown Janeway. New York: Schocken 1996.

Wolin, Richard. *Walter Benjamin: An Aesthetics of Redemption*. Berkeley: University of California Press, 1994.

Wyschogrod, Edith. *An Aesthetics of Remembering: History, Heterology, and the Nameless Others*. Chicago: University of Chicago Press, 1998.

Yerushalmi, Yosef. *Zakhor: Jewish History and Jewish Memory*. Seattle: University of Washington Press, 1984.

Young, James E. *The Texture of Memory: Holocaust Memorials and Meaning*. New Haven: Yale University Press, 1993.

Zelizer, Barbie. *Remembering to Forget: Holocaust Memory Through the Camera's Eye*. Chicago: University of Chicago Press, 1998.

———, ed. *Visual Culture and the Holocaust*. New Brunswick: Rutgers University Press, 2001.

Zizek, Slavoj. "Neighbors and Other Monsters." *The Neighbor: Three Inquiries in Political Theology*. Edited by Zizek, Slavoj, Eric Santner and Kenneth Reinhard. Chicago: University of Chicago Press, 2005. 134–90.

Index